All
Consuming
Images

STUART EWEN

ALL
CONSUMING
IMAGES

The Politics of Style

in Contemporary Culture

BasicBooks
A Division of HarperCollins*Publishers*

Arc lamp on p. 44 and AEG logo on p. 214 from Tilmann Buddensieg and Henning Rogge, *Industriekultur: Peter Behrens and the AEG*, trans. Iain Boyd White (Cambridge: The MIT Press, 1984). Reprinted by permission.

Fame on p. 95 from Martha Cooper and Henry Chalfant, *Subway Art* (New York: Holt, Rinehart & Winston, 1984). Photographed by Henry Chalfant.

"O, man in the street" reprinted from *Democracy* by Louis H. Sullivan by permission of the Wayne State University Press.

Evolution Charts on pp. 146–47 and p. 182 copyright © Raymond Loewy International Ltd.

Library of Congress Cataloging-in-Publication Data

Ewen, Stuart.
   All consuming images: the politics of style in contemporary
   culture/Stuart Ewen.
   p. cm.
Bibliography: p. 287.
Includes index.
   1. United States—Popular culture—History—20th century.
2. Life style.   I. Title.
E169.12.E93 1988   88–47684
306'.4'0973—dc19   CIP
ISBN 0–465–00100–9 (cloth)
ISBN 0–465–00101–7 (paper)

95 96 97 98 HC 12 11 10

FOR LIZ

When your hair turns to silver,
I'll still call you desert flower.

—MOON MULLICAN, *Jolé Blon*

Contents

3

Image and Power in a Changing World

4

The Politics of Style in Contemporary Culture

Acknowledgments

Work on this book began in the last months of 1983. From that time, many people have given me sustenance, providing me with intellectual guidance, helping me to see more clearly, listening as I struggled to make sense out of an often confusing subject, nudging me on. I want to thank and make mention of those whose openness, advice, and friendship contributed to the strength of this study and analysis of style.

Much of the research for this book was done at the New York Public Library, the Wexler Library of Hunter College, and at the Butler and Avery libraries of Columbia University. In each case, these libraries and their staffs were extraordinarily helpful. The staffs of the National Institute for Research Advancement in Tokyo, the Walker Art Center in Minneapolis, the Japan Society in New York City, and *PRECIS* magazine all provided receptive ears to some of the earliest rumblings of this project.

Along the way, the thoughts and insights of many writers have provided guidance and inspiration. Among these, Walter Benjamin and John Berger must be mentioned; unknowingly—and without being forewarned—they contributed much to the pages that follow.

I also want to thank the members of the Media and Culture Roundtable and Salon in New York City, and of the Massachusetts Institute for a New History (MINH) in Truro. As I pursued this project, both groups provided me with unbroken circles of friendship and advice.

Several students at Hunter and at the CUNY Graduate School contributed to this project and its realization. Adrienne Ryder and Bridget Fidler Hughes were excellent researchers and scouts. Jean Milman was "best girl" for some of the taped interviews I conducted. Chris Wink provided important insights on modern architecture. Discussions with Sooze Walters and Betsy Wheeler also lit the way. Catherine Bass helped in the final preparation of the manuscript. As the book went through the paces of production, my "homeboy" Andy Mattson's editorial assistance was invaluable as well.

In 1986 and 1987, nearly one hundred students at Hunter College participated in the Style Project, providing autobiographical testimonies that illuminated my understanding of the relationship between style and subjectivity. I am grateful to all of them and want to extend particular thanks to the following: Michael Heard, Maral Najarian, Victoria Tejeda, Denise Howell, Jane Driesen, Ruth Zimmerman, Marcus Salgado, Anita Albrizio, Lisa Esposito, Linda Morales, Cecile Hayes, Eddie Rockis, Fay Stombler, Sally Jones, Stefan Jordanow, and Shane Hadge.

Among my colleagues and friends at Hunter College, several were important to this book's completion. Serafina Bathrick, Ancil Deluz, and Larry Shore ventured with me often in pursuit of the elusive *image*. For the summer of 1987, Fulton Ross assumed many of my chairpersonly duties, allowing me to focus—entirely—on the tasks at hand. Carlos Hortas's interest, generosity, and understanding aided me as well. As the visual component of this book took shape, Stephanie Mack offered considerable help in assembling permissions to reprint previously published images.

Discussions with many people provided powerful nourishment for this book. Allessandra Latour's architectural sensibility was useful to much of my work. Roger Wunderlich provided me with valuable bibliographical suggestions. Samuel J. Cohen enlightened me with his nearly sixty years of experience as an American merchandising pioneer. Stephan "Van Dam" Muth—who became an industrial design *phenom* as this book was being written—talked with me often, providing insight and information. Joel Kovel discussed the psychoanalytic dimensions of style with me, offering me a clearer understanding of my subject matter. Conversations with Dick Hebdige in the early stages of this book were extremely helpful in focusing on the topic of *style*. In ongoing discussions, over a period of years, Herb Schiller has helped to keep me in touch with the unavoidable relationship between image and power. Nell Gutman made important contributions to the pictorial dimension of this book. As *All Consuming Images* moved into production, Suzanne Wagner proved to be the book's enthusiastic champion. On several occasions, R. M. helped me make it through the hour of the wolf.

I would also like to thank Billboards of the Future for allowing me to print several illustrated entries from the forthcoming *Encyclopædia Billboardica*.

Suggestions and warmth were given freely in discussions with Linda

Gordon, Allen Hunter, Elaine Scott, Paul Breines, Ros Baxandall, Eric Perkins, Dan Schiller, Jim Mann, Phyllis Ewen, Susan Davis, Josh Freeman, Obie Bing, Andrando del Mondo, Steve Gorelick, Harry Scott, Steve Brier, Wini Breines, Mae Gamble, Fran Wunderlich, Chuck Reich, Julie Kaye, and Gail Pellett. I also want to thank my associate Archie Bishop who kept his eyes open for me throughout the duration of the project.

My sons, Paulie-Dee and Sam Travis Ewen, did their best to keep me honest . . . and young. Scotty and Sol were also there in the crunch.

From the time this book was the germ of an idea, my friend and editor Steve Fraser has been with me, encouraging and demanding. We share a lot of history together, and now this. My care and respect for him have only grown.

Most of all, there is Liz Ewen, my *compañera*. She is the midwife of this book. She pulled me through an often difficult labor.

All
Consuming
Images

Shoes
for Thought

Ⅰt was December, and the fall semester at Hunter College was coming to an end. To prepare students for an upcoming final examination in "Introduction to Media Studies," my team-teaching colleagues and I were conducting a "review session."

The course, which examines the rise and significance of the mass media within an emerging world market society, had—for many of the students—raised important questions about the relationship between image and power in the modern world. There was an understandable feeling of anxiety in the room, but at the end of an hour-and-a-half session my colleagues and I felt that we had done our best; we wished the students well on the final, and called the session to a close.

I left the lecture hall and headed for my office with the weight of last-minute "things to do" on my mind. Riding down the escalator, however, I glanced behind me and noticed one of the students from the class coming swiftly down the moving stairs behind me, waving and trying to catch my attention. I stopped at the third floor landing and waited for him to reach me.

Out of breath, and with the familiar look of final exam jitters in his eyes, he approached me. "Professor Ewen, Professor Ewen," he gasped, "Can I ask you one more question?"

"Sure," I responded, attempting to soothe his nerves.

"One more question," he repeated, and then, in dead seriousness, he continued. "Professor Ewen, where did you get your shoes?"

I had just spent the better part of two hours reviewing course material with students in the class, and my *shoes* were—for this young man—of utmost importance.

My first reaction, hopelessly professorial, was "why bother?" On reflection, however, I took heart. This kid, with ingenuous clarity, had absorbed the essence of the course. In the contemporary world, where the mass media serve as increasingly powerful arbiters of *reality,* the primacy of style over substance has become the normative consciousness. My shoes *were,* after all, what the course was all about. On some level, they are what this book is all about.

The subject matter of this book is *style.* I began work on this topic early in 1984, inspired, to some extent, by my being asked to contribute an article to a collection of essays entitled "Beyond Style," to be published by *PRECIS,* an academic architectural journal.[1] When I was first called to do the piece, I explained that I felt unqualified, not being a student or practitioner of architecture or city planning. The editor of the journal protested, explaining to me that style was—after all—what I had been writing about for the previous ten or so years, and that if he had wanted an architect to write the piece, he would have asked one. My response was a tentative "Oh, yes, I see," and I agreed to consider writing the piece. This was the beginning, and I have been pursuing the topic—often with great frustration—ever since.

This frustration hit me on the first day that I set out to "research" the topic. I walked out of my house, to the local subway station, with the purpose of taking the train up to the Butler Library at Columbia University. At the entrance to the station, I glanced and then stopped to look at the newsstand next to the station doors. Among the hundreds of slick and colorful magazine covers, the word "style" appeared again and again. On news magazines, sports magazines, music-oriented magazines, magazines about fashion, architecture and interior design, automobiles, and sex, "style" was repeated endlessly. It seemed to be a universal category, transcending topical boundaries, an accolade applied to people, places, attitudes, and things. Still not sure what style was, I proceeded to the library with the knowledge that I was on the trail of a hot topic, a universal preoccupation, a key to understanding the contours of contemporary culture.

What I encountered at the library was sobering. Looking through the card catalog I understood that this would be a daunting topic. Unlike the newsstand, the card catalog offered few clues. There was a predictable reference to "See Fashion, Clothing," but I had spent more than a year in those sections of the stacks devoted to costume, the history of fashion, and fashion merchandising, and sensed the limits—as well as the utility—of the materials found on those shelves.[2]

In the card catalog there were also some references to works on literary style—William Strunk, Jr., and E. B. White's *The Elements of*

Style, to name the best known of them.[3] This was not what I was looking for either, I thought to myself, realizing that I was about to tackle a subject that was, at best, amorphous; a subject that had no clear shape to it, and lacked the kind of concreteness that has shaped the catalogs of knowledge that scholars and students depend upon for intellectual guidance.

Style was definitely more than a question of fashions in clothing or in literary expression. It was part of an ether, a general sensibility that touched on countless arenas of everyday life, yet was limited by none of them. It was something intangible yet important, everywhere and nowhere, inchoate. This intangibility, this slipperiness, has pursued me throughout the writing of this book.

One idea that I encountered again and again in my early library work was the notion of "style" as employed by art historians, or by historians of architecture. Within the conventions of these disciplines, style is a visual motif, characteristic of a particular era. Usually employed to describe the ornamental tastes of privileged elites, this notion of style sees it as a unified expression of an age. Some describe it as a "ruling taste." Thus the "Romanesque" style shaped the structures and artifacts of wealthy monasteries at a time when these monasteries ruled over much of Europe. The rise of the "Gothic" style, in European commercial towns, marked the emergence and outlook of a time influenced by incipient merchant princes, and so forth. Each style is a break from the past, signaling a new way of seeing and of depicting. It is a given within most such discussions of style that style is of little concern to the common lot of humanity, that style is neither a prerogative or property of ordinary people. The notion of "vernacular style"—so relevant in modern society—holds little sway within such discourses.

This conception of style is both perceptive and confounding. The idea that style is a way that the human values, structures, and assumptions in a given society are aesthetically expressed and received is a powerful insight. I think it is impossible to write an intelligent book on the subject of style without acknowledging it as an expression of the time that produces it. Yet limiting "style" to the objects and artifacts of elites is too narrow a focus for understanding its place in contemporary culture. Although notions of style are still often linked to prestige, style today is a preoccupation of nearly all sectors of society. It draws its inspirations from anywhere and everywhere, and the varied assortment of styles that passes before our eyes appears to be anything but a unified expression.

In writing this book I have learned about style from a lot of people. Collectively, their contribution to this book has been to underscore the variety of often contending ways that people see and understand style.

In talking with friends about the subject, all of them were intensely interested and helpful. Each had their own sense of style, shaped by their own interests and experiences. Each felt that their definition of style had to be included in the book, in order for the book to be true to its subject. "You'll be talking about music . . . jazz, of course," came one instruction. "You simply can't write on this subject without coming to terms with Boy George," counseled another. "Did you see the article about the return of Victorian decor?" inquired a third friend. From the day I began this book, until the day I submitted it to my editor, such advice was forthcoming if not always solicited.

Beyond the clashing variety of definitions by which friends and ac-quaintances approached the problem of style, I was confounded by another dilemma. The concept of style, in their descriptions, was often informed by a current fad, or accoutrement, or mode of behavior, which had—often with great publicity—entered the environs of my elusive subject matter. At first I grew anxious at every suggestion, con-vinced that I was leaving something out. With time I realized that any book about style which attempts to be *up to date* is doomed. Style is often defined by its currency, but it is also defined by its consumption. One of the main points of a style is that it will not remain current. To invest a study of style with moment and timeliness, one must avoid the pitfall of trying to be "fashionable." Though the general phenomenon of style has a kind of continuity, its particular representations are, at best, ephemeral.

In order to get a better grip on people's uses and experiences of style, I conducted an "experiment" with some of the students in my class "Myths and Images in the Mass Media." I asked them to write an essay entitled "What Style Means to Me." The ground rules were these:

1 No dictionary definitions.
2 No academic or research papers.
3 Be autobiographical. Draw on your own experiences and feelings about the subject.

The results of this assignment were astonishing, among the best set of papers I have ever received from students. At many colleges this kind of assignment might yield the experiences and perspectives of a rela-tively homogeneous group of people, but Hunter College's student body is extraordinarily diverse, drawn from the crazy quilt of neighbor-hoods and biographies that make up the population of New York City. More than half are black and Hispanic; nearly 40 percent speak a language other than English at home; many are recent immigrants; the age range is similarly diverse. The Style Project, as I came to call this collection of written testimonies, revealed an enormously varied set of sensibilities.[4]

For Ruth Z———, style provided a way "to be different," to break with the codes of a strict upbringing:

> I went to Catholic school for twelve years. In grammar school, I wore a uniform for eight years. I used to try to rebel against this in little ways, such as not wearing the tie I was supposed to, or by wearing the wrong type of collar. . . . It was a way of finding myself a little freedom, a way of fighting the system in a small way.[5]

For Jane D———, much of her life was a succession of styles to emulate, from which she constructed "an identity-of-sorts." At the "private all-girls" high school she attended in upstate New York, she lived in an "atmosphere" that was "very much like a cross between an L. L. Bean and a Ralph Lauren ad." Later, in college in Boston, she found a sense of belonging in "the alternative, seemingly underground life-style" of the "punk scene."

> I cut my hair very short and wore black clothes constantly. (Wearing black made it easy to spot my friends and be spotted by them. . . .) While I was rebelling against society in general, being the nonconformist in that sense, I was also conforming with the smaller group of people that became my friends.

Still later, in Manhattan, Jane moved on to the "clubs" where the crowd was "more trendy . . . more fashion conscious."

> Everyone (including myself) would get really dressed up; the main status symbol besides fashion was who got into the clubs and got their drinks for free. I learned the way these people danced, what they wore, what they said, the music they listened to. It was a lot easier to put on this mask than it was to stop and find the person underneath.

Michael H———, who grew up in the South Bronx, wrote of the style of the streets—rap music and breakdancing—a ritual that he and his friends understood as their own. In Michael's words, "I found a sense of style that suggested how people tell their own stories and find meaning in their lives":

> I grew up listening to rap music and breakdancing. It was considered "hot" in the South Bronx. . . . Both arts are aggressive. They're about competition and gaining attention. Both arts started at what we called "jams." They are parties found on the streets, in parks, or in community

or dance clubs. Breakdancing dealt with at least two people who faced each other and did "moves" while everyone else formed a circle and either cheered or booed. The audience really determined the winner by cheering one on more than the other. The festivity could get embarrassing for the one who "got served" or lost, and it sometimes led to fights. Rapping basically worked on the same principle, but verbally and musically. Violence wasn't so much the style of the art, nor the goal. It would only happen from time to time because of the audience members the festivity would draw, and because of drugs.

With these two arts, I think style here is saying "look at me, I can dance—so give me attention." "Listen to my story, about myself, life, and romance; and listen while I tell it to the beat of the music. There's poetry here, and I'll tell you anything to music without missing a beat."

Michael also revealed the amusement that he and his friends experienced when, later on, rapping and breaking moved beyond the block, becoming something different, part of a more commercial style; losing the context which gave it meaning. "In fact, I found it funny to hear it played on the radio, see it on television, and to see nonghetto dwellers so amazed at it downtown."

For some, style was part of a way that they "imagined" themselves, entered into fantasies about themselves. Victoria T—— spoke of "style" as listening to classical music while studying, revealing, in the process, the hunger *to be an image* that some people experience. "It's hard for me to explain," she related, "but it makes me feel like . . . it's background music to a movie I'm part of. Since my dreams and desires are of being in a movie, I feel pleasure and ease with classical music."

Also about the retreat into image—though on a far more somber note—Maral N—— wrote of "style" on the Green Line, living in a bombed-out building amid a war zone in Beirut. Quoted at length here, her testimony—a cool and haunting sequence of diary entries beginning New Year's Eve, 1983—provides a macabre collage of everyday banalities, high-style patter, and unfathomable ruin:

Roger comes to pick me up. I open the door and see him in a gray blazer. I recognize it. It's the one he was so excited about. He ordered it from France via a steward. He must have paid a fortune for it. . . .

My left cheek is swollen, I have a tooth infection. While observing Roger, I decide to change my leather dress. I put on my old baggy UFO jeans, a hot pink sweatshirt and my dad's gray blazer. . . .

We go down and Elie opens his new, metallic blue BMW's door. He has a casual suit on. He introduces me to his girlfriend who looks at me as if she was seeing a ghost. She has a black lace shirt and a yellow satin miniskirt. On our way to the party, Roger tells me about this new expensive boutique. He promises to take me there. As we are leaving my neighborhood, we hear shootings. Elie puts his hand on the horn and accelerates the car which goes like a rocket through the dark, narrow and empty streets. . . .

. . . after spending three days hiding in our first floor neighbor's apartment, I go up to my house and try to call my cousin Nathalie who lives down the street. Her mother answers the phone and with a funny voice says, "Nathalie is staying over her aunt's house." Knowing how strict is my uncle, I don't believe her. . . .

Nathalie calls. "Guess what? . . . I had a nose job." I go over to her house and listen to her mother's endless stories. "He's one of the most well known plastic surgeons. . . ."

Nathalie and I go to Ashrafieh, looking for the Lacoste blue and white striped, large cut T-shirt. Finally we find it at CHEZ BANNOUT. Nathalie pays 120.00 LL for the T-shirt and also buys a pair of Le Coq tennis shoes. . . .

Once again I'm trapped in the house. The bullets and rockets are keeping me company. The neighbors are gone to their chalets or country houses. I keep eating and reading. I get the L'Orient Le Jour . . . turn the first pages so I wouldn't see the pictures and articles of the latest fightings. I spend hours in the balcony, looking for a window to open. . . . I look around, inspect the buildings and find new holes. I feel nothing. I see the nothingness around me. I can't feel. I wonder if it's death. . . .

We come back from my father's funeral. We leave our house door open. People keep dropping in to express their condolences. . . . My mother's multi-millionaire cousin's wife talks about coffins: "When my darling husband died, we bought the most expensive coffin. . . ." I remember that they were not able to bury him. When they were in the cemetery, a very heavy fighting broke up between the Christian and Moslem militias. When they were about to go back there, after four weeks, they found the unburied coffin eaten by worms. . . .

I gained so much weight that my clothes won't fit me. I can't afford buying new clothes. I keep searching in the closets and wear retro things. . . .

I counted the shells that exploded in my street last night: 66. I'm amazed that our building is still standing.

In Maral N——'s diary, the juxtaposition of style-consciousness and war assumes a powerful literary dimension. The fissure between the world of images and the reality they inhabit is astounding yet, given the extremity of circumstances, comprehensible. As Maral reflects now, living in the United States, "Looking at the obsession of appearances of the Lebanese from a distance, I see what I couldn't see [then]: it might be the only satisfaction left for them, except the satisfaction of killing someone. . . ."

This testimony has its own eloquence. Within a book about style, its insights move from the rubble of Beirut into the frame of our own experiences. Though her contrast of style and substance is unusually stark, she implicitly offers some suggestions about the delusionary, yet compensatory powers of style and consumption which may, at the end of the day, prove instructive.

In the testimony of Marcus S—— style was about how he saw himself as part of an ethnic group, for him a shared source of rhythmic identity. In a way not dissimilar to the approach of art and architectural historians, Marcus S—— saw style as a coherent expression of a particular way of life, of a particular cultural sensibility:

> I begin to think about those experiences since childhood to this present day, that have influenced my idea of style. I begin to notice that those experiences are influenced by culture . . . "Black American Culture." Because black culture is closest to me, I am more readily capable to identify with those forms of cultural expression that give meaning to me when talking about style. . . . For example, although Black Americans speak and write the same language as other Americans, the way black people construct the English language is different from other groups in America. This difference is often depicted by certain rhythms in the language. Through this rhythm . . . a style is created that separates it from other groups who speak the same language.

For Denise H——, a young black woman, style was anything but coherent. Denise saw her "style" as a pastiche of diverse and contending images, as "the freedom to do and be what I want, the *way* I want. Let me explain":

> I have reddish-brown dreadlocks (hair a la Bob Marley and the Ras Tafarians who revere Ethiopian Emperor Haile Selassie I), but am a member (soror or sister) of the bourgeoise Black sorority Alpha Kappa Alpha, Inc. I am a member of the Daughters of Africa, but am also a two-time captain of the Hunter College Cheerleaders. I go to the member-exclusive avant-garde dance club the "Paradise Garage," but am also a Special Education teacher for the New York City Board of Education. My parents belong to many Black civic organizations, and with their tennis on weekends and

suburban way of life are totally bourgeoise (bourg'y), yet I have a ring in my nose. I look like Whoopie Goldberg (or so I've been told), but my . . . cousin is Diahann Carroll. . . .

These stories are resources rarely encountered within the confines of scholarly or academic works. When one does run across them in print, it is most often in literary writing. A pregnant example—Ralph Ellison's description of a man he observed in Harlem—provides a reflective rumination on the eclectic phenomenon of style that I have tried to write about in this book. Ellison's words provide an illuminating postscript to those of Denise H——:

> I am reminded of a light-skinned, blue-eyed, Afro-American–featured individual who could have been taken for anything from a sun-tinged Anglo-Saxon, an Egyptian, or a mixed-breed American Indian to a strayed member of certain tribes of Jews. This young man appeared one sunny Sunday afternoon on New York's Riverside Drive near 151st Street, where he disrupted the visual peace of the promenading throng by racing up in a shiny new blue Volkswagen Beetle decked out with a gleaming Rolls Royce radiator. . . .
>
> Clad in handsome black riding boots and fawn-colored riding breeches of English tailoring, he took the curb wielding—with an ultra–pukka-sahib haughtiness—a leather riding crop. A dashy dashiki (as bright and as many-colored as the coat that initiated poor Joseph's troubles in biblical times) flowed from his broad shoulders down to the arrogant, military flare of his breeches-tops, while six feet, six inches or so above his heels, a black Homburg hat, tilted at a jaunty angle, floated majestically on the crest of his huge Afro-coiffed head.
>
> As though all this were not enough to amaze, delight, or discombobulate his observers—or precipitate an international incident involving charges of a crass invasion of stylistic boundaries—he proceeded to un-limber an expensive Japanese single-lens reflex camera, position it atop the ornamental masonry balustrade which girds Riverside Park in that area, and activate its self-timer. Then, with a bullet leap across the walk, he assumed a position beside his car. There he rested his elbows upon its top, smiled, and gave himself sharp movie director's commands as to desired poses, then began taking a series of self-portraits. . . .
>
> I . . . know that his carefully stylized movements . . . marked him as a native of the U.S.A., a home-boy bent upon projecting and recording with native verve something of his complex of cultural identity. . . . Viewed from a rigid ethno-cultural perspective, neither his features, nor his car, nor his dress was of a whole. Yet he conducted himself with an obvious pride of person and of property, inviting all and sundry to admire and

wonder in response to himself as his own sign and symbol, his own work of art. . . . The man himself was hidden somewhere within, his complex identity concealed by his aesthetic gesturing. And his essence lay, not in the somewhat comic clashing of styles, but in the mixture, the improvised form, the willful juxtaposition of modes. . . .

Whatever his politics, sources of income, hierarchal status, and such, he revealed his essential "Americanness" in his freewheeling assault upon traditional forms of the Western aesthetic. Whatever the identity he presumed to project, he was exercising an American freedom and was a product of the melting pot and the conscious or unconscious comedy it brews. Culturally, he was an American joker. If his Afro and dashiki symbolized protest, his boots, camera, Volkswagen, and Homburg imposed certain qualifications upon that protest. In doing so they played irreverently upon the symbolism of status, property, and authority, and suggested new possibilities of perfection. More than expressing protest, these symbols ask the old, abiding American questions: Who am I? What about me?[6]

Each of these vernacular representations of style is a product of the particular history, contradictions, and experience of the person who is telling it, or (in Ellison's piece) the person whom it is describing. Every story could be pursued to reveal many things about the particular individuals and groups that are spoken for: the way people express themselves, the way they conform, the way they rebel.

At the same time, however, as I read through these and other accounts, I encountered certain similarities among them. At some point in nearly every one of them, the question of style was linked to consumption, and to the power of the mass media to convey, magnify, refract, and influence popular notions of style. Each biography was inextricably woven into the fabric of a society where the use and consumption of style has become a fascination of the millions, an inchoate earmark of "democracy," a central feature of everyday life. It is this question—the prominence, significance, and consumption of style, as a modern historical phenomenon—that this book attempts to trace.

Stuart Ewen

NEW YORK CITY
JANUARY 1988

I

In the Eye's Mind

CHAPTER ONE

" ... Images Without Bottom ... "

Style, hard to define . . . but easy to recognize.

—Magazine advertisement
for Hathaway blouse

Each week on television, a taut-faced woman named Elsa Klensch hosts a program titled "Style." The prime focus of the show revolves around the new designer collections, transporting us to major fashion shows around the world, but there is more.

Some features center on the homes of the people in the world of fashion design: castles in the countryside near Rome; converted farm houses in rural Connecticut; fabulous playpens overlooking Paris. Still other items deal with the daily lives of people employed in the "world" (one dare not call it *industry!*) of fashion. We follow a tawny Milanese mannequin through her regular two-hour body and facial treatment at Sergio Valente. We observe a busy New York model, rollerskating and taking tap-dance lessons; intimately sharing her longing to "make it" in the musical theater. We glide through the byways of Tokyo with Toko, a slender fashion model with "the most famous Japanese face in the world." Her spare time, we learn, is divided between shopping for her new apartment and practicing traditional Japanese Buddhism. Materialism and its spiritual rejection coexist without conflict.

Accompanying commercials blend right in, telling us of the slimming value of Tab cola, or of the way that Henry Grethel clothing will lead us into accidental and anonymous romantic encounters with beautiful women—or men—in elegant hotel rooms.

13

We see that style is about beautiful mouth-watering surfaces, but we see more. Beyond displaying surfaces, the uninterrupted message of the television program is that style makes up a way of life, a utopian way of life marked by boundless wealth. The people we view apparently inhabit a universe of bounty. They wear dresses costing thousands. They live in castles. Their encounters with interior designers lead to unrestrained flights of fancy. Their desires, their fantasies, their whims are painlessly translated into objective forms. There are no conflicts. In the name of "good taste," there is no mention of cost. There is no anxiety about affordability.

This way of life is marked by an endless succession of material objects, yet it is a life that curiously seems to float beyond the terms of the real world. This is essential to the magic of style, its fascination and enchantment. Part of the promise of style is that it will lift us out of the dreariness of necessity.

At the other end of the tunnel of television, however, sits the viewer: cheaper clothes; no castles; bills piling up; no stranger to the anxieties of desire placed within the constraints of possibility. The viewer sits, watches, embedded in the finite terms of daily life. From this vantage point, the viewer is engaged in a relationship with style. It is a relationship that offers a pledge, a pledge repeated across the panorama of American consumer culture again and again, day in and day out. Everyday life in its details (clothing, house, routine objects, and activities) can, through the sorcery of style, be transformed. Without ever saying so explicitly, the media of style offer to lift the viewer out of his or her life and place him or her in a utopian netherworld where there are no conflicts, no needs unmet; where the ordinary is—by its very nature— extraordinary.

Style today is an incongruous cacophony of images, strewn across the social landscape. Style may be borrowed from any source and turn up in a place where it is least expected. The stylish person may look like a duchess one week, a murder victim the next. Style can hijack the visual idiom of astronauts, or poach from the ancient pageantry of Guatemalan peasant costumes.

An advertisement for Neiman-Marcus (1984), one of the most fashionable department stores in the United States, reveals style's ability to constitute what Herbert Marcuse once described as a "unity of opposites." In an ad for women's clothing, the newspaper display offers readers a choice between two stylistic polarities.

One possible direction is "Attitude," a cool and self-confident expression of aristocratic taste. The typeface here is elegant and conservative. Above is a photograph of a woman, a poised Parisian, perhaps, wearing a broad-brimmed *chapeau* and *haute couture* coat. Her delicate hand caresses the brim of her hat; her skin is milky white; her eyes are passive, and vacant. Below her, the words:

ATTITUDE IS disposition with regard to people or things.

ATTITUDE IS wearing the correct thing at the correct hour.

ATTITUDE IS a seam.

ATTITUDE IS exactly sized. ("I wear a size 6")

ATTITUDE IS a mode.

ATTITUDE IS dressing to please someone else.

ATTITUDE IS an evaluation.

ATTITUDE IS strolling the avenue.

ATTITUDE IS Neiman-Marcus.

On the same page, on the other side of a sharp, jagged line, lies another vision of style: "Latitude." Far from the "cultured" refinement of the aristocrat, this is about breaking the rules, violating taboos. The typeface here is scrawled, in bold graffiti strokes. Above is a picture of another woman, a languid and brooding Semitic type, wearing the head scarf of a Palestinian and a loose-fitting desert caftan. She reclines; her arms fall back above her head. Her skin is olive, glistening with moisture, and her dark eyes look off to the side, gazing in the direction of forbidden desires. Below her, the words:

LATITUDE IS freedom from narrow restrictions permitting freedom of action.

LATITUDE IS changing the structure of a garment, however, whenever, the mood hits.

LATITUDE IS a slash.

LATITUDE IS whatever feels comfortable.

LATITUDE IS a mood.

LATITUDE IS dressing to please yourself.

LATITUDE IS an evolution.

LATITUDE IS loving the street life.

and, once more,

LATITUDE IS Neiman-Marcus.

Colliding world views are translated into style, images to be purchased. As disembodied images, they can be easily reconciled, both

IMAGES WITHOUT BOTTOM

15

available from the same source. As the ad concludes, we are instructed that style may fall on "the left or right" of a "strongly defined line," yet depending on the "moment or imagination," either may be appropriate. Style makes statements, yet has no convictions. "Our stocks," the advertisement concludes, "are full of both looks. Ask any N-M salesperson for a little direction—or just say the word. Attitude. Or Latitude." Obedience or self-determination, conservative or radical, Brahmin or Untouchable, Superego or Id; any of these dualities may be purchased, simultaneously, in the world of style.

If the style market constitutes a presentation of a way of life, it is a way of life that is unattainable for most, nearly all, people. Yet this doesn't mean that style isn't relevant to most people. It is very relevant. It is the most common realm of our society in which the need for a better, or different way of life is acknowledged, and expressed on a material level, if not met. It constitutes a politics of change, albeit a "change" that resides wholly on the surface of things. The surfaces, themselves, are lifted from an infinite number of sources.

The imagery of elite culture is an ongoing aspect of style. A magazine advertisement for Benson & Hedges "Deluxe Ultra Lights" places two large, gold-edged packages of cigarettes in front of a sweeping spiral staircase, draped in muted tones of ivory and pink. Halfway up the stairs a woman in a beaded evening gown, dragging a white mink stole up thickly carpeted stairs, has her cigarette lit by an elegant gent in a black tuxedo. Meanwhile, in another ad in the same magazine, an unseen hand pours Chivas Regal scotch into a sparkling crystal slipper. Each image reeks of money, offering the consumer a democratic promise of limitless possibility while, at the same time, projecting the sheltered prerogatives of an elite few. Assuming the iconography or "attitude" of elites may, for some, represent a change for the better, an elevation of status. More and more, however, style offers other visions of change, drawn from an endless repository of images.

ELLE magazine presents a photo-feature, entitled "Paramilitary Mode." Sultry, daring members of a "pricey platoon" display the potential allure of military gear. "Wake up to the fun of fatigues," challenges the text, as an enticing woman, preparing for "combat," removes her button-fly pants, revealing camouflage panties upon her forward-thrust hip.

TAXI, a slick magazine on "fashion, trends and leisure living," presents a profile of Ennio Capasa, a "rising star" among fashion designers. His "Japanese-influenced collection," comments the magazine (quoting the *New York Times*), "looks like what one imagines a rebel against totalitarianism would do to make drab clothes individual and the stulti-

Within European traditions of elite culture, an ornately framed portrait of oneself was a conspicuous sign of status, of having *arrived* in the world. Today, such signs of status have been *democratized,* available to anyone able to make the correct, stylish purchase. At left, *Portrait of a Man* by Lucas Cranach, 1532. At right, an advertisement for a Christian Dior men's suit, 1987.

fying sexy." Political transformation and liberation come through "with energy and force," part of a bold, sensual new look.

An advertisement for Esprit jeans argues that "denim and jeans-wear" are "social equalizers." Warring on the elitist tyranny of "silks and satin," the ad continues, Esprit jeans offer an "Elegance" that is "anti-fashion and anti-luxury." To underscore the political egalitarianism of the product, the jeans are modeled by two "real" young women—not professional models—whose credentials are listed to create an atmosphere of intelligence, physical and spiritual health, and firm social commitments. Both blonde and blue-eyed—conforming to the Aryan, photogenic ideals of the fashion trade—these two *really care.* Cara Schanche of Berkeley, California (another symbol of youthful idealism), is an "English Literature Student, Part-time Waitress, Anti-

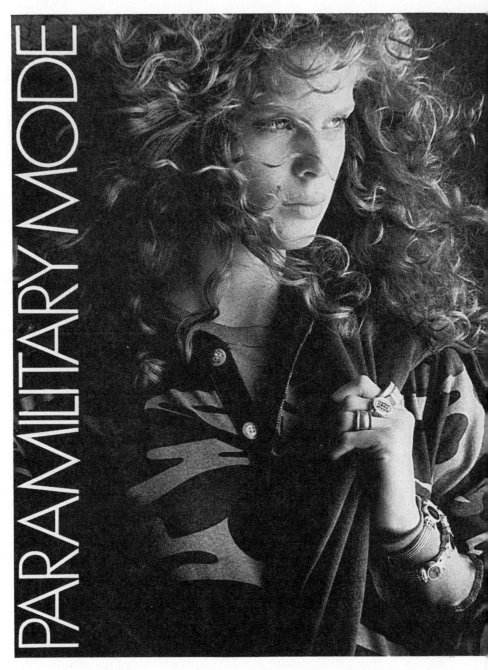

PARAMILITARY MODE

War is beautiful because it initiates the dreamt-of metalization of the human body. War is beautiful because it enriches a flowering meadow with the fiery orchids of machine guns. War is beautiful because it combines the gunfire, the cannonades, the cease-fire, the scents, and the stench of putrefaction into a symphony.

—EMILIO MARINETTI, as quoted by Walter Benjamin in
"The Work of Art in the Age of Mechanical Reproduction"

Racism Activist, Beginning Windsurfer, Friend of the Dalai Lama." Her soulmate in style, Ariel O'Donnell of San Francisco, is a "Waitress/Bartender, Non-professional AIDS Educator, Cyclist, Art Restoration Student, Anglophile, Neo-Feminist." In the world of style, ideas, activities, and commitments become ornaments, adding connotation and value to the garment while they are, simultaneously, eviscerated of meaning.

Another ad, for Bloomingdale's "Fall '87 Collection," draws its idiom from an indiscriminate clatter of social, political, and artistic references. "Courage comrades," begins the ad. "Back-to-School's anything but a bore for young Post-constructivists. We condone conspicuous clothes with working-class conviction. . . . And a fundamentalist belief in French Connection, The Fall '87 Collection. . . . Juniors moves into a new age at Bloomingdale's. From counter culture to sophisticated, sexy, fast forward fashion for progressive thinkers." Ideas and concepts—socialism, fundamentalism, conspicuous consumption, new age—meld into an effervescent swirl of inchoate activity, a fashion statement, implying everything, signifying nothing. Here, amid the polymorphous collage, we are tantalized by empty promises of transgression.

If the "life-style" of style is not realizable in life, it is nevertheless the most constantly available lexicon from which many of us draw the visual grammar of our lives. It is a behavioral model that is closely interwoven with modern patterns of survival and desire. It is a "hard to define . . . but easy to recognize" element in our current history.

Often silently, at times unacknowledged, style works on the ways that people understand and relate to the world around them. Its influence can be seen within the insecure, but nonetheless formative, boundaries of adolescence, when the search for *identity* accelerates. Anita A——, now a twenty-four-year-old college student, confides,

> When I was in high school I cut out an advertisement from a magazine and hung it on my wall. The ad read "Create An Image" in big bold white letters. . . . I don't remember what the ad was for, and I never really cared. . . . I simply wanted to remind myself to work on my style. . . . I used to be really taken by someone who could cause that intense silence just by entering a room. I was often captured by their style.[1]

Lisa E——, twenty, feels that style "is closely related to advertising." "My elements of style," she readily admits, "are what's spread across the pages of *Vogue, Elle* and *Glamour* magazines." She explains,

> Right now I'm in the middle of a style change. I'm making myself miserable as I wait for my hair to grow out from an extremely short, close shaven

cut. That haircut was my favorite. It was easy to care for. It looked great on me. I was always complimented . . . so why change it? The androgenous, short-haired look of Annie Lennox has been replaced by the more feminine locks of Paulina Porizkova. Her image is everywhere nowadays. It's her image that is making me desire longer hair. So I will add that to me.[2]

For others, style is seen as a powerful mode of self-expression, a way in which people establish themselves in relation to others. Michael H——, who grew up in the South Bronx, spent much of his childhood and adolescence playing basketball. For him, style was an essential part of the game, part of winning:

> I played the game from sun-up til sundown. It's never enough to just score the ball in the basket, or to simply block someone's shot. There's got to be style added to it . . . finesse, control, aggression. When a basketball is dunked in the basket, especially while an opponent is present, it says a statement and a sense of style. "Get off of me, and take this!" is the clear message. To block an opponent's shot and send the ball into another area of the park or gym is very threatening and shows style.

Michael's sense of "style" has been shaped by the choreography and competition of basketball, but it has also been mediated by items from the marketplace. Michael discusses the use of commodities in the process of establishing and expressing cultural meanings:

> When I grew up I wore basketball sneakers and *Lee* jeans. I wore my hair sometimes in braids or in waves, and I walked with a bop. It's a cultural statement that my friends and I identified with while growing up. . . . It's the "thing" to wear basketball sneakers in the ghetto.[3]

For a newcomer to the United States, the preponderance of marketplace style can initiate a moment of personal crisis. For Linda M——, a young woman who grew up in Peru, in a culture that she describes as "traditional," her encounter with "style" in metropolitan New York accentuated a fissure of meaning. In Peru, she explains, style was understood as "the way in which the inner being of someone is expressed." Here, in the United States, style has a "very different meaning . . . which comes from the external world rather than from the inner one":

> Not only tastes are being shaped, . . . but also perceptions of one's own self. . . . The interaction of people and environment is being turned inside out.
>
> My personal experience has been a difficult one. There are ways in which I feel anachronic in a modern society. . . . I found a tremendous difference in my perspectives of life and that of most people in a commer-

cialized society. . . . Only now I seem to begin to understand why life seems so meaningless to many people in a big society up to the point where they prefer to drug themselves not to bear with an empty reality which displays a glamour of images without bottom, without real meaning. . . .

If style . . . has become something people think they could buy, then what we are losing is man himself. We are betraying our own self, we are selling our own inner being and replacing it for a more suitable one for "modern society."[4]

The phenomenon of style within contemporary American society is varied and complex. It registers different meanings to different people, or among different communities. Yet what Linda M—— says, about "a glamour of images without bottom," cannot help but strike a chord with anyone who has observed, or lived in, the shadow of the managed image. In so many arenas of life, style has become the *legal tender*.

Style, more and more, has become the official idiom of the marketplace.* In advertising, packaging, product design, and corporate *identity*, the power of provocative surfaces speaks to the eye's mind, overshadowing matters of quality or substance. Style, moreover, is an intimate component of subjectivity, intertwined with people's aspirations and anxieties. Increasingly, style has emerged as a decisive component of politics; political issues and politicians are regularly subjected to the cosmetic sorcery of image managers, providing the public with a telegenic commodity. Democratic choice, like grocery shopping, has become a question of which product is most attractively packaged, which product is most imaginatively merchandised. How has this ubiquitous primacy of style come about?

Precisely because style deals in surface impressions, it is difficult to concretize, to discern its definitions. It forms a chimerical, yet highly visible corridor between the world of things and human consciousness. Investing profane things with sacred meanings, however, is an ancient activity, a universal preoccupation of our species. This, in and of itself, does not define style, nor does it situate style within the particular conditions and contradictions of contemporary life.

The ornamentation of life has been practiced within traditional cultures for millennia; the tendency to invest such embellishments with intricate, powerful, and often mysterious webs of interpretation has also been common. Often interwoven within mythological and magical be-

---

*Here, as elsewhere throughout this book, the term *marketplace* is employed as a euphemism for commerce. Today, as the market is often indistinguishable from society itself, there is no longer a market-*place* in its original and localized sense.

lief systems, decorative objects asserted astonishing powers. They could explain the world as it was, ratify established patterns of kinship and power, or express visions of something beyond the conventional terms of existence: a horror or a consolation.

Yet within such traditional societies, the role of imagery and decoration differed significantly from the volatile phenomenon of *style* in modern life. Traditional imagery stood for an unchanging or cyclical world, frozen in time and space, hierarchical and static, where everyone knew his or her assigned place in the "great chain of being." Modern style speaks to a world where change is the rule of the day, where one's place in the social order is a matter of perception, the product of diligently assembled illusions. Today, style is one way by which we perceive a world in flux, moving—apparently—ever forward, whereas traditional societies' use of imagery invoked a sense of perpetuity, which conformed to a general outlook on life.

The power of style, and its emergence as an increasingly important feature in people's lives, cannot be separated from the evolution and sensibility of modernity. Style is a visible reference point by which we have come to understand life *in progress.* People's devotion to the acceleration of varying styles allows them to be connected to the "reality" of a given moment. At the same time they understand that this given moment will give way to yet another, and another, and that as it does, styles will change, again and again. A sense of rootedness or permanency is elusive in the world of style, and it is perhaps this quality, more than any other, that locates style in the modern world. On the one hand, style speaks for the rise of a democratic society, in which who one wishes to become is often seen as more consequential than who one is. On the other hand, style speaks for a society in which coherent meaning has fled to the hills, and in which drift has provided a context of continual discontent.

But the question of style cannot be limited to the realm of subjectivity. Style is also a significant element of power. Style, today, is inextricably woven into the fabric of social, political, and economic life. It is the product of a vast and seamless network of industries. The production of sumptuous images, for the very few, was once limited to the sacred workshops of the medieval monasteries; now, the production and marketing of style is global, touching the lives and imaginations of nearly everyone. Design, of one sort or another, is affixed to almost every conceivable commodity, and style is now "ladled out" from what the art critic Herbert Read once disparagingly termed a continuous and "glorified soup kitchen." It is to the historic development of that "soup kitchen," and to its implications, that we now must turn.

CHAPTER TWO

Goods
and Surfaces

We are surrounded by emptiness, but it is an emptiness filled with signs.

—HENRI LEFEBVRE, *Everyday Life in the Modern World*

SKINNERS
OF THE VISIBLE WORLD

In 1859, amid a century marked by technological wonders, Oliver Wendell Holmes published the first of three articles he would write paying homage to what he understood to be the most remarkable achievement of his time: *photography.* Photography, the prominent New England man of letters rhapsodized, "has fixed the most fleeting of our illusions," and has permitted them, as never before, to endure before our eyes. The momentary glance, the ineffable memory, the detailed and textured surface, could now be lifted from its particular place and time, separated from the powerful grasp of the material environment, yet still remain real, visible, and permanent. For Holmes, the process of photography had effected an earthshaking, previously unimaginable "conquest over matter." The photograph, he asserted, was a *"mirror with a memory."*[1]

This ability to capture and preserve the disembodied countenance of things was, for Holmes, changing the physics of perception, inducing a metamorphosis in the way people would see and understand the world. Before photography, he explained, the features of a person, a place, or an object were inalterably bound to their unique material substance. True, paintings could fasten upon the effigies of the material world, but they were, at best, costly and skillful depictions, time-consuming representations wrought by the careful hand of an artist. Now, with the birth of photography, the physical environment could be forced to yield its manifold appearances directly. Form could be separated from matter. A new reality, shaped by the flourishing of dematerialized surfaces, could take hold.

For Holmes, photography signaled the beginning of a time when the "image would become more important than the object itself, and would in fact make the object disposable." Holmes foresaw a time when surfaces would be routinely appropriated from any conceivable source, and would then take on an autonomous, yet objective, life of their own. *"Form,"* he proclaimed, *"is henceforth divorced from matter. In fact, matter as a visible object is of no great use any longer, except as the mould on which form is shaped."*[2] The cord between aspect and materiality had been severed.

In his essays, Holmes delineated a world in which surfaces were assuming "the effect of solidity," and where the play of images within the vaporous ether of perception was coming to signify an ever-more potent and provocative arena of *truth.* Photography gave substance to the idea that images could be the conclusive expression of reality on the one hand, and exist autonomous of that reality on the other. Technically reproduced surfaces were beginning to vie with lived experience in the structuring of meaning. The image offered a representation of reality more compelling than reality itself, and—perhaps—even threw the very definition of *reality* into question.

Intrinsic to Holmes's analysis was his prescient understanding that the ability to reproduce the disembodied appearance of things portended the coming of a vast and mobile market in images, such as the world had never before seen. Freed from the encumbrances of matter, the *look* of the visible world could now be easily, and inexpensively, reproduced:

> Matter in large masses must always be fixed and dear; form is cheap and transportable. We have got the fruit of creation now, and need not trouble ourselves with the core. *Every conceivable object of Nature and Art will soon scale off its surface for us. Men will hunt all curious, beautiful, grand objects, as they hunt cattle in South America, for their skins and leave the carcasses as of little worth.*[3]

With remarkable, if unwitting, clarity, Oliver Wendell Holmes had laid out the contours by which the phenomenon of *style* operates in the world today. Holmes was writing of photography, yet his perception that people would soon navigate the world, skin it of its visible images, and market those images inexpensively to people, reflected a keen understanding of what, in the twentieth century, would stand as a palpable indicator of material progress. For people who, in another epoch, would have been unable to afford it, the acquisition of *style* represented a symbolic leap from the constraints of mere subsistence.

STYLE AND
SOCIAL MOBILITY

If the nineteenth century saw the flowering of style on a mass scale, the seeds of the modern market in style were sown centuries before. The rumblings of this development, soft at first, began to be heard in Europe, in the late Middle Ages, as mercantile trade began to stir the caldron of town life. After a period when cultural life had been dominated by wealthy monastic estates, an increase in merchant activity, and in highly skilled, urban handcrafts, transformed the once-marginal towns into hubs of economic and cultural energy. Challenging the rooted, feudal patterns of agrarian self-sufficiency, the towns became vibrant arenas for an incipient, increasingly mobile money economy. Crafts, previously controlled by the monasteries, now gravitated into the towns, into the hands of free and relatively independent artisans. Manufacture, formerly the domain of monastic power, was now beginning to produce goods for *sale* to a growing market of landed and urban customers.

As the exchange in goods became more and more common, and as the financing of burgeoning production became necessary, merchant enterprise flourished. Against the still imposing panorama of feudalism, the beginnings of a market society were unfolding. Implicit in these beginnings was the rise of a mobile form of wealth which challenged the very social fabric of feudalism. Whereas the old order was predicated on the notion of an eternally fixed system, the new town life represented a society predicated on change: the growth of manufactures, the expansion of markets, the circulation of wealth, *progress.*

Wealth and power under feudalism were depicted as God-given rights of those that ruled; the emerging wealth of the towns was merely a product of entrepreneurship. Merchants and artisans, who stood at the heart of this new development, composed a population of mobile individuals, navigating throughout society, operating beyond the margins of feudal custom.

Yet the power of feudal tradition still held sway within merchant life.

Fueled by their desire for franchise and status, the merchant class mimicked and appropriated consumption practices of the nobility. Commercial activity made luxurious items more readily available than before and provided prosperous merchants the wherewithal to acquire them. Although the merchants' fortunes were a product of commercial enterprise, their consumption patterns were designed to obtain the imagistic trappings of landed heritage. The results of this tendency characterized—to a large extent—the genesis of the bourgeois ideal of style on into the nineteenth century. *Conspicuous consumption,* as Thorstein Veblen would name it, was the mark of status. In a world where nobility still ruled, the merchant class seized upon symbols of excess which had customarily been prerogatives of landed elites.

Alongside the acquisition of land, other items entered the field of bourgeois consumption. Elaborate clothing, a commonly understood mark of power, was now available to a successful merchant. This caused the nobility some consternation. Before the rise of merchant wealth, the sartorial rights of nobility were assured by the fact that only they could afford to acquire sumptuous garments. Painstaking and delicate needlework was at their disposal. With the expansion of mercantile wealth, however, the nobility began to erect legalistic means to protect their privilege. From the 1300s on, the old feudal order began to establish "sumptuary laws," specific guidelines governing the wearing of apparel. Even within the detailed proscriptions of the law, however, the rising prominence of the bourgeois was evident. A law adopted in Augsburg, in 1530, for example, noted that "only princes, knights and their ladies were permitted to wear brocade" and "velvet garments were for patricians," but the law also allowed members of the "upper bourgeoisie" "three ellens of velvet to decorate their headdresses."[4]

Aspiring merchants also fueled the development of a broader market in art objects. Earlier in the Middle Ages, intricate crafts were the product of a localized, "household" economy; artful objects, for the most part, were produced for the pleasure and grandeur of landowners. Beautiful illuminated manuscripts and ornamental handicrafts rarely changed hands, except "in the form of occasional presents or in the execution of direct commissions given to particular craftsmen."[5] With the expanding market in artisan crafts, however, art became a prestigious item to purchase. The trade in art objects began to grow; style was becoming something one could acquire.

The emerging commerce in appearances is well illustrated by the proliferation of "deluxe edition" manuscript books which came with the rise of the commercial towns. Before this period, books were articles of "supreme luxury," treasured possessions of feudal nobles. The labor involved in producing one illuminated manuscript was enormous. Months, sometimes years, were spent creating these sacred objects of beauty. Ownership of books was an incontrovertible sign of one's status in the world, and—given the religious nature of most texts—one's closeness to God. Clearly, these volumes were collected more for the admiration they inspired than for their literary use, and book craft and design accentuated this display function.

With the emergence of a bourgeois market in style, however, interest in such one-of-a-kind treasures became more widespread. To feed a market of hungry consumers, new workshops were established to produce illuminated and decorative Books of Hours, ornately illustrated religious calendars which, in the past, were extraordinarily rare specimens of beauty. Even before the development of the movable-type printing press, Flemish artisans modernized the labor process in order to satisfy the mimetic desires of parvenu taste. Marcel Thomas, keeper in the Department of Manuscripts, Bibliothèque Nationale, Paris, described the intricate division of labor that prevailed in these new, market-oriented workshops:

> The trade in these Books of Hours was the virtual monopoly of certain specialist workshops, and in these, above all, an ingenious division of labour allowed time to be saved and made possible proper mass production. Ateliers of this kind existed in Flanders, and . . . illuminators would produce identical stock scenes for each of the main religious festivals (the Nativity, the Annunciation, etc.) while scribes copied out the different calendars of the various dioceses, so that they could then be joined on to those sections of the Books of Hours which did not vary from diocese to diocese.
>
> Illuminators even perfected a process which permitted them to make several copies from one original.[6]

To prosperous townfolk of the fourteenth and fifteenth centuries, the ability to acquire such items of beauty was a sign that, from all appearances, one had *arrived*.

Another example of the emerging market in style is found in the expanding industry of religious iconography. By the fifteenth century, religious art, historically associated with monasteries and cathedrals, could be brought into the home.[7] The gravitation of religious art from the sanctity of the cathedral to the secular and personal realm of the home may be understood as a matter of style as well as of religion.

On a qualitative and functional level, style embodied a significant transformation. Previously, dominant imagery had spoken on behalf of the

The continual association between the nobility and God was intrinsic to the feudal hierarchy and the traditions of imagery it generated. In this fifteenth-century manuscript page from the Duke de Berry's *Très Riches Heures,* that association is still clearly drawn. While the one hundred forty-sixth psalm (illuminated in gold) intones that the afflicted should "Put not your trust in princes," the illustrator dressed David's piety in the medieval vestments of nobility.

hierarchic world view of feudalism. It was a representation of a worldly, and presumably heavenly, chain of being. Even the clothing of nobility and clergy belonged more to an office than to a person. It represented a certain station in the broad range of fixed stations that encompassed the whole of humanity.

With the bourgeois market in style, however, images became—more and more—marks of individual, autonomous achievement. They became property, possessions, things that reflected upon the person who owned them, more than on the intricate web of obligation and power that constituted society. Where images and things had once connoted one's place within an immutable network of social relations, they were now emerging as a form of social currency in an increasingly mobile commercial world.

When the burghers of the late Middle Ages decked themselves with the veil of aristocratic style, they established a pattern that would advance over the centuries to follow. The installation of style as a device by which people sought to strengthen an unsure footing in the world was a decidedly modern evolution, one which in the twentieth century is easily recognized. Yet despite this familiarity, the style of these merchants was in significant ways different from the scope or texture of style that we experience today.

One of the most dramatic differences was in access. In the contemporary world the sirens of style are far reaching; their song touches nearly every imaginable commodity; they are regularly employed by people as part of an idiom of everyday life. During the formative period of a money economy, however, style was still a province of elites. It was a conceit of those relatively few merchants whose expanding wealth allowed them to obtain the iconography of prestige. For the overwhelming majority, peasant life and poverty set the boundaries of existence. Even with the growth of cities, most townspeople lived in squalor. In a hand-to-mouth world, material goods were scarce; they were simple vernacular products, made from readily available resources, and crafted at home.

Inseparable from the question of access to style lay that of production. Today's style market is geared to the rhythms of mass production, inextricably linked to the proliferation and promotion of standardized goods. Before the nineteenth century, such a connection would have been unimaginable. Style was defined by elegant handicrafts, each produced individually, from conception to completion. To be a person of style—aristocrat or bourgeois—implied the ability to pay for and command the patient skills of artisans in the satisfaction of one's desires.

By the seventeenth century, a market in style had become a fixture of European elite culture. In the reign of Louis XIV, the monarchy struck a deal with mercantile capitalism, establishing France's supreme position as a marketer of style. The king's principal financial advisor was Jean Baptiste Colbert, the son of a cloth merchant from Reims. Colbert stitched his merchant roots to the splendor of the court and "gathered together all the plans and expedients of his predecessors for a prolonged attempt at establishing an entirely self-sufficing national economy." At the heart of this enterprise lay Colbert's ingenious strategy for French economic development. "With our taste," he declared, "let us make war on Europe, and through fashion conquer the world."[8] Central to his notion of taste was the promotion of the French style industries, industries marked by an ability to construct and communicate an aristocratic veneer. Since that time the predominance of French *haute couture* has been legendary. As illustrated by the case of Colbert in the court of Louis XIV, the "skinning" of the aristocratic world was, ironically, achieved by the very force that was—in the long run—undermining its historic dominion: an advancing, mobile market economy.

To a large extent, Colbert's innovations represented a culmination more than a beginning. The ability to coordinate luxury markets was predicated on the already established presence of such markets in French society and elsewhere. By the sixteenth century, Western European markets were filled with refined and delicate goods: silk and woolen cloth, fine pottery, spices, rare woods for inlaying furniture. These and other items contributed to an increasingly affluent life-style for those capable of purchasing it.

The variety of goods that poured into Western European markets, and which increasingly defined European standards of luxury, were dependent—to a large degree—on the development of European expansion into resource-rich areas of the world. The rise of European colonialism, and the establishment of plantation slavery in the Americas, made certain key luxury items increasingly available to an enlarged, status-conscious market of *nouveau riche* consumers. The growth of international shipping, and the "precocious industrialism" of slavery, as anthropologist Sidney Mintz has characterized it, made the importation and mass production of former rarities more and more possible. The world was yielding an ever-widening variety of skins, multiplying the variety of styles to be consumed.

Among the extravagances of royalty that began to enter the marketplace were items which, at first, may appear to have little to do with style: tea, coffee, cocoa, tobacco, and sugar. An examination of the last of these, however, illuminates the significance of colonialism and slavery in an emerging bourgeois style market.

Before the fourteenth century, sugar had been a substance of unimaginable rarity. Coming from the Middle East, as a spoil of the Crusades, it entered the lives of nobility in small and treasured parcels; its consumption was an unmistakable mark of exclusivity. By the sixteenth century, however, sweets were crossing the boundaries of bourgeois life, seducing the senses and affirming the social position of mercantile wealth. The sugar plantations of the Caribbean were adding refinement to the lives of an expanding middle class. Just as feudal aristocrats had placed sugar trinkets on their tables as symbols of their power, now wealthy commoners decorated their dinner tables with "subtleties" made of sugar:

> While kings and archbishops were displaying magnificent sugar castles and mounted knights, the aspiring upper classes began to combine "course paste" men-of-war with marzipan guns to achieve analogous social effects at their festive tables. Some of these people were probably only newly ennobled; others were prosperous merchants or gentry.[9]

By the eighteenth century, the "transformation of regal subtleties into bourgeois entertainments" was relatively complete, revealing the curious capacity of style to serve as a mark of privilege and a device of democratization simultaneously. Sugar had become an entrenched middle-class habit. Britons prided themselves in their daily, afternoon dose of stimulants (tea) and sugar. Confectionery cookbooks appeared, offering recipes that exploited the display possibilities of sugar. The elaborately decorated wedding cake had become institutionalized in bourgeois custom; a multitiered monument to middle-class prosperity had been erected.[10]

THE TRIUMPH
OF THE SUPERFICIAL

By the beginning of the nineteenth century, with the rise of factory production, the ability to standardize goods found an ever-widening sweep of applications. The era of merchant capitalism was giving way to that of industrial capitalism.

The mechanical reproduction of styled goods, previously possessions of extreme wealth, signaled the beginnings of a mass market in style. The possibility of what Warren Susman has termed a "culture of abundance" was rearing its head. This development constituted the flowering of a provocative, if somewhat passive, definition of *democracy.* The revolutionary conception of democracy that had flourished during the eighteenth century had been predicated on the notion of an active citizenry, shaping their world for the common good, rejecting the symbols and prerogatives of elite power in favor of social equality and natural rights. The new *consumer democracy,* which was propelled by the mass production and marketing of stylish goods, was founded on the idea that symbols and prerogatives of elites could now be made available on a mass scale. The values of elite culture were simultaneously upheld and undermined by this peculiar variant of democracy.

The impact of industrialism on the character and scale of the style market was prodigious. Industries previously characterized by artisanal handcrafts, and by a relative scarcity of output, were now able to turn out enormous quantities of goods. Elegantly worked surfaces, once the product of slow and deliberate skill, were now the product of high-speed, less-skilled, factory processes.

Using the methods of mechanical production, factories applied stamping, pressing, embossing, and other methods to leave the look of hand-working on the surfaces of their goods. The historian of architecture and design Siegfried Giedion reminds us that "pressing, stamping, casting result in standardization and, closely connected therewith, the interchangeability of parts," yet the surfaces of many of these early products did everything they could to deny their industrial origin.[11]

In Europe, and in the United States as well, a widening middle class was able to purchase mass-produced imitations of aristocratic style. "Pressed glass" bric-a-brac had the semblance of cut-glass patterns molded onto its surface; "profile cutting lathes" and "stenciled painting" gave mass-produced furniture the suggestion of fine hand-carving.[12] Clocks, once the extravagantly tooled possessions of the few who could afford to own them, were mass produced by the early decades of the nineteenth century. For the members of an expanding middle class, the historically coded look of wealth was coming within their means.

This trend toward embossed ornamentation gave mass-produced style a powerful appeal, one that continues to beckon. By the 1830s, according to the historian of industrial design Arthur J. Pulos, "the application of art and style" to the surfaces of manufactured goods had become "important to their marketing." Before the nineteenth century the term *design* had referred to the planning of a product from its inception: laying out of patterns, choosing materials, constructing, correlating the object's contours to its eventual function, and the application of ornamentation. By the 1830s, the term *design* was assuming a modern definition, describing the superficial application of decoration to the form and surface of a product. The notion of decoration was becoming more and more distinct from the overall plan of production.

This separation of form from substance became a characteristic paradox of nineteenth-century industrialism. By the latter half of the century, the notion of design as the application of a mystifying mask had become established as a principle of the age. The Viennese historian and cabaret entertainer Egon Friedell defined the ruling ethic of the period, and of the twentieth century as well, as a "delight in the unreal." In a broad panorama of the late nineteenth-century style market, Friedell offers a vivid, if chaotic, characterization of this "delight":

Every material used tries to look like more than it is. It is the era of a universal and deliberate swindling in the use of materials. Whitewashed tin masquerades as marble, papier mache as rosewood, plaster as gleaming alabaster, glass as costly onyx. The exotic palm in the bay window is impregnated or made of paper, the tempting fruit in the epergne is of wax or soap. The rose shaded lamp over the bed is just as much a "property" as the cosy log fire in the grate: neither is ever used. On the other hand, the illusion of a roaring fire is intensified by the use of red tinfoil. The sideboard boasts copper vessels, never used for cooking, and mighty pewter mugs out of which no one drinks. On the wall hang defiant swords, never crossed, and proud hunting trophies never won. Should, however, any utensil serve a particular purpose, this must in no case be obvious from its shape. A magnificent Gutenberg Bible is discovered to be a work-box, and a carved cupboard an orchestrion. The butter knife is a Turkish dagger, the ashtray a Prussian helmet, the umbrella-stand a knight in armour, and the thermometer, a pistol. The barometer takes the form of a bass-viol, the bootjack of a stag-beetle, the spittoon of a tortoise-shell, the cigar-cutter of the Eiffel Tower. The beer-jug is a monk, made to open, who is guillotined at every gulp; the clock is an instructive model of an express engine. . . . [13]

Architecture was deeply affected by the separation of surface and substance. Up until the nineteenth century, formal architecture made regular use of "load-bearing walls," walls that—in addition to any decorative motif they might have—provided the support system of the building, held the building up. Even though it was common to apply neoclassical or other facades to brick wall surfaces throughout the eighteenth century, walls served an important structural function. In designing them, an architect had to combine purposes of engineering and ornamentation simultaneously. Even when ornate facades were used to cover a wall surface, they required the time-consuming skills of stone cutters to produce. There was a connection, a symbiosis, between the intricacy of the image and the method of craft being used to fashion that image.[14]

By the 1830s and 1840s, however, these interconnections between image, structure, and method of construction were, in large degree, severed. "Modern" methods of construction, employing an inner structural frame that held the building up, began to be used more and more frequently. Developed in the United States in the 1830s, these new kinds of buildings originally had wooden "balloon frame" structures which were then covered with a "skin." By the 1840s, the balloon frame construction of buildings became a standard approach to industrial architecture, as wood was replaced by iron in the infrastructure.

Central to this new approach to construction was the fact that walls no longer played a structural role. They became decorative "curtains," to be hung and attached onto the structural frame. As walls lost structural significance, however, their ornamental aspect escalated. Like the household objects that transmitted a cacophony of appearances in this era of the "unreal," external wall panels were also being stamped out in a multiplicity of often discordant styles. With the development of industrially manufactured cast-iron panels, embossed to suggest the look of other places and times, the disembodied skin became a regular feature of modern architecture.

With the rise of the balloon frame and the curtain wall, the enterprises of the engineer and architect became increasingly separate, often at odds with one another. While the engineer's task was one of making a building structurally sound, the architect was becoming what one industrial designer has called a "merchant of whimsy."[15] The eclectic and pretentious quality of much nineteenth-century architecture betrays this commitment to surface as an end in and of itself. In Chicago, often considered the birthplace of modern architecture, cast-iron building fronts, molded to look like various historical styles, were the vogue between 1855 and 1870. After this period, other materials were used. In each case, however, there was an intrinsic tension between the *look* of a building—which attempted to reproduce a style originally achieved by the chisel of a preindustrial craftsman—and a method of construction which was only hastening the degradation or annihilation of the decorative crafts.

Style in architecture was becoming a matter of pure appearance. Substantive issues were more and more inconsequential. There was an all-consuming effort to capture the multifarious auras of elegant grandeur, and to employ those auras to construct a veneer of cultivation. The Renaissance was there for the taking; other ostentatious motifs multiplied as well. Romanesque, Rococo, Baroque, Italianate, each provided a florid shell, an eye-catching alternative reality.

Nowhere did the triumph of the superficial leave its mark more powerfully than at the Columbian Exposition of 1893. Held in Chicago, as a tribute to the vigor of American industrialism, the fair constituted an orgy of facade. Even promotional literature for the exposition noted the ironic tension between the fair's neoclassical official image and the context of the American Midwest: "How sweet it is to think that great things and great thoughts cannot die; that out of the raw young life of the prairies should spring this lovely bit of Grecian genius."[16] The entire fair was a flimsily constructed masquerade. Iron frameworks were covered by iron and wood sheets. Facades were then applied, molded out of staff, a concoction of cement, plaster, and jute fibers.

If the substance of the fair's construction was uniform and cheap, its surfaces recalled a precious symphony of styles. The "White City," the focal point of the fair, was a tribute to the Renaissance.

The Midway of the fair, on the other hand, appropriated a wide and

The separation of form from substance is particularly evident in this (circa 1900) photograph (*top*) of a street of New York row houses. From the street, each house is a unique tribute to a different historical period and source. From the side, as is evident in the picture, we see that these architectural motifs are simply an overlay to a shared structure. Recently some postmodern architects have turned the concept of the facade into an explicit architectural element, a humorous visual commentary. This is apparent in the "peeling front" showroom (*bottom*), designed for Best Stores by SITE architects.

diverse world of imageries, placing the triumph of American industrialism at the center of a global context:

> The Midway in effect formed a colossal sideshow, with restaurants, shops, exhibits, and theaters extending down a huge corridor, six hundred feet wide and a mile long. . . . Here the Beaux-Arts neo-classicism of the Court of Honor [the White City] gave way to Barnumesque eclecticism, refined order to exuberant chaos. Fairgoers threaded their way on foot, or in hired chairs among a hurly-burly of exotic attractions: mosques and pagodas, Viennese Streets and Turkish bazaars, South Sea Island huts, Irish and German castles, and Indian tepees.[17]

The entire world, in its various visual incarnations, was there for the taking. What Oliver Wendell Holmes had seen as the intrinsic outcome of photographic technique had been elevated to the level of a social principle.

A trade in stylishly emblazoned surfaces had been established as a cardinal component of an American consumer society in formation. The rapidly expanding inventory of industrially produced goods was being routinely camouflaged by a suggestive aesthetic veil. The interior life of nineteenth-century industry was marked by low wages, long hours, and severe standards of discipline; meanwhile the outer face of industrial society was developing an ingenious ability to stamp an alternative way of seeing—one that evoked a sense of abundance—across its visible exterior.

PICTURES OF REFINEMENT

The implementation of mass-produced style was not limited to the surfaces of material goods or monumental environments. The "delight in the unreal" found one of its most seductive arenas of expression in association with new techniques of visual representation. In a society that was reaching new levels of appreciation for the ephemeral power of images, the simultaneous developments of chromolithography and photography opened up astonishing new avenues of mass impression.

Propelled by the development of cheap yet dazzling color dyes, and by printing techniques brought to the United States by immigrant German and Russian printers, the proliferation of chromolithographs, from the 1840s onward, reached across the barriers of caste and class. Within the framework of pre-nineteenth-century life, oil paintings, like luxurious clothing or objects, were designations of status. Their absence from the lives of common people were part of the fact of class, as was their presence in the homes of those who displayed them as property.

Access to the sumptuous image was limited to those few able to enjoy what John Berger has called the "special relation between oil painting and property" that has endured for hundreds of years.[18]

Although original oil paintings continue, even today, as emblems and possessions of wealth, chromolithography was able to capture some of their luster, depth, and richness of color. Many chromolithographs were brilliant reproductions of paintings previously unknown and unseen by their now democratized audience. Chromos transported the visual trappings of *high* art into that democratized, emerging consumer marketplace. Late nineteenth-century advertising and packaging made continual use of chromolithography. Packages of cigarettes, soap, flour—the stuff of daily life—were covered with alluring images ranging from sultry women to gorgeous depictions of nature, town life, royalty, and historical settings. The world of products was now initiating a highly visible and relatively inexpensive appeal to the popular imagination. Superficially ornate goods were linked to broadly disseminated images, creating an interwoven fabric of mass-produced style.

As style reached out to a more broadly defined "middle class" of consumers, the *value* of objects was less and less associated with workmanship, material quality, and rarity, and more and more derived from the abstract and increasingly malleable factor of aesthetic appeal. Durable signs of style were being displaced by signs that were ephemeral: shoddy goods with elaborately embossed surfaces, advertising cards, product labels. If style had once been a device by which individuals tried to surround themselves with symbols of perpetuity, now it was becoming something of the moment, to be employed for effect, and then displaced by a new device of impression.

This ephemerality finds no better example than in the fad for disposable paper products that developed in the United States during the 1870s. Chromo technology was used to imprint dazzling, luxuriant looks upon disposable paper goods. Paper "waistcoats, bonnets, aprons, hats, tapestries, curtains, carpets," all items which in their original form represented delicate and time-consuming craft, were now mere visual gestures toward craft, to be used, and then thrown away.[19]

The symbolic province of elegance had been democratized. Colorful art had been the customary privilege of the rich; now the dissemination of chromos began, on a symbolic level, to break the monopoly of possession. Only the quality suffered. The market in chromolithographs spread rapidly. They were merchandised by mail, distributed door to door, used by advertisers, and offered as premiums. They could be purchased in galleries as well. Amid the gray tonalities of industrial life, chromos appeared as a tangible rupture in the customary, exclusive privileges of the upper class. Chromos were a dramatic enactment of democracy, albeit a democracy of images. Their dissemination broke through the symbolic boundaries of an old and restrictive order, and at the same time paid homage to the cultural property and traditions of that order.

More than any nineteenth-century development, perhaps, the rise of photography amplified the power of image over substance as an earmark of modern style. Developed in France, already noted for its market in luxuries, photography became—almost immediately—a prime medium of pretension.

Before photography, portraiture had been linked to the traditions of easel painting. A portrait was an acknowledged possession of wealth. Men would have themselves, their families, occasionally their mistresses, and their property painted as a tribute to their own existence, as a visualization of the riches at their command. Just as owning certain kinds of objects was understood as a mark of personhood, a portrait was a sign of social franchise. With the birth of photography, during a period in which style was beginning to be industrially mass produced, portraiture boomed. Portrait studios flourished from the 1840s onward, in the United States, as more and more people sought to acquire the emblems of station. Miniature portraits, known as "tin-types," were sold at these studios for a mere two cents. Holmes, writing in 1863, remarked on the new, democratic potential implicit in photographic portraiture:

> Prices have . . . come down to such a point that pauperism itself need hardly shrink from the outlay required for a family portrait-gallery. . . . A portrait such as Isabey could not paint for a Marshal of France—a likeness such as Malbone could not make of a President's Lady, to be had for two coppers—a dozen *chefs d'oeuvre* for a quarter of a dollar![20]

Studios were fitted with props to invest the people being photographed with the accoutrements of wealth and status. Customers would have themselves photographed in fine clothing (often provided by the studio), against elegant surroundings (a painted, theatrical backdrop). When the portrait was ready, and mounted in an ornately embossed pasteboard frame or album, people would bring home a bona fide testament to their eminence, regardless of circumstances. The portrait, as composed by the photographer and packaged in an ornamental frame, suggested a connection to the traditions of handcraft and high art. Actually, such portraits were products of large-scale enterprises which often employed a sophisticated, industrial division of labor.

This tension between image and reality is evident in Holmes's description of a visit to one of New York's largest portrait mills, the Broadway studio of Messrs. E. and H. T. Anthony. The account discusses the manufacture of products for the packaging of photographs, in a large, steam-powered plant:

> The luxurious album, embossed, clasped, gilded, resplendent as a tropical butterfly, goes through as many transformations as a "purple emperor." It begins a pasteboard larva, is swatched and pressed and glued into the tradition of a chrysalis, and at last alights on the center table gorgeous in gold and velvet, the perfect imago.
>
> Each single process in the manufacture of elaborate products of skill oftentimes seems and is very simple. The workmen in large establishments, where labor is greatly subdivided, become wonderfully adroit in doing a fraction of something. . . . A young person who mounts photographs on cards all day long confessed to having never, or almost never, seen a negative developed, though standing at the time within a few feet of the dark closet where the process was going on all day long.[21]

Everything about the look of the product was at odds with the material process of its production. This general pattern was coming to characterize much in the way of industrially produced style, but it was perhaps most fitting in the realm of photography, where the ability to exaggerate experience, to create believable imagistic fictions, stood at the heart of its power to depict and transmit style.

CHAPTER THREE

The
Marriage Between
Art and Commerce

I

INTEGRATED VISIONS

n the United States, and throughout much of industrialized Europe, the years between 1890 and the 1920s saw qualitative changes in the organization of industries and in methods of production. Industrial corporations grew into giant enterprises, implementing an increasingly mechanized system of mass production.

In the midst of these changes, culture itself was undergoing a fateful transition. If *culture* can be understood as the accumulated stock of understandings and practices by which a given people live and maintain themselves in a given society, the industrialization of daily life may be said to have, in large measure, displaced the customary fabric of culture. Increasingly, resources of survival were being produced by modern systems of mass manufacture. As this mode of production demanded broadened national or international markets, corporations made expanded use of advertising, among other merchandising techniques. Advertising not only sought to inform people about the availability and appeal of industrially produced goods, it also contributed to a restructured perception of the resources and alternatives that were available to people in their everyday lives.

Partly as a response to unprecedented marketing needs; partly to establish a uniform and easily recognizable corporate identity; partly in response to avant-garde tendencies in the arts, giant industrial corporations began to develop multipurpose styling divisions in the first decades of the twentieth century. A pioneer in this development was Walter Rathenau, head of Allgemeine Elektricitäts-Gesellschaft (AEG), the huge German electric company that had been founded (as Deutsche Edison Gesellschaft) by his father, Emil, in 1883.

By 1907 AEG had become one of Europe's great industrial corporations. It "had a capital value exceeding 100 million marks and employed some 70,000 people. Its sales catalogs listed hundreds of different products."[1] Rathenau, according to his friend Franz Blei, was a man possessed and disturbed by the chaotic social world that had emerged alongside the apparatus of corporate industrialism. Rathenau held the "passionate conviction that spiritual content and form could be given to the chaotic and inert body of trade and industry."[2]

For Rathenau, it was necessary to invent a new definition and application of style, one not rooted in the past, but derived from "the techniques of mass production and . . . the widespread dissemination of industrial products." What made Rathenau unique was his implementation of this idea within the bureaucratic structure of a modern corporation. Believing that a new style, an industrial aesthetic, could be a "means of alleviating the devastation that industrialization had wrought on such basic areas as labor, production, housing, and human relations," Rathenau commissioned Peter Behrens, an architect and designer, to create a uniform corporate *look* for the AEG. Behrens's assignment was "to redesign the company's buildings, products, and publicity material," from a huge "turbine hall down to tiny publicity seals."[3] Between 1907 and 1914, Behrens created what he called an "artistic context," designed to encompass all elements of the corporation. This was the beginning of the consciously promulgated "corporate image," a uniform reminder that in a world of the ephemeral, the corporation is a constant.

In the nineteenth century, an indiscriminate reverence for the grandiosities of the past had given rise to a shoddy imagistic chaos. By the early twentieth century, the industrial exigencies of coordination, standardization, and control were beginning to find aesthetic expression, part of a move toward more coherent corporate design strategies. Behrens's work at AEG created the prototype for industrial design departments to come. He understood that design could not be limited to a particular building or commodity. In order for design to project a new "spiritual content," it was necessary to erect an imagistic panorama: a new symbolic totality, constituted by an interconnected, cross-referenced, visible world.

This integrated vision was remarkably inclusive in its application.

Behrens designed lamps, table fans, humidifiers, motors, dental drills, light switches, clocks, electric kettles, electric heaters, and numerous other products. His designs also shaped the factories in which these products were manufactured, the exhibition pavilions in which they were displayed, and the advertisements by which they were promoted. In each case, Behrens's designs were infused with the look of the "modern." Clean lines and a strictly regulated geometry replaced the encrusted ornamentation that had marked many industrial products to that time. Where ornament did appear, it was spare and understated, its links with the past for the most part severed.

CONSUMER
ENGINEERING

In the United States, during the years that Behrens worked at AEG, the instrumental use of style as a business device was also gaining adherents and practitioners. Speaking to the Chicago Commercial Club in 1907, Daniel H. Burnham, the architect and chief designer of the Columbian Exposition, asserted an intimate and important link between style and profitability. "Beauty," he advised his audience, "has always paid better than any other commodity, and always will."[4] By 1915, the marriage between business planning and aesthetics had already shaped the visible aspect of commerce.

One of the most ubiquitous examples of this development was advertising. Writing in 1914, Walter Lippmann commented upon the flowering of advertising as a sign that businessmen were attempting to "take charge of consumption as well as production." Inextricably linked to the development of consciously styled products, advertising projected images of these products, and of the "happy" consumers who purchased them, across the horizons of everyday life. A seductive, imagistic panorama had been installed above the American landscape:

> The eastern sky [is] ablaze with chewing gum, the northern with toothbrushes and underwear, the western with whiskey, and the southern with petticoats, the whole heavens . . . [are] brilliant with monstrously flirtatious women, . . . When you glance at magazines . . . [a] rivulet of text trickles through the meadows of automobiles, baking powders, corsets and kodaks.[5]

Business was coming to embrace advertising as the "ignition system of the economy, the dynamo of mass dissatisfaction and the creator of illusions in a most materialistic world."[6] Advertising was becoming es-

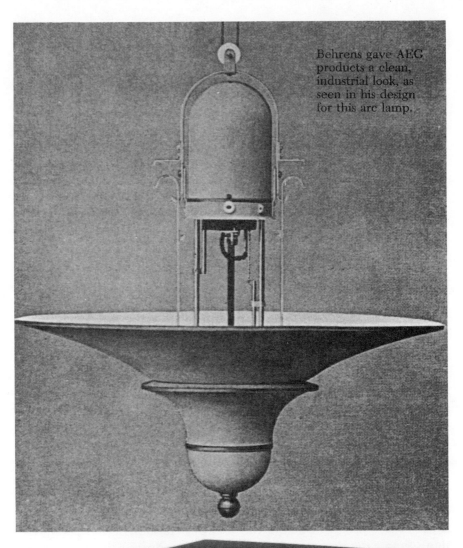

Behrens gave AEG
products a clean,
industrial look, as
seen in his design
for this arc lamp.

The influence of
consumer engineering
can be seen in this 1936 radio,
designed by Walter Dorwin Teague.

tablished as what C. Wright Mills once called "the prime means of acclaim."[7]

From the 1920s onward, advertising agencies broadened their field of action, organizing multifaceted merchandising campaigns for clients. A central figure in the development of this coordinated image-management was Earnest Elmo Calkins, of the Calkins & Holden advertising agency. Calkins intuited that the success of merchandising depended on the ability to construct an unbroken, imagistic corridor between the product being sold and the consciousness (and unconsciousness) of the consumer. Following this logic, Calkins created an agency that linked a diverse but interrelated range of "creative services," including product design, packaging, aesthetic counseling, and, of course, advertising. Calkins assembled an extraordinarily talented and innovative staff, including Egmont Arens, a leading product and package designer, and Walter Dorwin Teague, who, along with a few others, would become one of the most influential industrial designers from the 1930s on. While at Calkins & Holden, between 1929 and 1933, Arens coined the phrase "consumer engineering" to describe what was entailed in a complex, coordinated merchandising effort.

Central to consumer engineering was the notion that style, or, as Calkins called it, "beauty," was the "new business tool," whose intelligent use could generate sales and profits. Following in a path laid by Walter Rathenau and Peter Behrens at AEG, Calkins delineated many of his ideas in "Beauty The New Business Tool," published in *The Atlantic Monthly* in 1927. In the article, Calkins offered a historical account of the systematic integration of business and aesthetics. In the early days of industrialism, he noted, the use of beauty was piecemeal, or disregarded as an economic factor. Where goods were decorative they lacked "integrity"; they celebrated the values of another time, while ignoring the signals of the machine age. Calkins himself was enamored with modern art—"the new art," he called it—and he believed that even more than realism, this art contained enormous powers of "suggestion." Advertising artists, influenced by these modern artistic developments, pioneered in the transformation and aestheticization of business. The youthful advertising industry, Calkins argued, "seized upon the power of the artist to say things which could not be said in words, and thus a large group of men trained in artistic standards was brought to work in close conjunction with factories producing goods." This mixture left its mark across the wide tableau of American commercial life.

The first step toward making the advertising attractive was to make the goods attractive. It was frequently necessary to introduce the article sold into the advertisement, or at least its package, and most products and packages were so ugly or so commonplace *they spoiled the picture; and thus began that steady, unremitting pressure on the manufacturer to make his goods or packages worthy of being placed in an artistic setting.* Bales and boxes and cans and wrappers and labels and trade-marks were revised and redesigned.[8]

The first merchandise to be affected by these make-overs were fashion goods and cosmetics. Then, General Motors (GM) began to implement general design strategies in the production of automobiles, leading to the development of the GM "Styling Section," under the directorship of Harley Earl. General Electric coordinated the design of their image and products as well. Phonographs and radios, two important fixtures in the new way of life that was emerging, were also seductively styled. Moving beyond product design and labeling, advertising now entered the realm of retail environments:

> These better designed goods and packages demanded a better environment in which to be sold, and thus we have a revolution in the furnishing of shops and stores. The old-fashioned store was a stereotype—a long, narrow room with two windows and a door in front and in back, counters down the full length on both sides. . . . Today the store has given way to the shop* . . . The shop front, the tinting of the walls, the furniture, the arrangement of goods—everything has been transformed. . . . Everything is done to create a setting for the new style of goods. You see this in every industry.[9]

Continuing his rhapsody on a totally administered environment, Calkins discussed the innovative uses of color and light in the creation of a sensuous commercial atmosphere. Behind all of these stylistic metamorphoses lay the bottom line: *sales.* "Beauty is introduced into material objects," he explained, "to enhance them in the eyes of the purchaser. The appeal of efficiency alone is nearly ended. Beauty is the natural and logical next step. It is in the air."[10]

Ultimately, Calkins's approach was not one of combining efficiency and aesthetics. A product's efficiency, its durability, was, for Calkins, a stumbling block to sales. Beauty, according to Calkins, would allow for the undermining of the efficiency factor, stimulating compulsive consumption. He wrote that "this new influence on articles of barter and sale is largely used to make people dissatisfied with what they have of

*The term *store* connotes a place where goods are simply stored; the arrival of the term *shop* implies an increased focus on the act of consumption.

the old order, still good and useful and efficient, but lacking in the newest touch. In the expressive slang of the day . . . [these goods] 'date.' "[11]

By the end of the 1920s, the stylization of the marketplace was in full swing. It had influenced goods, packages, retail establishments, advertisements. It had also affected the orientation of the popular mass media. Previously, style had been a concern in publications geared toward a primarily wealthy audience; the 1920s witnessed the flowering of style in magazines aimed at a mass market. Robert S. Lynd, the sociologist, noted that the "increased emphasis on style was encouraged by advertising and editorial content in periodicals and newspapers" of the 1920s. He continued,

> The *Ladies' Home Journal,* for example, after devoting but 16% of its non-fiction editorial content to fashion in 1918 and 1920, raised this to 28% in 1921 and to 30 in 1922–23, while popular magazines have increasingly taken over high style artists formerly used only by exclusive style journals such as *Vogue* and *Harper's Bazaar.* [12]

The play of surfaces was becoming a deliberate and decisive component of consumer merchandising, and a more general obsession of the consumer culture. Seventy years before Calkins's "Beauty The New Business Tool" appeared in *The Atlantic,* Oliver Wendell Holmes had predicted that the ephemeral surface would soon overwhelm the objective world in the pages of the same magazine. Holmes's vision had been prophetic. Vast new industries were now engaged in the process and business of generating evanescent meanings. This turn of events was not unnoticed by Egon Friedell, writing in Vienna in 1931. "There are no realities anymore," he lamented. "There is only apparatus. . . . *Neither are there goods any more, but only advertisements:* the most valuable article is the one most effectively lauded, the one that the most capital has gone to advertise. We call all this," he added, "Americanism."[13]

IMAGE AND DESIRE

In service of the emerging apparatus of representation, many corporations simultaneously employed a social scientific apparatus; for monitoring and analyzing mass psychology; for studying—among other things— the impact of images on the mind of the consumer. "Understanding the consumer's mind," wrote ad man Harry Dexter Kitson in 1923, comes

Overt appeals to erotic desire may appear anywhere, be attached to anything.

This subway poster for Chardón Jeans contains subliminal sexual promises. The first promise is contained in the product's name. New York graffiti writers picked up on this, and regularly painted out the first letter of Chardón, transforming it into a common euphemism for a male erection. The second suggestion can be found in the woman's face. Do you see it? Look carefully at the lower half of her face. See page 51 for the answer to this puzzle. . . .

down to the question of appealing to and enhancing desire. To do this, he proposed, it is necessary to create a context in which "pictures are painted before the consumer's imagination representing the pleasurable aspects of possession of the commodity."[14]

Such strategic thinking, however, went beyond making rational appeals to the consumer's desire for pleasure. Styling, it was increasingly argued, must speak to the unconscious, to those primal urges and sensations that are repressed in the everyday confines of civilization. Like art, psychoanalysis was being evaluated as a "new business tool." Roy Sheldon, who along with Egmont Arens wrote the definitive guide *Consumer Engineering* (1932), spoke of the "astonishing fruits" being borne by the work of Freud, Jung, Alfred Adler, Pavlov, and others. These pioneers in the areas of psychoanalysis and behavioral psychology, they asserted, were providing business with tools that could be used to its "active advantage."

An example of this approach is seen in Sheldon and Arens's instrumental discussion of the *sense of touch* which, along with smell, was the least acknowledged and most repressed of the senses in modern Western civilization. Taking cues from Freud's ruminations on "civilization and its discontents," they outlined a technique for product merchandising:

> If it is true that the exigencies of civilization have driven it [the sense of touch] below the surface, it persists in the unconscious mind as a powerful motivating force. Every day the average person makes hundreds of judgements in which the sense of touch casts the deciding vote, whether or not it rises into the consciousness. . . . undercover decisions [are] made by this sense. Such simple judgements as the acceptance or rejection of a towel, washrag, hairbrush, underwear, stockings, hinge upon how these things feel in the hands; their acceptance or rejection is motivated by the unconscious.[15]

Given this reality, they maintained, the study of human sensory systems and the integration of this study with merchandising practice was essential. Designs should be executed with an appeal to tactile senses. On some level, Sheldon and Arens saw style as a symbolic return of the repressed, offering consumers a subliminal promise of polymorphous gratification. Rather than verbal appeals in advertising, they were proposing a depth-psychological strategy, one that would promote "the exploitation of the 'sublimated sense' in the field of product design":

> Manufacturing an object that delights this [tactile] sense is something that you do but don't talk about. Almost everything which is bought is han-

dled. After the eye, the hand is the first censor to pass on acceptance, and if the hand's judgement is unfavorable, the most attractive object will not gain the popularity it deserves. On the other hand, merchandise designed to be pleasing to the hand wins an approval that may never register in the mind, but which will determine additional purchases. . . . *Make it snuggle in the palm.*[16]

By the 1930s, such approaches to emotion, desire, and the unconscious had become part of the jargon of the style industries. Harold Van Doren, a major industrial designer of the period, noted that "design is fundamentally the art of using lines, forms, tones, colors and textures to arouse an emotional reaction in the beholder."[17] The very meaning of aesthetics was changing. Once the study of beauty and its universal appeal, it was becoming, within the style industries, a study of art insofar as it could provoke and promote consumer response. At a time when the idea of "art for art's sake" was taking hold as a dominant faith among art critics, *art for control's sake* was becoming the dominant practice in the marketplace.

Jean Abel, of the Pasadena Architects School of Arts, wrote of the ideas of "simplification and control" as the paramount concepts governing "modern design." To Abel, designs should be accessible to as many people as possible and should be executed—deliberately—with specific responses in mind. To do this, designers needed to understand that design "speaks a scientific language, with universal laws and principles, governing elements." An effective use of this semiological "language," Abel insisted, could help artists and their employers achieve the "conscious control of ideas":

> The design of today is dynamic. In diagonal lines it moves with the speed and precision of the airplane. In geometric forms, it presents the cold calculating power of the adding machine. In color, it suffocates, chills, shocks or soothes through choices and combinations of hues, values and intensities. It invents strange realms, insane with distortion; or creates new worlds, ideal with release into new spaces, *hence the need of control.*[18]

Not all designers employed such a scientific (psychological or semiotic) approach; many worked more intuitively. From the 1930s onward, however, major figures in industrial design had internalized such instrumental thinking into their work. For Harold Van Doren, the role of the industrial designer was "to interpret the function of useful things in terms of appeal to the eye; to endow them with beauty of form and color; above all to create in the consumer the desire to possess."[19] For J. Gordon Lippincott, another designer, "the appearance of a product" had become "an integral feature in its success or failure" as "the industrial designer . . . seeks to imbue the consumer with the desire of ownership."[20] Raymond Loewy put it more concisely. Industrial design was "the shaping of everyday life with the marketplace in mind."[21]

In the commercial world of style, the fundamental assumption underlying the "shaping of everyday life" is that life must visibly change, every day. Roland Barthes called this phenomenon *neomania,* a madness for perpetual novelty where "the new" has become defined strictly as a "purchased value," something to buy.[22] What will appear next is not always predictable. That *something new* will appear is entirely predictable. "Style obsolescence," reported a major industrial design firm in 1960, "is the *sine qua non* of product success."[23]

In the 1930s, with the consumer economy in serious straits, styling and "style obsolescence" came to the forefront as methods designed to stimulate markets, and to keep them stimulated. Roy Sheldon and Egmont Arens counseled that "styles wear out faster than gears," and encouraged industry to utilize style to motivate purchases.[24] Earnest Calkins concurred, and suggested that even durable goods must be reconceptualized, and sold as if they were nondurables:

> Goods fall into two classes, those we use, such as motor-cars or safety razors, and those we use *up,* such as toothpaste or soda biscuit. Consumer engineering must see to it that we use *up* the kind of goods we now

When the woman's eyes are masked, a second face appears. This second woman is performing fellatio on the man whose body is being embraced.

Archie Bishop

merely use. Would any change in the goods or habits of people speed up their consumption? Can they be displaced by newer models: Can artificial obsolescence be created? Consumer engineering does not end until we can consume all we can make.[25]

Such thinking was catalyzed by the collapse of markets during the Depression, and it has persevered as the basic logic of consumer capitalism ever since. Though the long-term ecological implications of this trajectory may be disastrous, from a strictly merchandising point of view, it is *the air we breathe.* Style and changes in style, once part of a privileged competition among merchant princes, have become routine ingredients in almost everybody's lives, from the clothes we wear to our daily gruel. With the institutionalization of "style obsolescence," the perpetual challenge to offer *something new* became a cornerstone of business planning. While corporations, and political institutions, and people of wealth and power employ and project images of stability for themselves, daily life—for most other Americans—carries a visual message of unpredictability and impermanence.

Another of Oliver Wendell Holmes's predictions has come to pass. In 1859 Holmes had written that "every conceivable object" would soon "scale off its surface for us." Like animals in a trophy hunt, all manners of "Nature and Art" would be hunted down "for their skins," with the carcasses left to rot. To a large extent, this describes the practices of the style industries today. In their continual search for ever-evolving novelty, all manners of human expression and creativity are mined for their surfaces: their *look,* their *touch,* their *sound,* their *scent.* This booty is then attached to the logic of the marketplace: mass produced and merchandised. Visions of a preindustrial, more "natural" form of life are appropriated by the corporate food industry. Graffiti artists from the Bronx provide "the look" for Macy's new fall line. The "anti-style" of the punk subculture inspires the layout for a Warner Communications annual report. All faces are seen; few are heard from.

Whatever the "skin," or its vernacular origin, its meaning is most often compromised or lost once it enters the style market. The meaning that *will* remain constant, that *will* be expressed across the shifting tableau of style—regardless of the skins it appropriates—is the continual message of consumption. Art historians speak of *styles*—Gothic, Romanesque, neoclassical, and so on—as coherent embodiments of the epochs that produced them. The facades of style in contemporary culture, however, are ever-changing, often incoherent. It is this volatility that embodies the period we inhabit. Style is something to be *used up.* Part of its significance is that it will lose significance.

Archie Bishop

"Get Used," reads the inscription on the upper right corner of this Times Square billboard. Here it's the graffiti style that is getting *used*—to promote Macy's Fall '87 line.

Here a *campesino,* a poor Mexican farm worker, provides a picturesque backdrop for a fashion display in *TAXI,* a slick fashion magazine. Reduced to a "colorful" prop, his lived experiences become stylistic evocations, eviscerated of meaning.

Photograph by William Garrett

Black dress by Kikit. $140. Available at Bloomingdale's, NYC; Ann Taylor, NYC; Macy's, San Francisco. Kenya bag by Craft Caravan. $12. Available at Craft Caravan Inc., NYC.

2

Image
and Identity

CHAPTER FOUR

Chosen People

It's not what you own, it's what people think you own.

—Company motto of Faux Systems,
makers of the Cellular Phoney,
an imitation car phone that
looks like the real thing

MARKS
OF DISTINCTION

A personalized letter arrives by mail. It has the *feel* of quality, written on heavy-weight, cream-colored, linen stationery, embossed at the top in gold:

Dear Mr. ——:

Because you are a highly valued American Express © Card member, I am inviting you to apply for the Gold Card at this time.

I believe you've earned this invitation. You've worked hard and have been recognized for your efforts. And nothing is more satisfying than achieving your own personal goals.

Now it's time for you to carry the card that symbolizes your achievement—the Gold Card.

Only a select group will ever carry the Gold Card. So it instantly identifies you as someone special—one who expects an added measure of courtesy and personal attention. . . .

The Gold Card says more about you than anything you can buy with it. We think it's time you joined the select group who carry it.

Sincerely, . . .

An accompanying color brochure, adding sumptuous visions to laudatory words, invites Mr. —— to "Come into your element." Opening up the richly coated stock of the brochure, he finds the following scenario:

The close of a fine meal.

The presentation of the bill.

And you take out the Gold Card©.

It is a gesture that speaks volumes.

It says you are someone special—whose style of living requires very special privileges.

Someone whose financial credentials rank among the nation's highest.

Someone who appreciates—indeed, has come to expect—an extra measure of courtesy and personal attention.

In fact, the Gold Card in your name says more about you than almost anything you can buy with it.

American Express "membership" has already placed you above the throng. Now, the gift of Gold will distinguish you even more.

The promise of "unspoken prestige" that runs through this elegant packet of junk mail is one representative specimen of a promise that is repeated endlessly across the landscape of American consumer culture: *You will be seen. You will be noticed. The symbols you display, your most valuable possessions, will permit you to stand apart from the crowd. You will be noteworthy and honored. You will be someone. You will have "joined the select group."* Only the faint remnant of perforations—at the top and bottom edges of the personalized letter—suggests that this promise of individual identity is being made, simultaneously, to a mass of others.

This highly individuated notion of personal distinction—marked by the compulsory consumption of images—stands at the heart of the "American Dream." To a certain extent, this continuous offer of personal distinction may indicate an epic crisis of identity that lurks within the inner lives of many Americans. Nonetheless, the promise is also an essential part of the way of life that is anxiously pursued by people who are now, or wish to become, part of the great American "middle class." This vision of status is offered to us by mail, it is reiterated by advertising; it is fed by the style industries; it is reinforced and mythologized in the publicized biographies—fact or fiction—of "folk heroes" and celebrities. According to the dream, this privileged existence is open to anyone who really wants it. Those who do not believe in the dream, do not deserve it. Those who do believe, but have not yet achieved it, must try harder. The Gold Card, which "says more about you than anything you can buy with it," is but one step in the right direction.

This dream resonates through much of American social history. To a large extent it has left its imprint on the aspirations and discontents of people and cultures around the world. The notion that each individual has fair access to status and recognition, and therefore can escape the anonymity and conditions of the common lot, has shaped the meaning and understanding of American *democracy*.

The conviction that personal status looms as a ready possibility for everyone is a faith that was fueled by nineteenth-century industrialism. The proliferation of styled goods, which crossed into the lives of an increasing number of people, provided a spectacle of upward social mobility. To be sure, dreams of status had motivated merchant princes from the late Middle Ages, but the genesis of a new, mechanized productive apparatus extended the dream far beyond its historic association with economic elites. Now, noted Alexis de Tocqueville in the 1830s, the accoutrements of status were beginning to become available to people "whose desires grow much faster than their fortunes."[1]

In the United States, by the 1830s, even budding cities of the recently settled West boasted an up-and-coming merchant middle class. Historian Edward Pessen notes that these parvenus "went to great pains to match the lavish living of the older upper classes of the eastern cities, succeeding to a large degree." As might be expected, the conspicuous consumption of luxuries provided these people with much desired marks of position: "Many of them lived in 'villas.' Expensive furniture, overloaded tables, fancy dress for dinner, extravagant entertainment, elegant carriages, ornate cotillions led by dancing masters imported from the East, characterized merchant life in the 'frontier towns.' "[2]

Yet it was not merchants alone who were surrounding themselves with the trappings of luxury. A growing market in cheap *luxury* items allowed others to purchase the symbolic accoutrements of status. Historian Alan Dawley writes that in Lynn, Massachusetts, in 1870, there was a class of "white-collar employees who earned only subsistence salaries and who called their condition 'genteel poverty.' " Though their holdings were small, their vocations and their sense of "pride lay in the prestige of being close to the social elite." These people lived close to the economic edge, and their "ability to get along well in economic terms" (their "competence," it was called) was very limited; their patterns of consumption and style "imitated the more commanding presence and sumptuous raiment of the upper middle classes."[3] Counting clerks and schoolteachers among their ranks, these "white-collar employees" anxiously strove to assemble a stylistic affinity to wealth.

If factory industrialism was producing icons of material abundance for some, it was bringing misery into the lives of many others. As Dawley puts it, "wealth and poverty were increasing apace." As some people assumed the mass-produced mantle of improved circumstances, the "wealth" of the industrial workers was, for the most part, "measured negatively by the goods they needed but did not have."[4] Critics and defenders of the factory system acknowledged the widespread immiserization that accompanied the expansion of factory industrialism, the social costs that coincided with the middle-class "delight in the unreal."

The tension between surface and substance, intrinsic to nineteenth-century industrialism, was evident in a critique published in the *Fourth Annual Report* of the Massachusetts Bureau of Labor, in 1873:

> Those who look beneath the surface of things, with unprejudiced eyes, are painfully conscious that wealth, though year by year still on the increase, goes now into fewer hands; that the results of industry are very unequally divided; that the advantages which machinery and division of labor bring, have been altogether in favor of capital and against labor, and that these evils are dangerously increasing from year to year.[5]

Six years later, in 1879, an "editorial defending the factory system" carried the same general evaluation: "Machinery creates wealth; and a large part of the increase naturally falls into the hands of capital that employs the machinery. Colossal fortunes are piled up in a few years, apparently making wider the gap between rich and poor."[6]

The emerging colossus of factory capitalism was giving rise to two contrasting perceptions of social reality. In 1847, *Scientific American*, a journal of science, technology, and invention, articulated one perspective when it described factory industrialism as producing the accoutrements of a "democracy," one "which invites every man to enhance his own comfort and status." Equating democracy with consumption, the magazine contended that the unfolding world of mass-produced objects was providing "the vehicle for the pursuit of happiness." Mass production, according to this outlook, was investing individuals with tools of identity, marks of their personhood.

For those laboring in many of the factories, however, industrial conditions systematically trampled upon their individuality and personhood. Many of the factory workers were migrants from premodern cultures of agriculture and handcrafts. Individuals whose work patterns were rooted in the more "irregular and undisciplined" structures of preindustrial labor were now being subjected to the monotonous discipline of machinery, and strict work rules were designed to rid them of preindustrial habits, memories, and temperaments.[7] Remuneration for work of this kind was most often low, a mere subsistence.

Out of these two conflicting ways of seeing and experiencing the new industrial reality, there emerged two distinct ways of apprehending the very question of *status* and *class.* By the mid-nineteenth century, both of these contending outlooks were being articulated. One way of comprehending class focused on the social relations of power which dominated and shaped the modern, industrial mode of *production.* The other outlook—which has left an indelible imprint on the meaning of style in contemporary American society—gave rise to a notion of class defined, almost exclusively, by patterns of *consumption.*

For those whose definition of class was drawn from the social relations of production, the nineteenth century highlighted a growing and irreconcilable conflict between those who profited from the increasingly mechanized and consolidated means of production, and those whose lives, labors, and energies were being consumed in service of this new industrial apparatus. As artisan craft and small-scale manufacture fell to an emerging economy of larger scale, more and more people were being drawn into the ranks of the industrial working class. For this growing population of factory workers, industrialism was creating a downward spiral of poverty, and a meager subsistence which only compounded the degraded conditions and exploitation that they faced at the workplace. While the captains of industry were surrounding themselves with the trappings of status and wealth, the elements of style were of little consequence to the swelling numbers of factory operatives.

This was a working class very similar to the *proletariat,* described by Karl Marx and Frederick Engels during the same period. Writing in 1848, they depicted the modern working class as a "class of laborers who live so long as they find work and who find work only so long as their labor increases capital." Selling themselves "piecemeal," like a "commodity," their lives became more and more "exposed to all the vicissitudes of competition, to all the fluctuations of the market." The modern worker, they maintained, has become "an appendage of the machine, and it is only the most simple, most monotonous, and most easily acquired knack, that is required of him." The final indignity of his class position was that "as the repulsiveness of the work increases, the wage decreases."[8]

In mid-nineteenth-century America the gap between rich and poor was widening, and the wealth being accrued in factory capitalism was inextricably linked to the impoverishment of those whose labor was being drawn into its sphere of influence. *Class position* was part of the social relations of power that were emerging. *Class identity* was not a matter of individual choice, but of the position one inhabits in relation to the forces of production. This conception of *class,* elucidated by Marx and Engels, but shared by diverse others, encouraged people to look at groups of people not in terms of the individual claims they made for themselves, but in terms of where the stood within the *objective relations* of power. Such a consciousness of objective relations would, they believed, eventually give rise to a collective, revolutionary consciousness (and activity) among the expanding, international ranks of exploited workers.*

Such ideas spread in the United States, as well, during the rise of industrial and, then, corporate capitalism. Yet alongside this, another approach to the question of *class*—one resting on a flimsy, if seductive, foundation of appearances—was also taking hold. Within a society where, as Oliver Wendell Holmes had argued, inexpensively produced images were becoming more important than objects, it was increasingly possible to avoid dealing with objective relations. By the middle of the nineteenth century, the expanding market in appearances was helping to feed a notion of class defined primarily in *consumptive* rather than productive terms, highlighting individual, above common, identity. The idea of an American "middle class," constructed out of images, attitudes, acquisitions, and style, was emerging.

In eighteenth-century Europe, argues historian Karen Halttunen, "the term *middling class* referred to people who occupied a static social position between the extremes of peasantry and aristocracy, a position believed to offer only modest opportunities for advancement." In the teeming urban world of nineteenth-century America, however, "middle class" began to take on a new and volatile meaning, one which assumed that more and more people were engaged "in a passage from a lower to a higher social status."9

In an urban industrial world, where traditional hierarchical patterns of work and family life were disintegrating, and where new promises of economic opportunity were fueling the imagination, many people "imagined themselves on a social escalator to greater wealth and pres-

*For many living in the United States, or Western Europe, such an understanding of class may appear outdated, yet in many respects these insights into class continue to be relevant, if unappreciated. In today's world, where transnational corporations dominate a global market economy, multitudes in Southeast Asia, Latin America, and elsewhere are—like the nineteenth-century proletarians of Europe and the United States—being forcibly separated from traditional modes of survival; being drawn into the orbit of factory production; being paid bare subsistence wages. Within the "developed" economies of the West, the "competition" offered by these miserably paid workers of the Third World has driven down wages and benefits; the gap separating rich and poor has widened once again.

tige."[10] At the heart of this mobile dream, argues Eric Foner, lay the republican "middle class goal of economic independence . . . the opportunity to quit the wage earning class."[11]

For the most part, Halttunen maintains, this middle class "lived suspended between the facts of their present social position and the promise, which they took for granted, of their economic future. In reality," she continues, "the middle-class escalator was at least as likely to go down as up. Whether rising or falling, however, middle-class Americans were defined as men in social motion, men of no fixed status." This condition of flux, she adds, "was believed to include a vast majority of Americans who were neither very wealthy nor very poor."[12]

This middle-class commitment to the ideal of social mobility was fed by the expanding market in appearances that characterized nineteenth-century industrial life. Mass-produced fashions, furniture, and other symbolic accoutrements of a privileged station were anxiously assembled by those who strove to avoid what one mid-nineteenth-century advice writer called the *"shame of being thought poor."*[13] An industry of advice literature began to emerge, offering would-be *arrivés* the proper behavioral techniques and etiquette by which they might complete their projects of pretension.

The obsession with appearances ran deep within this new middle-class life and affected the most minute details of existence. Proper attention to current fashions was complemented by intricate instructions on how to position one's hands or head, and how to move about in a proper "genteel" manner. Middle-class homes were marked by front rooms, parlors, adorned with overstuffed furniture, pianos, and other recognized symbols of prosperity. Back rooms, where people retreated from the primacy of display, were more plainly furnished.

The priority of facades was becoming a characteristic feature of American middle-class life. *Godey's Lady's Book,* a magazine which itself served as a middle-class guidepost in the mid-nineteenth century, bemoaned the extent to which pretense had become a cardinal element of middle-class behavior:

> The exterior of life is but a masquerade, in which we dress ourselves in the finest fashions of society, use a language suited to the characters we assume;—with smiling faces, mask aching hearts; address accents of kindness to our enemies, and often those of coldness to our friends. The part once assumed must be acted out, no matter at what expense of truth and feeling.[14]

It was with a sense of irony that Harriet Beecher Stowe described the contortions that middle-class women in the process of trying to establish the social credentials of a leisured existence, one ostensibly dependent on servants:

> When we have company! there's the rub, to get out all our best things and put them back,—to cook the meals and wash the dishes ingloriously,—and to make all appear as if we didn't do it, and had servants like other people.[15]

When a rising middle class of merchants began to appropriate the marks of style from the late Middle Ages on, it was a tangible expression of their increasing power, both locally and globally. When they took on the vestments, titles, and properties previously monopolized by the aristocracy, it was because they had assumed a central, increasingly decisive position in the world. While political structures took time to acknowledge their franchise, these merchant capitalists were becoming men of power.

Industrial-, corporate-, and finance-capitalists of the nineteenth century also assumed style as palpable evidence of their power. The artifacts with which these people surrounded themselves were, for the most part, handmade, intricately crafted, constructed of rare and expensive materials, often one of a kind. While social critics and jealous defenders of aristocratic taste decried the garish displays of the robber barons, these capitalists had, in a very real sense, inherited the prerogatives of now-fallen elites.

The nineteenth-century mass-produced style, which gave shape to a democratized, "middle class" existence, was different. It was composed primarily of *kitsch:* cheap, mass-produced imitations of elite style. The ornate bric-a-brac described by Egon Friedell, or the ready-to-wear fashions that became increasingly available from the 1870s onward, were pale imitations of elite styles and were notable for their shoddiness.

Yet more important than its formal obeisance to the values of elites, this "middle class" pretension was more a social mask, claiming a power that was not there, than it was an achievement of real social power. The stylish ephemera of the new "middle class" existence was more of a symbolic fringe benefit, a *cultural wage,* which permitted its recipients to identify with the interests of the upper classes, while occupying a relationship to power that was more akin to that of the working classes. In its symbolic identification with power, this "middle class" performed, and continues to perform, a political function; it effects divisions among people who otherwise might identify with one another.

The ironic position of this middle class, committed at once to democratic mobility and to the imagery of entrenched elites, was captured

This page from the 1908 Sears Roebuck catalog is cluttered with "pressed cut glass" bric-a-brac—part of the early-twentieth-century, middle-class identity kit.

succinctly by the mid-nineteenth-century social reformer Orestes Brownson. "The middle class," he wrote, "is always a firm champion of equality when it concerns humbling a class above it, but it is its inveterate foe when it concerns elevating a class below it."[16]

Writing in 1873, Ira Steward—a weaver and leader in the Massachusetts movement for an eight-hour workday—offered a prescient description and analysis of this emerging "middle class" and its consciousness; his words seem even more trenchant today. In powerful contrast
with a notion of class rooted in the social relations of power, Steward
depicted a growing "class" of people whose fragile identity was wedded
to the consumption of goods, and whose troubled consciousness was
enforced by a thin veil of appearances.

In his essay "Poverty," included in the 1873 report of the Massachusetts Bureau of Labor, Steward made a striking and unexpected detour
from a discussion of pauperized wage laborers, and focused on the lives,
conditions, and psychology of what he called the "middle class." The
section deserves quotation at length:

> But has not the middle class its poverty—a poverty that should excite the
> most anxiety, and the most searching inquiry. . . .
>
> They are a large majority of the people, and their poverty is generally
> carefully concealed.* All who have barely enough to keep up appearances
> are just the ones to cover up the fact that they have nothing more. They
> are ranked among the middle classes; and their power to cover up their
> poverty, is made to argue that they are not poor.
>
> The middle classes have the strongest motives for never making any
> parade or public complaint of their poverty. To advertise one's self desti-
> tute, is to be without credit, that tides so many in safety—to their standing
> in society—over the shallow places where ready resources fail. To be
> without credit and without resources, is to be dependent upon charity
> whenever employment fails, or sickness prevents employment, and to
> depend upon charity is an advertisement of one's destitution and poverty
> that the public is very slow to forget. . . .
>
> To betray or confess the secrets of one's destitution, is also regarded, in
> some measure, as a sign of incapacity; for, as the world goes, the poor man
> is an unsuccessful man.

To dispel any evidence of their indigence, Steward observed, these
"middle class" poor participate in a continuous effort to erect the semblance of substantiality; to construct a stylish imago in order to maintain
a claim to social position; to secure those promotions which are available
to "white collar" employees; to qualify for credit. All of this scurrying

*Most probably Steward's reference to the "majority," here, does not include blacks or
immigrants, whose combined numbers were large, and who performed the most menial
and low-paid work.

for position, Steward noted, made access to credit all the more imperative:

> The poverty that publishes or argues one's incapacity, closes many a door to more profitable or advantageous situations or promotions. The more expensive and superior style of living adopted by the middle classes, must therefore be considered in the light of an *investment,* made from the soundest considerations of expediency—considering their risks and their chances—and from motives even of self preservation, rather than from the mere desire for self indulgence, or because the middle classes are not poor. Very few of them are saving money. Many of them are in debt; and all they can earn for years, is, in many cases, mortgaged to pay such debt,—"debt that increases the load of the future, with the burden which the present cannot bear."[17]

In the masquerade of elegance that shaped the lives of these "genteel" poor, Steward found pathos. In the haunted eyes of these people, the core of insecurity overwhelmed the surface of prosperity. In "the faces of thousands of well-dressed, intelligent, and well-appearing people," Steward perceived the "unmistakable signs of their incessant anxiety and struggles to get on in life, and to obtain in addition to a mere subsistence, a standing in society."[18]

It is difficult to gauge the accuracy of Steward's survey of the "middle class" soul, but such symptoms of anxiety were also the concern of the American medical establishment which, by the middle of the nineteenth century, began to observe and treat the advancing symptoms of ennui, phobia, and nervous exhaustion among their middle-class patients. Dr. George M. Beard, a physician who specialized in the treatment of "neurasthenia," attempted to make sense of the "causes of American nervousness." In terms that evoke Steward's insight about "middle class" restiveness, Beard concluded that the social priority of constructing *fronts* was giving rise to a state of "constant inhibition, restraining normal feelings, keeping back, covering, holding in check the atomic forces of the mind and body." Beard saw this suppression of emotion as a consequence of a society in which more and more people were continually jockeying for status, "to rise out of the position in which they were born . . . and aspire to the highest possibilities of fortune and glory. . . . In all classes," he continued, "there is a constant friction and unrest—a painful striving to see who shall be highest."[19]

Such concerns had been expressed by various commentators from the 1830s onward. In his narrative account of his life as a *Stranger in America,* Francis Lieber made note of an "appalling frequency of alienation of mind" among Americans; the result, he contended, of a "diseased anxiety to be equal to the wealthiest, the craving for wealth and consequent disappointment, which ruins the intellect of many."[20] During the Panic of 1857, when middle-class hopes were rocked by the volatility of economic factors, the Cincinnati *Gazette* confirmed a similar sense of widespread anxiety when it concluded that "we have been living too fast. Individuals, families, have been eagerly trying to outdo each other in dress, furniture, style and luxury."[21]

Democracy and privilege, once understood to be opposing forces, were becoming engaged in a strange and fitful unity. The "stress and agony and excitement" of what Erving Goffman would later describe as the "arts of impression management," were rife within Anglo-America.[22]

These discussions of the "middle class" and its anxieties have a remarkably current ring to them. They point to the emergence of a consumer society, filled with mass-produced status symbols, in which judgment about a person is not based on what one *does* within society, but rather upon what one *has*. Such an understanding of class has moved away from the conception rooted in the social relations of power, and toward a notion based, for the most part, on income and credit. "Middle class" status was becoming something founded purely on one's ability to purchase, construct, and present a viable social self. While this modern idea of class invested more and more people with the iconography of status, it also tended to mask the relations of power that prevailed within society.

In the late nineteenth century, when Ira Steward was writing, the ability to assemble a "middle class" identity was still limited to a white, primarily Anglo-American population. Working-class people, largely white immigrants and blacks, had little access to the goods or necessary income to make this social presentation of self possible. In the twentieth century, with the growth of vast consumer industries and, for many, improved income, times of prosperity have been marked by increasing numbers of people entering the orbit of "middle class" existence. With these developments, Steward's prescient characterization of a "middle class" existence, shaped by the acquisition and display of stylish goods, has provided the predominant definition of class and aspiration in American society. The term *middle class,* like the term *consumer,* has become, for the most part, an appellation of citizenship.

This development reached its height in the twenty years after the end of World War II, when a period of economic boom drew unprecedented numbers into the ranks of the middle class. In the process, and with the assistance of anticommunist ideology, the alternative definition of class began to ebb in the public vernacular. Although many still

A 1907 advertisement for the Washington Shirt Company in Chicago.

lived in severe poverty, the most visible representation of social life depicted the "increased bunching of Americans around the middle-income levels, the increased blurring of occupational distinctions, and the increased adoption of middle-class living styles by families of diverse occupational background."[23] By the late 1950s, *Fortune* magazine asserted, nearly all Americans had the option of "choosing a whole style of life":

> A skilled mechanic who earns $7,500 after taxes may choose to continue living in "working class" style, meanwhile saving sizable sums for his children's college education; or he may choose to live like a junior executive in his own $17,000 suburban house; or he may choose to live in a city apartment house otherwise occupied by business and professional men. When the American "masses" have options of this breadth, . . . it is scarcely an exaggeration to suggest that we have arrived at a landmark in all the history of human freedoms.[24]

The force behind this historic turning point, the editors of *Fortune* explained, can be found in the work of the "status-symbol school of sociologists," who held the following convictions about contemporary human behavior:

> (1) people constantly express their personalities not so much in words as in symbols (ie: mannerisms, dress, ornaments, possessions); (2) most people are increasingly concerned about what other people think of them, and

hence about their social status. Thus the taste of many Americans is expressed in symbols of various social positions. . . . people tend to buy things that symbolize their aspirations.[25]

Feeding and responding to this increasing concern with the symbols of status, consumer industries and the advertising establishment surrounded more and more goods with the cloak of prestige. Throughout the 1950s, nearly all sectors of consumer goods manufacture moved to invest their products with superficial but recognizable marks of status, giving rise to what author Thomas Hine has called a "populuxe" culture.[26] In 1958, advertising man David Ogilvy translated this general tendency into a concise merchandising axiom: "It pays to give a product a high-class image instead of a bargain-basement image. Also," he added, "you can get more for it."[27]

What was coming to fruition, for unprecedented numbers of people, was a society in which mass-produced, stylized goods were functioning as an intricate system of personal certification, an "identity kit." As Joan Kron has argued in *Home-Psych,* her book on the psychology of interior design, the utility of such "middle class" certification was inextricably linked to the growing anonymity of modern life:

> As more and more people leave the protection of closely knit communities and move into neighborhoods of strangers, the house becomes a credential as well as a haven. Just as we need the intimate relationships that a house can shelter, we need the respect and esteem provided by a home we create in our own image. And we must forgive ourselves for caring about the opinions of others and trying to influence them. . . . We all use material things to stand for us. That's the system.[28]

Within the so-called yuppie (young urban professional) culture of the 1980s, we find the ultimate expression of such a "middle class" ideal, as well as its inherent anxieties. Amid a declining standard of living for many, these young professionals—many of whom are employed by the new "information industries"—scramble to surround themselves with the ever-changing "latest" in designer clothing, consumer electronics, and other commodified symbols of the *good life*. As they frenetically pursue this semiotic world of objects, they perform a role written for them, by Ira Steward, more than one hundred years before. Life is a tightening snare of credit and debt; all connection to society, or to social responsibility, is forsworn in favor of individual acquisition and display; stress and stress-induced conditions are endemic; *loneliness* and *emptiness* are common in their accounts of everyday life. In their ongoing presentation of self, it is essential that one's inner self, one's inner feelings, remain masked. This pose is well expressed by a 1984 television commercial for Dry Idea deodorant. "Never answer the phone on the first ring," begins the first in a series of instructions:

Never say, "I'll be right over."

Don't ever let 'em see you sweat.

It doesn't matter how anxious you are. . . . Never let 'em know you're anxious.

That's what *Dry Idea* is all about.

Such instructions are a common legacy of twentieth-century American life. In 1933—following a decade in which consumer industries had flourished, and in which mass-produced goods had extended their influence over the lives of many Americans—sociologist Robert Lynd commented dryly upon the rise of the *commodity self*. Discussing the "people as consumers," Lynd's words indicate the extent to which the tension between inner self and outer image had become a routine fixture in everyday life:

The process of growing up and of effective adult living consists in adjusting one's individual tensions by weighting them with values sufficiently congruous with the accepted values of society and at the same time with the urgent personal needs of the individual to enable him *to present some socially tolerable semblance of an integrated front in the business of living. Within each of us this exciting drama is played out in our every waking and sleeping hour until the end of the picture.* [29]

FIRST IMPRESSIONS

The development of consumer capitalism in the United States was fueled by a series of massive migrations—from within and without—which supplied a cheap, continually replaceable work force. Over time, these migrations also created a population whose hopes for a better life became the building blocks out of which a responsive, mass market of consumers would be constructed. With an immigration of millions between the late nineteenth century and 1920, the meaning and power of style underwent prodigious changes.

Immigrants from foreign lands came, during these years, primarily from Eastern Europe and the southern tier of Italy. In addition to these Europeans, there were also millions of migrants—black and white—

who came from rural poverty to burgeoning industrial cities, seeking employment and improved conditions.

In these cities—New York City, particularly—the iconography of style was touched and molded by a new multiplicity of influences. If the meaning of style had previously emanated from the consumption patterns of European elites, new, more democratic influences now began to assert themselves. With its infusion of different nationalities and cultures, and as a center of global commerce, the metropolis became a battleground, a vibrant cacophony of contending and cross-fertilizing cultural meanings. This heterogeneity and swarming energy, along with the relative tolerance of metropolitan life, turned the city into an always-moving repository of images, a perpetually expanding, and changing, inventory of "looks" and expressions. The jagged and vital quality of urban life has given shape to the definition of style ever since. Nearly anything that bubbles to the surface of the city can find its way into the style market.

Yet the city was more than a stylistic resource. It was also an environment that made style into an essential tool for everyday life. For people coming from agrarian or small-town artisanal roots, the move to urban industrialism posed a shock of world historic proportions. Uprooted from familiar patterns of work, kinship, and community, and also from customary ways of comprehending the world, they now entered a terrain that included countless strangers. Social life itself was being transformed from something known, set and transmitted by custom, into something increasingly anonymous; custom was inadequate to provide measures and lessons for survival.

In the shadow of this dislocation, people's customary conception of *self* was challenged. First, life became an experience of repeated and regular encounters with the unknown. As one navigated this vast new world of strangers, one quickly learned that to the eyes of countless others one becomes a "stranger" oneself. Anonymity was not only the characteristic of others; it was also becoming a component of subjectivity, part of the way one came to understand oneself. Part of surviving this strange new world was the ability to make quick judgments based, largely, on immediate visual evidence. The city was a place where surfaces took on a new power of expression. The very terms of everyday experience required, as part of the rules of survival and exchange, a sense of *self as alien,* as an object of scrutiny and judgment. From this vantage point, immigrants learned that matters of dress and personal appearance were essential for success in the public world. Writing in 1902, Jane Addams described the imperative of dress among urban working girls:

The working girl, whose family lives in a tenement, or moves from one small apartment to another, who has little social standing and has to make her own place, knows full well how much habit and style of dress has to do with her position. Her income goes into her clothing, out of all proportion to the amount which she spends upon other things. But, if social advancement is her aim, it is the most sensible thing she can do. She is judged largely by her clothes. Her house furnishing, with its pitiful little decorations, her scanty supply of books, are never seen by the people whose social opinions she most values. Her clothes are her background, and from them she is largely judged.[30]

In an environment where being labeled a "greenhorn" left one open to swindles and mockery, assuming the look of an "American" was a device of survival. Leonard Covello, who immigrated as a boy from Italy, described his acquisition of acceptable American attire before anything else. "My long European trousers had been replaced by the short knickers of the time, and I wore black ribbed stockings and new, American shoes. To all outward appearances I was an American," he confided ironically, "except that I did not speak a word of English."[31] The visual vernacular of style was the lingua franca of the city.

With the guidance of various Americanizing forces and institutions, young people began to learn that when one applied or interviewed for a job, or sought acceptance in school, it was important to make a good impression. This reality gave rise to a divided self. "Family obligations" and traditional codes of behavior were often enforced in the home, but outside the home these young people were seduced by the American social environment. If Ira Steward's "middle class" was torn between the longing for status and the struggle for the legal tender, these new Americans experienced a similar dissonance in their lives, this one marked by a toe-to-toe struggle between cultures.

For example, Pauline Young, a social worker writing in *Survey* magazine (15 March 1928), spoke of a sixteen-year-old son in a family of Jewish immigrants from Poland: "Jim is in almost daily contact with two divergent cultures: the older Jewish culture symbolized by the home, and the newer American culture symbolized by the school, industry and the larger community." Within the context of the home, she related, "family obligations . . . are still set in the foreground, and individual members are expected to conform to family tradition." Alongside this, however, was the opposing pull of the new world he inhabited:

In the larger community . . . Jim tends to become an "American Citizen." The English language and the associations at school open up to him a new world of social practices, customs, attitudes, and social values. This newer culture fosters, moreover, traits of independence, personal resourcefulness, individuality, and cultivates desires for personal distinction.[32]

This example repeated itself again and again. The old world of the parents was rooted in a continuity, an ongoing connection among closely tied people over generations. Familiar cultural resources were drawn upon, to navigate and envision the possibilities and limits of everyday life. The new world, on the other hand, demanded a sense of self that was malleable, sensitive to the power of increasingly volatile surfaces. Addressing the historical transformation of individual identity, historian Warren Susman described it as a shift from the importance of "character" (intrinsic self) to the importance of "personality" (a moldable, extrinsic self).[33] In this transition, the problem was invariably who one *was*. Who one could *become* was the solution. In the finding of solutions, the emerging consumer culture would gladly oblige.

Patterns of courtship were also affected by this transformation. The customary cultures of these immigrants and migrants were—for the most part—shaped by patterns of traditional patriarchal authority. Courtship, marriage, and sexuality were often arranged by parents, as agreements and exchanges between families from the same village or locale. Now, relations of love, sexuality, and matrimony were drawn from the new world of strangers. Young people, as they left the radius of the family, had unprecedented opportunities to develop relationships beyond the gaze of parents and matchmakers.

This mobility left a painful dent in the surface of the old culture. One Jewish matchmaker, interviewed by the New York *Tribune* in 1898, complained that the new American styles of courtship were leaving his business in ruin:

> Once I lived off the fat of the land, and most marriageable men and women in the quarter depended on me to make them happy. Now they believe in love and all that rot. They are making their own marriages. . . . They learned how to start their own love affairs from the Americans, and it is one of the worst things they have picked up.[34]

This independence from habitual constraints required new tools of negotiation. Greenhorns were confronted in the streets with new patterns of adornment which signaled and beckoned toward a more independent mode of existence. A collision of cultures can be seen in one social worker's description of an encounter between a recent immigrant girl and her American counterparts:

> Each morning and evening as she covers her head with an old crocheted shawl and walks to and from the factory, she passes the daughters of her

Irish and American neighbors in their smart hats, their cheap waists in the latest and smartest style, their tinsel ornaments and their gay hair bows. A part of the pay envelopes goes into the personal expenses of those girls. Nor do they hurry through the streets to their homes after working hours, but linger with a boy companion "making dates" for a movie or an affair.

"Inevitably," wrote the social worker, "the influence of the new life in which she spends nine hours a day begins to tell on her."[35]

Here we see a second change in the definition of *self*. As people became what Raymond Williams calls "mobile individuals" they experienced a break from old patterns of hierarchy and authority, rooted for many in the history of feudalism and the conventional structures of a localized, agrarian existence. This break was both disorienting and promising. It cast people adrift from known and internalized strategies of survival, but it also posed the seductive possibility of greater autonomy and freedom, of democracy.

The industrial society that these people confronted was simultaneously oppressive and liberating. The machine, and its relentless rhythms, supplied the modern context for misery and exploitation, but it also contained an ability to reproduce—on a mass scale—pregnant images and symbols of luxury, abundance, and distinction, powerful suggestions of privilege and franchise. Styled objects, once the province of an upper class, now became reproducible, if only as surface images.

To some extent this development was triggered by the mass production of chromolithographs, as objects of desire and alluring tools of commerce. Extended access to style was also effected by the great public expositions of the late nineteenth century, where urban dwellers could come to witness the wonders of industrialism on display. Exposition halls—their plaster and horsehair surfaces molded to imitate the grandeur of Renaissance palaces—offered the public entry into environments traditionally inhabited by elites. The democratic privilege suggested by such spectacles can be heard in a promotional claim made for the Columbian Exposition: "We are all princes, for the time being, in this little realm."[36]

Perhaps the most significant area in which stylized goods became common possessions of working-class people was that of fashionable, mass-produced clothing. From the 1880s onward, men's and women's garment industries began to mass produce inexpensive fashions, cut to imitate the ornamental elegance of upper-class styles. Coming from societies where the prerogatives of dress were intimately connected to one's elevated class position, European immigrants, in particular, perceived the availability of mass-produced fashions as a mark of social mobility, of materially improved circumstances. People who had previously been denied access to images of magnificence now found them in reach, for a price.

Beginning in the nineteenth century, and catapulting in the twentieth, a wide-ranging consumer market in style was reaching deeply into nearly all aspects of life. Style was in the process of being transformed from a prerogative of the few to an amusement of the millions.[37] Though the implication of exclusivity and privilege would remain, the expressive and connotative arena of style was becoming an essential part of the modern vernacular. With this alluring access to fashion, old world notions of quality and durability gave way to new world priorities of consumption and frequent changes in style. This transformation of values between mothers and daughters was described by a social worker, Sophinisba Breckenridge, in her 1929 book, *New Homes for Old:*

> In her [daughter's] main contention that if she is to keep up with the fashions she need not buy clothing that will last more than one season, she is probably right. It is also natural that this method of buying should be distressing to her mother, who has been accustomed to clothes of unchanging fashions which were judged entirely by their quality.[38]

In such a broad milieu of strangers, style was a dramatic necessity. One was repeatedly made aware of *self as other,* of one's commodity status within a vast social marketplace, and style provided its user with a powerful medium of encounter and exchange. Whereas contacts between people had once been familiar, the city was unfamiliar, and daily life, at times, seemed threatening.

In the face of this apparently "hostile" environment, style allowed one to put up a front, to protect one's inner self. As a kind of armor for city life, style taught people that they could gain comfort from self-estrangement, from erecting a visible line of defense for a subjectivity that often experienced a sense of jeopardy. As a basic lession in *modernization,* immigrant and migrant workers learned to be "presentable," to rely on the tools of presentation while navigating the treacherous waters of everyday life. True moderns, they were learning to internalize the dictum of Bishop Berkeley, that "to be is to be perceived."[39]

In its mimicry of upper-class elegance, as well as in its piracy of emerging forms of popular expression, the marketplace of consumer goods, from the early twentieth century onward, provided instruments for the construction of a self—a surrogate self, perhaps—to be seen, to be judged, to simultaneously scale and maintain the wall of anonymity. In worlds of work and love, status and aspiration, the assembly of "self" was becoming compulsory for ventures into the society at large. The appeal of "style" was not a matter of aesthetics alone; it was also a functional acquisition of metropolitan life.

This can be seen in the story of one woman, a Russian immigrant, who described her own relationship with style. In Russia she wore the customary clothes of the poor, made crudely out of scraps of cloth. "It was not a question of style," she explained, "but of how to cover one's body in those days." When she came to America in the 1920s, one of the first articles of clothing she bought was an item she had admired from afar while still in Russia: a leather jacket, a "symbol of both the Revolution and elegance." Yet when she wore this prized acquisition while looking for work, she discovered that employers would not hire her; they, too, understood the political connotations of the jacket. They were afraid its wearer might cause problems, as a unionist or agitator. Employers were looking for signs of docility, adaptability, and conformity in their prospective employees. Finally, the woman was forced to make a concession to the codes of the job market:

> I dressed myself in the latest fashion with lipstick in addition, although it was so hard to get used to at first that I blushed, felt foolish and thought myself vulgar. But I got the job.[40]

Style provided an extension of personality on a physical plane, leaving its mark on the sundry accessories of life: personal apparel, the home, even the foods one ate. In a world where scrutiny by unknown others had become the norm, style provided people with an *attractive otherness,* a "phantom objectivity" (to borrow a phrase from Georg Lukacs), to publicly define oneself, to be weighed in the eye's mind.

A central appeal of style was its ability to create an illusory transcendence of class or background. While hierarchy and inequities of wealth and power were—in many ways—increasing, the free and open market in style offered a symbolic ability to name oneself; to become a "lady" or a "gentleman," a "Sir" or a "Madam." Mass-produced, often shoddy, nevertheless style seemed to subvert ancient monopolies over the image that had predominated in the cultures out of which many of these "greenhorns" were drawn. If style was essentially a matter of surface and mystification, it was—and continues to be—a surface that offered a democratic charm.

CHAPTER FIVE

"The Dream of Wholeness"

Personality is an unbroken series of successful gestures.
—F. SCOTT FITZGERALD,
The Great Gatsby

DEFINING PERSONHOOD

The genesis of style, from a birthright of hierarchical elites to a diversion for "the masses," can easily be interpreted as a process of symbolic democratization. This was certainly a part of its impact. By the early twentieth century, large numbers of people, whose parents could not have imagined donning the trappings of distinction, were parading down city streets in wardrobes of elegance. Writing in 1929, the social critic Stuart Chase observed that although style still retained its connotations of high status, it was—at the same time—leaving its mark on all ranks of society:

> The function of clothes as a badge of social rank is enormously expanding over all classes in America for both sexes, but particularly for women. Only a connoisseur can distinguish Miss Astorbilt on Fifth Avenue from her father's stenographer or secretary. An immigrant arriving on the Avenue from the Polish plain described all American women as countesses. So eager are the lower income groups to dress well in style, if not in quality, as their economic superiors, that class distinctions have all but disappeared. To the casual observer all American women dress alike. The movement to cut down the margin of class distinction . . . has made great headway.[1]

The appeal of style, however, was not simply a matter of putting on airs. Three early studies of fashion motivation—by G. Stanley Hall

(1898), L. W. Flaccus (1906), and George Van Ness Dearborn (1917)—indicated that anxieties about self-image, and the hunger for self-expression, contributed to people's use of style within their daily lives. On the one hand, style (particularly clothing) was seen as a device for blending in, conforming to the expectations of the society at large. Being noticed approvingly was something to be desired, but being overly "conspicuous" was something to be avoided, even feared. The *correct* use of style was seen as a way of avoiding "adverse criticism," of being acceptable to others.[2]

Alongside this defensive use of images, however, style was also understood as a tool for constructing personhood. Style was a way of saying who one was, or who one wished to be. The emerging market in stylized goods provided consumers with a vast palette of symbolic meanings, to be selected and juxtaposed in the assembling of a public self. Writing on fashion images, Roland Barthes described this array of meanings as "psychological essences," each an objectification of some subjective quality. The fashionable person, for Barthes, is a quantitative assemblage of objective elements, all of which combine to present the semblance of an integrated subject.

Writing from the vantage point of the 1960s, Barthes, saw "the accumulation of . . . psychological essences" as constituting and projecting a "dream of identity," or even more suggestively, "a dream of wholeness."[3] The utility of style in this regard is to find for oneself, and for others, the evidence of meaning in one's life.

The assembling of a commodity self, this "dream of wholeness," implies a sense of partialness and fragmentation that resides just beneath the surface. The appeal of style in twentieth-century cultures cannot be separated from the conditions of the human subject it addresses. We can not, in evaluating the patterns of individual style, disregard the fact that over the past century, an ongoing lament has been that of aloneness, isolation, invisibility, and insignificance; a desperate thirst for recognition, often expressed as a desire for fame. A great deal of modern literature speaks eloquently of a crisis of the spirit; a condition of anomie and diminished meaning. Amid the democratic puffery of the modern age, the self grows dimmer. Behind these feelings lies a constellation of objective circumstances, the social world we inhabit.

The repeated pledge of *progress* is greater freedom for the individual, yet actual choice over the conditions of existence, the domain of freedom has been—in many ways—reduced. Nowhere has this narrowing of freedom been greater than in the modern structures of work.

From the late nineteenth century onward, the organization and management of work has, in large part, been designed to promote corporate and institutional interests at the expense of individual or even group initiative among workers. Conceptual and decision-making powers have been systematically removed from people not only in production, but in the "white collar" industries of distribution, promotion, service, and bureaucracy.

A pioneer in this attack on the human subject was Frederick W. Taylor, the father of "scientific management." At the center of Taylor's managerial strategy stood a commitment to the systematic observation of human behavior in the workplace, and the subsequent standardization of behavior in order to control the workforce more effectively.

Developing his techniques in the steel industry, Taylor devised an approach to management that was predicated on "the dictation to the worker of the precise manner in which work is to be performed."[4] The conceptualization of the overall job to be done—from start to finish— was appropriated by management. Workers were seen, ideally, as pliable instruments within the production process; automatons who would perform routinized elements in a grand, managerial scheme. This required a systematic stripping away of all aspects of production that had previously depended on the judgment and discretion of the workers. Skills were divided up into a sequence of simple procedures, to be taught to the workers and monitored by management:

> The managers assume . . . the burden of gathering together all of the traditional knowledge which in the past has been possessed by the workmen and then of classifying, tabulating, and reducing this knowledge to rules, laws, and formulae.[5]

The connection between a worker's mind and hand was to be broken, or as Taylor put it, "all possible brain work should be removed from the shop and centered in the planning or laying-out department."[6] Ultimately, Taylorism was a technique designed to assert absolute, managerial control over the productive sphere. Harry Braverman, in his classic study of *Labor and Monopoly Capital* (1974), summarized Taylor's managerial strategy in three principles:

1 Dissociation of the labor process from the skills of the workers.

2 Separation of conception from execution.

3 Use of this monopoly of knowledge to control each step of the labor process and its mode of execution.[7]

Taylor's strategy of management was not simply aimed at increased productivity; the very patterns of working-class culture were in its sights. Throughout the nineteenth century, as American capitalism built its industrial base, the factory system had drawn its labor force from people whose sensibilities were formed by "artisan culture and . . . peasant and village cultures." Herbert Gutman has shown that "quite diverse patterns of collective lower-class behavior (some of them disorderly and even violent)" were drawn from these preindustrial cultures, in opposition to the disciplines of factory labor. Insofar as the United States gathered a cheap labor supply from successive waves of migration, the tensions between preindustrial cultures and factory were continuous:

> Even though American society itself underwent radical structural changes between 1815 and the First World War, the shifting composition of its wage-earning population meant that traditional customs, rituals, and beliefs repeatedly helped shape the behavior of its diverse working-class groups.[8]

Customary work rhythms, common understandings, community bonds, and cultural practices; all of these aspects of lower-class life meant that much of nineteenth-century industrial history was marked by a contest—between workers and owners—for control over the productive apparatus.

Given this historical context, Taylor reasoned that in order to achieve his managerial goals it was necessary not only to wrest from workers the control of their crafts, but to approach workers in a way that would minimize the possibilities of resistance. The key here was to undercut historic patterns of association and solidarity, to individuate the workforce.

> In dealing with workmen under this type of management, it is an inflexible rule to talk to and deal with only one man at a time . . . since we are not dealing with men in masses, but are trying to develop each individual man to his highest state of efficiency and prosperity.[9]

Taylorism envisioned a society in which there was consolidation and cooperative planning among those who ruled; for those working within the system, it fostered conditions of individuation, social competition, and dependency. Taylor's dream depended on a population that had been eviscerated of its cultural resources, community bonds, and knowledge of craft.

Scientific management, from its beginnings, engendered widespread working-class hostility. Nevertheless, it provided a general strategy which, in the long run, became the basic American approach to the structuring of labor processes. As Harry Braverman said, "its fundamental teachings have become the bedrock of all work design."[10] Increasingly, over the course of the twentieth century, most people's labor has become the hard shell surrounding other people's thought.

The routinization of work has not been limited to the productive sphere. As industrial society gave rise to retail, service, and clerical occupations, work patterns in these fields have similarly entered the orbit of managerial attention.

In contrast to factory labor, many of these jobs involve the selling of commodities and services and they depend upon skills of human relations and persuasion. Before the rise of giant enterprise and the emergence of national distribution markets, these "sales" activities were practiced by independent drummers and itinerant peddlers. There was an intimate connection between aspects of personal charm and the processes of selling. This can be seen in D. W. Griffith's description of "a most welcome visitor . . . an old Jewish peddler" who visited his family regularly when Griffith was a child in Oldham County, rural Kentucky:

> "He . . . carried an enormous load on his back as he walked through the countryside." He usually paid for room and board by barter—some tinware or crockery in exchange for a night's stay.
>
> Griffith recalled him as an indifferent businessman, spreading out his wares and allowing the family to pick over them, but never pushing the sale of anything very hard. One late winter evening he stopped with the Griffiths and after dinner . . . took out an accordion and "began to play strange airs," apparently Jewish folk songs. Between songs he paused to tell stories of his travels, and the children loved it all—not the least because they were allowed to stay up past their usual bedtimes.[11]

Such a story evokes a society where mass production, and the frantic need to generate responsive markets, had not yet taken hold. The peddler was not merely a carrier of goods, but a link between the isolation of a Kentucky farm and the wider, more traveled, world; he was a storyteller, an educator, a welcome guest.

The development of a modern consumer culture, however, transformed the meaning of sales and promotion. As the engines of production were overflowing with a previously unimaginable mass of goods, corporate enterprises increasingly moved to systematize and routinize the processes of selling. Centralized planning was applied to tasks formerly in the hands of independent jawsmiths.

By the 1920s, and bolstered by the new "science" of motivational psychology, the routinization of the drummer was being promulgated by a growing sales apparatus. Personal behavior, and details of human interaction, were being scrutinized and packaged for the expanding number of people who worked in sales and related fields of "human relations." In his discussion of *Salesmanship for the New Era* (1929), Charles W. Mears encouraged prospective salespeople to break down their identity into its constituent parts and examine it as if it were seen in the mind of another:

> The salesman is on display. Everything about him may count; he cannot tell what small detail about himself the prospect may notice—hence the salesman must consciously go over himself and check up.[12]

The notion of *self as other,* as something to be molded and manipulated, was becoming a job qualification. Anything about one's *intrinsic self,* it was argued, might intervene in the achievement of a desired goal (sales), so it was essential to cultivate an *extrinsic self* to hold up constantly, to avoid the possibility of spontaneous rejection:

> On your first call and on your succeeding calls, until you have won . . . deeper recognition, you are under scrutiny and analysis on what may seem to you to be superficial or unimportant matters. . . . It is safe to say that the salesman must necessarily sell himself to the prospect, not merely the first time, but every time he calls.[13]

Personal traits, once the facets of a person's character, were now being mass produced as instruments of persuasion, masks to cover those aspects of character that might get in the way of sales.

By the 1930s, such approaches to human interaction were promulgated for both on-the-job purposes, and as a general approach for engaging with others. Dale Carnegie's *How to Win Friends and Influence People,* first published in 1936, provided a technical guide for human relations. "When dealing with people," Carnegie told his readers, "we are not dealing with creatures of logic. We are dealing with creatures of emotion, creatures bristling with prejudices and motivated by pride and vanity." Skills in "dealing with people . . . in human engineering," he argued, required an ongoing appeal to these emotions.[14]

Using anecdotes from his life and from the lives of other "successful" people, Carnegie amassed a catalog of techniques for "handling people," neutralizing and circumventing conflict, and getting what you want from others. In order to "make a good impression," Carnegie offered this simple advice:

> Actions speak louder than words, and a smile says, "I like you. You make me happy. I am glad to see you." . . .
> An insincere grin? No. That doesn't fool anybody. We know it is mechanical and we resent it. I am talking about a real smile, a heart-warming

smile, a smile that comes from within, the kind of smile that will bring a good price in the market place.

In order to achieve this "real" smile, Carnegie counseled:

> You don't feel like smiling? Then what? Two things. First, force yourself to smile. If you are alone, force yourself to whistle or hum a tune or sing. Act as if you were already happy, and that will tend to make you happy.
> . . .
> Everybody in the world is seeking happiness—and there is one sure way to find it. That is by controlling your thoughts.[15]

In this passage, and throughout most of the book, Carnegie advised the instrumental cultivation of a marketable self. Insofar as inner feeling undercut outer projection, inner feeling was dispensable.

Human emotions themselves were becoming objectified into discrete elements, raw materials within the standardized production of salesmanship. Writing in 1941, psychoanalyst Erich Fromm commented on the way in which shows of affection had been appropriated as devices within the sales and service industries. Expression was being cultivated as a consumable style and sham was becoming the profitable norm: "Friendliness, cheerfulness, and everything that a smile is supposed to express, become automatic responses which one turns on and off like an electric switch."[16]

Personal characteristics, drawn from the reservoir of human experience, were becoming the techniques of false *personality*. In the process, the outer self was being separated from the realm of inner feeling, providing a subjective corollary to Oliver Wendell Holmes's celebrated split between images and objects. False friendliness was valued over genuine affection in an emerging choreography of commercialized relations. Integrity was becoming the stuff that legends are made of; something to stir the heart, send chills down the back, close the deal.

C. Wright Mills, in *White Collar* (1951), brilliantly summarized the trajectory of salesmanship in twentieth-century American life:

> In the new society, salesmanship is much too important to be left to pep alone or to the personal flair of detached salesmen. Since the first decade of the century, much bureaucratic attention has been given to the gap between mass production and individual consumption. Salesmanship is an attempt to fill that gap. In it, as in material fabrication, large scale production has been instituted. . . . The dominant motive has been to lower the costs of selling per head; the dominant technique, to standardize and rationalize the processes of salesmanship. . . .
>
> In selling, as everywhere, centralization has meant *the expropriation of*

certain traits previously found in creative salesmen, by a machinery that codifies these traits and controls their acquisition and display by individual salesmen. The rise of absentee selling, rooted in the mass media, has done much to spur these centralizing and rationalizing trends.[17]

Mills's summary offers a parallel between the realm of sales and human relations and that of the labor process within factories. In both areas, people were being stripped of customary practices and tools, of personal input in conceptualizing the job. Skills and initiative were being appropriated by centralized management, transformed into "rules, laws, and formulae." Ultimately, as direct selling methods gave way to "absentee" methods (packaging, advertising, product design), the application of salesmanship to everyday existence would employ, more and more, the use of disembodied images.

PATHWAYS OF FULFILLMENT: PHOTOGRAPHY AND CELEBRITY

In a highly mobile society, where first impressions are important and where selling oneself is the most highly cultivated "skill," the construction of appearances becomes more and more imperative. If style offers a representation of self defined by surfaces and commodities, the media by which style is transmitted tend to reinforce this outlook in intimate detail. They continually offer us visible guideposts, reference points to draw upon, against which to measure ourselves.

In urban centers, or in huge shopping malls, the visual juxtaposition of *style* and *self* is continual. Passing by shop window displays, broad expanses of gleaming plate glass, people confront a reflection of themselves, superimposed against the dream world of the commodity. An invidious comparison is instantaneously provoked between the "off-guard" imperfections of ourselves—suddenly on view—and the studied perfection of the display.

Similarly, commercial photography—in advertisements, fashion magazines, catalogs—offers visions of perfection which, though lifeless and object-oriented, provide us with models of appearance. For the still camera, the most photogenic subject is one that freezes well, one that can be ripped out of time, suspended, motionless. The ideal photographic model is one who is able to suggest action while standing still, who can imply inner substance or attitude through remote and superficial means. The idealized human becomes the plastic human, able to maintain a perpetual smile, not one whose beauty requires a lingering familiarity, an intimacy.

Writing about medieval France, Mikhail Bakhtin argued that classical aesthetics reinforced conceptions of an eternal, hierarchical social order. In its frozen perfection, the classical ideal of female beauty reinforced the supremacy of those who claimed an endless, God-given right to property and power. Repudiating popular notions—expressed in the "carnival" aesthetic that Bakhtin has described—which celebrate the beauty found in all people and in the cycles of nature, the classical paradigm spoke for a concept of beauty which was, by definition, exclusive, which—in its agelessness—stood above the forces of nature. That which is beautiful, the image silently argues, is the province of the few. In the cool, porcelain tone of this advertisement for Gucci No. 3 Parfum, we confront a depiction of beauty that has served the interests of exclusive power for centuries.

The stark perfection of the image is the outcome of a coordinated industrial process. Among those "creative" people who design and produce the images, or write the copy that accompanies them, managerial systems of observation and discipline have been installed. Artists, photographers, and writers are routinely subjected to the formulaic calculus of the bottom line: sales figures, audience testing, demographic patterns. The cash value of the imagination prevails as the dominant ethic.

The photographs that serve as the centerpiece of style are shot under carefully planned conditions. Photographers follow the detailed instructions of an art director. The photograph is then passed on to the touch-up artist, who will remove "a few stray strands of hair, smooth . . . a wrinkle, slim a model's leg," or do whatever else is necessary to create the effect of immaculate conception. According to Louis Grubb, one of New York's leading retouchers,

> almost every photograph you see for a national advertiser these days has been worked on by a retoucher to some degree. It's very, very rare that an art director will go directly from the chrome, the original native source. Somewhere along the line the photo retoucher's hand is applied. Fundamentally, our job is to correct the basic deficiencies in the original photograph or, in effect, to improve upon the appearance of reality.[18]

In order to depict the "dream of wholeness," fragmentation is often necessary. In the profession of photographic modeling, a model is often selected for the *perfection* of a particular part of the body. Danielle Korwin, the founder and owner of Parts Models, Inc., proudly proclaims, "Yes, we do handle all body parts. Everything from finely manicured hands and feet to pouting lips, weathered hands, even models with two differently colored eyes."[19] In the photographic presentation of style and beauty, these parts become the building blocks of a complete image.

In the pursuit of this ideal, photographers regularly draw upon an inventory of disembodied parts, in order to construct the semblance of wholeness. Advertising photographer Michael Raab explains that "it's difficult to get the foot, ankle and calf perfect on the same leg. Sometimes you have to strip images together to get all three perfect." An article in *Photo/Design* magazine, a trade journal for "the creative team" in advertising, instructs that "the 'part' has to be so perfect that many times the hand and face" in an ad must be an alloy of "two different models."[20]

From conception to execution, the photograph is carefully distanced from real experience. What is created is an image of a person in which all elements of spontaneity, or of individuality, have been removed. The

Louis Grubb

Before a printed advertisement appears, photographs are retouched to remove all *flaws*. At left, an advertisement as published. Above, a photograph marked for the retouching expert.

industrial process of commercial photography follows guidelines developed in Hollywood starlet factories, or "love-goddess assembly lines," where young actresses were transformed into generic, interchangeable, audience-tested ideals. The film director Cecil B. De Mille recalled the uniform beauty of the starlets: "They were stamped out of a mint like silver dollars." To De Mille, the problem was with the process:

> The girls themselves have nothing to do with this. Many of them are distinctive-looking and different looking when they arrive. But they don't come out that way. The eyes, the lips, the mouth, the hair, all are done in a certain typed way. Their faces look like slabs of concrete.
>
> Maybe the average Hollywood glamour girl should be numbered instead of named.[21]

Photogenic beauty rests its definition of perfection on a smooth, standardized, and lifeless modernism, a machine aesthetic in the guise of a human. Caught in time, it is a perfection that never ages, and experiences no mood swings. The idiosyncrasies of *character* are forged into the market-tested gleam of *personality*. Even for those—mostly women—whose faces and bodies provide the raw materials for these images, comparisons are invidious. Against the flat, clichéd view of reality that they portray in the fashion photograph, all elements of lived experience constitute potential flaws. This tension between *self as subject* and *self as object* places these people—perhaps above all others— in the position of being perpetual spectators of themselves, autovoyeurs, taking pleasure or pain from the wrinkle-free surfaces of their own hard shells. For Marlene Dietrich, commenting on seeing herself in *The Blue Angel* on television, it was an ironic sense of pleasure:

> I look at my face on the television screen, and I remember how every tooth was capped, how every inch of skin on that face and neck was dyed and shaped, and in spite of knowing all that, I sit back and say to myself, "That is *still* the most beautiful thing I've ever seen in my life."[22]

For others, *beautiful thinghood* becomes an affliction; the image of self stirs painful feelings of inadequacy. In a 1986 television interview, singer / actress Lanie Kazan spoke revealingly of a seven-year period of crisis, during which she fell victim to the corroding influence of her own publicity photos. Haunted by her inability to live up to, or embody, the air-brushed perfection of the image, she became housebound. "I went to bed in 1969," she related, "and didn't get up until 1976. . . . I would not come out until I looked like my photograph." The abstract, intangible quality of her packaged self was more than even she could bear.[23]

Similarly, rooms or living spaces are conventionally sanitized by the photography of style. Most often they are devoid of people, devoid of evidence that people have been there; cold, uncluttered (or stylishly cluttered); there is no intimation of any significant action outside the frame. These forbidding environments, literally "disembodied," become models for the home as it *should* look. Against such austere shrines, the merest evidence of human life becomes a certain sign of disarray. The potency of these visual guidelines can be seen in the readers' photographic responses to a "home beauty contest" held by the magazine *Metropolitan Home* in January 1983. Invariably, photographs of rooms were submitted "in a perfect imitation of design magazines' " style of photographic representation.[24]

Such tributes to the power of photography have entered into the design of objects themselves. Writing in 1948 in *Arts and Architecture* magazine, Alfred Auerbach noted the emergence of what he called "KODAK modern," an approach to furniture design that considered how the piece would appear in a photograph as the top priority. Everything that practitioners of "KODAK modern" create, he lamented, "is undertaken with an eye for the camera. Is it photogenic? Will it look well in *House Beautiful* or *House and Garden?*"[25]

Photography's powerful ability to mediate style is rooted in its simultaneous affinity to *reality* and *fantasy*. As Oliver Wendell Holmes had observed, the power of the disembodied image is that it can free itself from the encumbrances posed by material reality and still lay claim to that reality. At the same time that the image appeals to transcendent desires, it locates those desires within a visual grammar which is palpable, which *looks real*, which invites identification by the spectator, and which people tend to trust. According to John Everard, one of the pioneers of commercial photography, it is this trust that makes photography so forceful as an advertising medium. Writing in 1934, Everard admitted that

> there seems little doubt that the old fallacy that the camera cannot lie greatly strengthens its appeal. In the hands of a man of technical ability and moderate artistic sense, it is now a pliant medium. It can emphasize qualities of delicacy, elegance of line, mystery and glamour, and yet retain the persistent atmosphere of reality. Cameraland is the land of dreams come true.[26]

As is the case with Everard, people involved in the creation and depiction of style can be very candid and incisive about the work they do. James B——, a photographic stylist whose work appears in major ad campaigns, retail and wholesale catalogs, and "shelter" (home decorating) magazines, discussed the definitions of his work:

I create the image that people want to see. It's up to me to fake people out. . . . Basically you lie to people. You create . . . a picture and then they adapt to that picture. You can bring people up in taste level, you can bring them down in taste level, just by what you create, what you put into it. . . . And it's just pulling together elements which work with whatever you're trying to sell.[27]

What B—— describes is an ongoing dynamic of the consumer culture. After a brief acknowledgment of what "people want to see," he arrives at the heart of the matter. Style is a process of creating commodity images for people to emulate and believe in. Such emulation, though, is not without its costs. As frozen, photogenic images—in ads or style magazines—become models from which people design their living spaces, or themselves, extreme alienation sets in. One becomes, by definition, increasingly uncomfortable in one's own skin. The constant availability of alternative styles to "adapt to," to purchase, thrives on this discomfort. The marketing engines of style depend on anomic subjects seeking to become splendid objects. The extent to which objects seem so promising may be but an index of the extent to which the human subject is in jeopardy; destined only to be defined as a *consumer.*

The personal lives of celebrities, closely monitored and continually represented in the disembodied images of the mass media, perform a function similar to that of commercial photography. Like the alluring commercial photograph, the phenomenon of celebrity cannot be separated from the image machinery of contemporary consumer culture.

By the mid-nineteenth century, the ability of the mass media to endow individuals with an honored, public status was already evident. The Russian film director Sergei Eisenstein wrote of the fame and fan behavior that centered on the person of Charles Dickens as people read the widely distributed, monthly installments of his stories. Emphasizing the cinematic quality of Dickens's novels, Eisenstein saw them as engaging the interests and fantasies of an emerging mass audience:

They compelled the reader to live with the same passions [as film]. They appealed to the same good and sentimental elements as does the film . . . they alike shudder before vice, they alike mill the extraordinary, the unusual, the fantastic, from boring, prosaic and everyday existence. And they clothe this common and prosaic existence in their special vision.

Illumined by this light, refracted from the land of fiction back to life, this commonness took on a romantic air, and bored people were grateful to the author for giving them the countenances of potentially romantic figures.

In the lives of Dickens's heroes, people saw obstacles that were familiar and adventures that piqued their fantasies. They began to see their own lives elevated to new, even epic, levels. The enormous popularity of Dickens's writings was matched by the celebrity that he began to attain. Eisenstein quotes Stefan Zweig, in a description of the "three-quarters of a mile" long lines of people who waited for tickets to a Dickens reading in New York:

> The tickets for the course were all sold before noon. Members of families relieved each other in queues; waiters flew across the streets and squares from the neighboring restaurant, to serve parties who were taking their breakfast in the open December air; while excited men offered five and ten dollars for the mere permission to exchange places with other persons standing nearer the head of the line.[28]

Anyone who has ever lined up to get tickets to a rock concert will recognize the scene. Like Bruce Springsteen, Dickens evoked the heroism of the "common" people, while an emerging media machinery made the heroism available, and the author *known,* in ways that were peculiarly modern.

According to historian Lewis Erenberg, the phenomenon of celebrity gained momentum at the turn of the century, when urban elites ventured across the tracks and "discovered" the appeal of cabaret life. Once shunned as a place of lower-class degeneracy, the cabaret and its performers gained respectability, stretching the boundaries of upper-class style. Performers whose previous audiences had been local, often working class, and largely ethnic, began to transcend their provincial roots, emerging as "objects of emulation" among a wider, more "respectable" orbit of people.[29] The cultural diversities of urban life, the grass roots of industrial society, were attaining an unprecedented legitimacy among the arbiters of "culture." As performers began to reach a wealthy audience, with influence over the dominant means of communications, they were catapulted to positions of notoriety and admiration; they became *known.* A corridor between anonymity and fame was being built. The reciprocity between the reservoirs of popular culture and what C. Wright Mills once called "the prime means of acclaim" was under way.

By the 1920s, the movies, and then radio, provided a machinery of glory that was, up until that time, unimaginable. Audience identification with emerging "stars," along with a growing apparatus of press agentry, combined to produce a public display of personal life that was intricate and enveloping in its detail, vernacular in its expression. In a society where everyday life was increasingly defined by feelings of insignificance and institutions of standardization, the "star" provided an accessible icon to the significance of the personal and the individual. Hortense Powdermaker, writing on the star system of Hollywood, spoke of the "close-up" shot as a monument to intimacy; each pore, each line on the face, each expression becomes memorized as the possession of the spectator. Fan magazines and newspaper columnists filled in the details:

> The details given by columnists of what the star eats for breakfast and whether or not he sleeps in pajamas, gives not only the fan but the regular movie-goer and reader of newspaper columns a feeling of great personal knowledge about his favorite actor.[30]

The fact that many of the stars' "candid" thoughts are written for them, most of their "intimate" life orchestrated by publicity agents, rarely tarnished the image.

In his classic essay "The Work of Art in the Age of Mechanical Reproduction," Walter Benjamin maintained that when a painting or other work of art is reproduced, and made generally available, it loses something. It loses "its presence in time and space, its unique existence at the place where it happens to be." It also loses, he argued, its "authenticity . . . its testimony to the history which it has experienced . . . [its] traditional value" within a given "cultural heritage."[31] Although the reproduction of an art work makes its acquisition more democratic, the reproduction is also less sacred. Ripped from its original context, its original meanings are lost. Benjamin called that which is lost in the reproduction of art the "aura." What was special in the original—its aura—is liquidated, fragmented, deconsecrated in the copy.

The phenomenology of celebrity is nearly the opposite. If great art loses its aura in the marketplace of mass impression, the individual life of the celebrity achieves an aura through mass reproduction. In their ability to magnify, and to create near universal recognition, the mass media are able to invest the everyday lives of formerly everyday people with a magical sense of value, a secularized imprint of the *sacred*. If the reproduction of the Sistine Chapel allows the artwork to be downwardly mobile, the reproduction (of the face, voice, gestures, personal habits) of the celebrity is often a case of upward mobility. It should be added that the celebrity, "seen in the flesh," becomes more captivating the more she or he has been mechanically or electronically *reproduced*.

The impact of this development has been double-edged. According to C. Wright Mills, the apparatus of fame has created "channels through which those at the top could reach the underlying population." To Mills it was a force of "the power elite":

Heavy publicity, the technique of the build-up, and the avaricious demand of the media for continuous copy have placed a spotlight upon these
people such as no higher circles of any nation in world history have ever
had upon them.[32]

No contemporary analysis of social and economic power can avoid
the devices of press agentry and image management as means for
"engineering" mass constituencies and popular consent. At the same
time, the phenomenon of celebrity cannot be reduced to that. If anything, the ongoing message of the celebrisystem is that through its
channels the "underlying population" can achieve the status of "those
at the top." In Nashville, Tennessee's music district, where the names
and faces of country and western stars are emblazoned in a crazy-quilt
tribute to upward mobility, one also finds several small-scale recording
studios which are "open to the public." Across the front of one—similar
to the others—is the following sign:

Your Dream Come True
You, Recording in Nashville
"You Provide the Voice, We Provide the Music."
Record a Memory Today
You came to see the stars. . . . Here . . . you are the star.

Celebrities, though they shine above us, are also—many of them—
very much like us. Identification is easy. The whole story of their success
is that they came from "the mass." They were once unknown. In a
society where conditions of anonymity fertilize the desire "to be somebody," the *dream of identity,* the *dream of wholeness,* is intimately
woven together with the desire to be known; to be visible; to be docu-
mented, for all to see.

Previously unknown, the celebrity was often also previously poor.
The combination of anonymity and poverty are often ritually linked in
the telling of the success story. In Nashville's Country Music Hall of
Fame, as well as in the other, more personalized museums that tell the
stories of various country music stars, the trajectory from rags to spectacular riches is layed out from room to room. Room one is filled with
origins: wooden shacks on the banks of the Mississippi or in the hills of
Appalachia; guitar whammers sittin' on rickety front porches; old
church music; rural poverty. Room two is beginnings: local followings;
old handbills; makeshift instruments (an occasional cigar-box banjo); old
cigar butts; homemade clothes; an indication of "things to come," a
fancy, hand-tooled guitar strap. By the end there are the golden Cadil-
lacs, maroon Rolls Royces, a mint green T-bird, never driven. The star
is visible. The colorful, ornate performing clothes reinforce this. In the

The graffiti writer who decorated this New York subway car in 1981 uses "Seen" as his tag-name.

Hall of Fame, the final scene is filled with props from country-western Hollywood movies: boots worn by Sissy Spacek in *Coal Miner's Daughter,* the car from *Smokey and the Bandit.* Hollywood acclaim is still close to the summit.

The affinity between audience and celebrity stands at the center of this story, and of its popular appeal. Celebrity links the extrication from poverty to extrication from the mass of "unknowns." It speaks to common conditions, and to common discontents. It is perhaps no surprise that in 1924, as the celebrity apparatus was moving into high gear, a survey of the "dreams" of adolescent girls evoked the following responses:

> "Many times have I had dreams of having the world at my feet."

> "I have dreamed of . . . charming millions, winning fame and fortune."

> "I was before a large audience. . . . It was a great success."

> "The whole world applauded me."[33]

Celebrity forms a symbolic pathway, connecting each aspiring individual to a universal image of fulfillment: to be someone, when "being no one" is the norm. Whereas the beginnings of celebrity often begin with a local, word-of-mouth following, invariably, becoming "someone" is a gift bestowed upon people by the image machine. The myriad stories of chance meetings and lucky breaks fuel the belief, for many, that it "may happen." Each success feeds the hopes of millions who will never make it.

Nevertheless, the phenomenon of celebrity reflects popular longings. In celebrities, people find not only a piece of themselves, but also a piece of what they strive for. Warren Susman discussed the appeal of Babe Ruth in terms of how Ruth could play a game of rules and statistics—the tools of modern regimentation—and come out of it as a self-determined individual. To Susman, Ruth was both a product of the modern machinery, and one who, simultaneously, transcended it.

This transcendent, and critical, quality is an aspect of many celebrities. Stevie Wonder, big-time recording artist, is also a voice of freedom against the centuries of racism in the United States. Marilyn Monroe, a product of the Hollywood "Dream Factory" (and also, perhaps, its victim), also spoke to women's sensual longings, and vulnerability, subjectively. Springsteen chants the dreams, and the betrayed hopes, of working-class people at work, at war, in love. Charlie Chaplin, one of the first "stars," was also the ironic critic of industrial regimentation and fascist vanity. These critical aspects of each of these celebrities is, unquestionably, part of their bond with their audience.

Yet it is the instinct of the image industries, as has been discussed, to systematically "skin" the surface of everything. In the process, even the critical content gets boiled down for its most valuable element: *style*, to merchandise, to consume. Along the way, the consumption habits of the celebrity generally become part of the picture, completing the circle, providing models.

Despite Babe Ruth's appeal as a transcendent individual in a standardized world, Susman noted that Ruth was "also an ideal hero for the world of consumption":

> Ruth enjoyed spending money as well as earning it. An incorrigible gambler, and for large sums, he never seemed concerned about winning or losing. He loved expensive and fancy clothes. . . . His gluttony became equally legendary; he often overate and overdrank to the point of actual severe physical illness.

Consistent with his proclivities for consumption, "Ruth found a way of making all of this pay; he made himself into a marketable product," hiring a press agent, doing product endorsements, appearing in movies, and sometimes—for a fat fee—just appearing live, for people to see "in the flesh."[34] In the process, his *style* provided a formulaic prototype for the bombastic "sports hero" against which future athletes would be measured.

Similarly, Stevie Wonder's *style* is transformed into a "look," for clothing to be sold, for hair-care products and styling salons; a "sound" for AT&T commercials. Meanwhile, the recording industry may try to maximize receipts by scouting the neighborhoods for talent that will appeal to the same "market segment" as Wonder.

This is what happened to Marilyn Monroe. Her popular appeal gave rise to a parade of look-alikes, standardized reproductions for popular consumption: Jayne Mansfield, Mamie Van Doren et al. Long after Marilyn died, her face and figure retain their commodity value. She has been transformed into costly artworks (now available in reproductions for your home) by Andy Warhol. An imitator strikes that *inimitable* pose—dress blown up by a rush of air from a grate on the sidewalk—in a newspaper ad for summer dresses "guaranteed to give you chills all over. . . . $29.99–$39.99."

The Springsteen look, sound, and pose have been lifted and transferred to ads selling trucks, cars, and blue jeans. It is the instinct of the style market to capitalize on something *hot,* to turn popular desires into demographics.

Along the way, the surface reigns supreme. Meaning is transformed. The case of Charlie Chaplin, and his film *Modern Times,* is typical. The film is a scathing indictment of industrial capitalism, a critique of an increasingly regimented industrial society, a bitter and poetic examination of modern life and alienation. In *Modern Times* we confront a factory world which increasingly usurps human initiative. Within the scope of the film, people are trapped beneath the thumb of productivity, their bodies and souls shaped and overwhelmed by the assembly line. The priorities of such a world submerge human needs; misery and homelessness abound. People are seen as useful only if they can be plugged into the productive apparatus. Otherwise they are tossed aside, like garbage.

Another theme of the film confronts the relationship between media and power in this modern world. Those in authority, those with their hands on the controls, utilize the media of communication to exercise their power. Those who labor, poor folks, remain—within the film—voiceless.

Alongside this grim vision of industrial encroachment, Chaplin's *Modern Times* is also rebellious, visionary. Against the robotic rhythms of factory life, it is a call for poetry, action, resistance. It offers a critique of work itself, suggesting that pleasure is a more meaningful goal for human life. Against the monotony of a mechanical civilization, Chaplin evinces a politics of spontaneity, a manifesto for sensuality and positive disorder. At film's end, Chaplin—a former factory worker—and his beloved "gamin," take to the road; walk away from the strictures and disciplines of industrial society.

Many young people of the 1980s have never seen *Modern Times,* made in 1936. Surveys of my students consistently reveal that most have never seen the film, have never seen *any* Chaplin film. But his skin remains.

Today Charlie Chaplin (a look-alike) and "Modern Times" (the phrase) have returned to the public eye. In this incarnation, however, the Little Tramp is selling computers for IBM. In the IBM ads we once again see Chaplin as a victim of industrial chaos, overwhelmed by the assembly line. But this time, the solution is different. Beleaguered Charlie is saved by the computer, the quintessential modern instrument of order, control, surveillance. Here the frenetic conditions of modern life are solved by modern technology. The 1936 film had pointed an idealistic *way out,* the ad points the *way back in.* The critique has been turned on its head, packaged, and used against itself.

If some celebrities appeal to an audience's critical concerns before being skinned and transmuted into a consumable style, many require little alteration. Much of celebrity is style from beginning to end; conceived, at birth, as something to be sold. The systematic link between celebrity and consumption was established, in the United States, during the 1920s and 1930s. The fan magazines and newspaper columns that covered Hollywood dovetailed with the movies to offer a seamless tableau of fashions, hairstyles, favorite foods, personal habits, reading interests, decorating ideas, and recreational interests, not to mention sexual proclivities, all of which were visible, many of which offered appealing alternatives to the stuffy residues of Victorianism, or the greenhorn habits of immigrant parents.

By 1939, Margaret Farrand Thorp, in a study of the relationship between America and the movies, noted that the consumption patterns of Hollywood (on and off screen) had become a "standard of reference" for popular consumption, "making it possible for the housewife in Vermont or Oregon to explain to her hairdresser, her dressmaker, or her decorator, the ideal that she is striving to realize."[35] The interaction between celebrity life-style and popular—mainly women's—consumption was fueled by the regular features appearing in fan magazines:

> One obvious way to resemble your ideal is to dress as she does and no fan magazine is complete without its fashion department devoted to the costumes of the stars both on and off the screen. . . .

[Fan magazines] . . . will fill in for you all the little intimate details that make a personality real, that make identification close and exciting.
. . .

The imitative fan is almost always feminine but sometimes she wants to establish a sense of intimate friendship with a male adored one. There are two good channels for that, food and house furnishing. No issue of a fan magazine is complete without a favorite recipe of Clark Gable or Tyrone Power or some other of the galaxy. . . . Interior decoration offers further possibilities for sympathetic magic.[36]

By 1930, this connection had become institutionalized in merchandising. Bernard Waldman, a New York garment executive, transformed the celeb/fan affinity into a business when he began turning out copies of a wedding gown that appeared in the film *King of Jazz*. This was the beginning of the Modern Merchandising Bureau, which spun off a number of trade names that specialized in cinematic fashion: Cinema Fashions, Screen Star Styles, Cinema Modes, and so on. This, along with an already established tradition of celebrity endorsements, provided a framework for the connection between celebrity style and the mass production and distribution of style. In big cities, Thorp reported, many other forces contributed to the kaleidoscope of style; in small towns, however, Cinema Fashions were particularly influential. "There," she wrote, "the movies have little else to compete with as dictators of fashions."[37]

Just as the escape from anonymity, and the expression of popular longings, created a meaningful avenue between regular people and celebrities, the status of *consumers* was also a powerful link, and—on some level—their status as wage earners was another.

The "life-styles of the rich and famous," their consumption habits, provide an enticing and ever-visible form of popular entertainment in the United States. From the 1920s, when the glitter of Hollywood stardom first sparkled, Americans have watched—in awe—as a wondrous and unrestrained celebrity shopping spree has unfolded before their eyes.

In a consumer society, the lives of the celebrities are not merely guideposts from which people can take their stylistic cues. They also embody every consumer's dream of what it would be like if money were no object. In "the magnifying glass of the mass media," wrote C. Wright Mills in 1956, we see "all the expensive commodities, to which the rich seem appendages. . . . money talking in its husky, silky voice of cash, power, celebrity."[38] The luminaries, their clothes and cars and villas and vacation yachts, represent a consumerized interpretation of personal freedom—a "middle class" ideal—multiplied exponentially; beyond comprehension, but never so far as to undermine a glimmer of hope in the mind of the spectator. The dream of abundance, the principle of appearances, circulates in the lives of celebrities as it circulates in the desires of those maintaining—or attempting to construct—the semblance of a "middle class" life.

Celebrities, collectively, supply us with the most accessible vision of what wealth means. Yet while their lives provide a vernacular depiction of *wealth,* they also tend to mask the relation between wealth and power. Though celebrities are routinely described as "fabulously wealthy," they are linked to their audience by the fact that for both, consumption serves as the primary expression of their power, or lack of it. True, celebrities can go to the movies without having to wait in line, can get the best table in the house at a moment's notice. Yet these are essentially consumer aspirations; to purchase without restraint, to enjoy the envious glances of those around them. In critical ways, however, most celebrities stand in a similar relation to meaningful, decision-making power over society as do the "unknown" people who admire them.

Few celebrities are the ones "who really run things." Among the assembled audiences of American society, the names and faces and activities of finance capitalists, transnational corporate leaders, political policymakers, or those who operate the machineries of mass impression, are—for the most part—unknown, invisible.

As consumers, most celebrities are also *employees.* Their value, their celebrity itself, is sold "piecemeal," like a "commodity." Their fame and their fortune is "exposed to all the vicissitudes of competition, to all the fluctuations of the market." Like the factory worker, or the clerical worker, or the mid-level functionary of a corporate or government bureaucracy, a celebrity is "an appendage of the machine." The machine, in this case, is the media industry, the "prime means of acclaim."

In this sense, although their pay is enough to make them the uncontested "aristocracy of labor," their exploitation, their status as commodities, is more visible than in other areas of employment. They, literally, are the commodity being sold; fabricated, most of the time, on an elaborate, cultural assembly line.

The studio system in Hollywood established the standards of production during the 1930s. The Central Casting Corporation supplied extras to the various studios, while promising "stars" were signed on as exclusive properties, *owned* by one of seven major studios. As the "star" system generated certain identifiable *types* which movie fans (markets) responded to, potential "stars" were scouted out and given contracts insofar as they conformed to certain industry standards. A promotional machinery then went into gear, projecting faces and names into the spotlight, generating celebrities. Some caught on, some did not. As Hortense Powdermaker noted, Hollywood types were often selected according to specific physical attributes: "comely legs . . . bust . . . husky sensuous voice"; a handsome male star was "colloquially referred to as 'the penis.' "[39] The *division of labor* was complete; the body of the laborer was broken down, and evaluated, according to its constituent parts.[40] Though their glamorous lives took precedence in the press releases and glossies, these celebrities were owned, typed, and operated by the studio bosses.

Not only were actors hired according to standardized types; the movies they starred in were produced according to standardized models—film genres—which still predominate over most films and television shows. With some exceptions, the market-tested formula is an earmark of celebrities and the media they inhabit.

The studio system no longer exists. It has been transcended by a somewhat less centralized image machinery that is far more vast, more diverse in its applications. Through it all, the commodity status of celebrity remains. To be known is to be sold.

It is this objectification of the person that, most probably, explains much of the turmoil and grief, the identity crisis that often accompanies stardom. Perhaps celebrities, too, become uncomfortable in their own skins as they, in the eyes of others, become frozen images; as their faces and bodies and mannerisms become icons; always the personage, never the person. It is difficult to be a disembodied image.

Celebrities last as long as the people continue buying. If celebrity declines—as it often does—they become part of an enormous, cultural garbage pile; worthless, forgotten, or retained in the mind as pieces of trivia. It is on this level, as they are faithfully kept in the popular memory, that the link between the known and the unknown is most poignant.

THE DECORATION
OF INDEPENDENCE

A young male model looks out at us. He lounges across the right-hand side of a two-page magazine spread. He wears an open shirt, exposing a lean, defined torso; he wears a face of seriousness and integrity.

He speaks to us:

I hate this job.

I'm not just an empty suit who stands in front of a camera, collects the money and flies off to St. Maarten for the weekend.

I may model for a living, but I hate being treated like a piece of meat. I once had a loud-mouthed art director say, "Stand there and pretend you're a human." I wanted to punch him, but I needed the job. . . .

Oh, yeah, about this fragrance [identified below as Perry Ellis, Fragrance For Men]. It's good. Very good.

When I posed for this picture, the art director, a real nice woman, insisted that I wear this while the pictures were being taken. I thought it was silly, but I said, "What the hell? It's their money."

After a while, I realized I like this fragrance a lot. When the photo shoot was over I walked right over, picked up the bottle, put it in my pocket and said, "If you don't mind I'd like to take this as a souvenir." Then I smiled my best f—— you smile and walked out.

Next time I'll pay for it. It's that good.

This is the fragrance for those men who hate work and are willing to say "f—— you" to their boss. Disgusted by "being treated like a piece of meat," sick of having his humanity suppressed, tired of meaningless consumption, this guy knows *and says* what he wants.

The industrial regimentation of the body, the rationalization of emotional expression, and the capitalization of the imagination are all aspects of commercial culture. Fragmentation and deception have been normalized within a society that is predicated on *freedom*.

In *Being and Nothingness* (1943), the French philosopher Jean-Paul Sartre approached the question of human freedom within the context of twentieth-century life. In contrast to eighteenth-century Enlightenment philosophers, Sartre did not perceive freedom as an inborn state of being, a natural right, a condition at birth. For Sartre, *being in itself* held no intrinsic meaning. Life in its "essence" was understood to be absurd. Freedom, Sartre argued, was realized in moving beyond the state of being; taking action. Active, self-determined engagement within the world, is what—for Sartre—constituted freedom.

Yet not *all* activity constituted meaningful freedom. The prescribed roles and rituals of society provided people with an arena of action that is not their own. Using the example of tradesmen, shopkeepers, Sartre spoke of how people in these positions tend to act according to ritual behavior more than self-motivated engagement:

The public demands of them that they realize . . . [their condition in the world] as a ceremony; there is the dance of the grocer, of the tailor, of the auctioneer, by which they endeavor to persuade their clientele that they are nothing but a grocer, an auctioneer, a tailor. A grocer who dreams is offensive to the buyer, because such a grocer is not wholly a grocer. Society demands that he limit himself to his function as a grocer. . . . There are indeed many precautions to imprison a man in what he is, as if we lived in perpetual fear that he might escape from it, that he might break away and suddenly elude his condition.[41]

The acceptance of these ceremonial expectations, even when they require "denying the qualities" that one possesses, Sartre contended, places life in an ongoing condition of "bad faith." Freedom is a condition of self-realization through action: *doing* within the world.

Held up against the structures of work as they have developed in the twentieth-century United States, and elsewhere, the implications of Sartre's argument are multiplied. The routines, fragmented gestures, and institutionalized shams that constitute much of what people *do for a living,* make the realization of freedom ever more elusive. In the context of a society that holds up the idea of personal freedom as its dominant ideology, the gnawing feeling of "bad faith" is compounded. It is here that Roland Barthes's "dream of wholeness" speaks most poignantly to the citizen—perhaps *consumer* is more appropriate—of contemporary culture. In style we find the "dream of identity" that, for so many, eludes them in the terms of their daily activity. We also find the *dream of action,* of *engagement;* the dream of being "oneself" and of having "this *self . . .* recognized by others."[42]

The bureaucratic work structures of the contemporary consumer culture militate against the freedom to act creatively, to realize oneself through engagement with the world. A sense of wholeness eludes the person whose daily tasks are encompassed by acts which have little meaning in and of themselves, which are fragmentary pieces within an enterprise that he or she cannot fully comprehend. Against the prominent backdrop of "personal freedom," the terms of reality can fill a person with an overwhelming, insatiable hunger: to act, to make meaning in one's life.

As the realms of work provide little nurture for the hunger, it is in "leisure" that many people look for satisfaction. One of the most available routes to satisfaction is consumption. While the preponderant work structures of consumer capitalism often bear the fruits of frustration, the images of consumerism continually acknowledge the desire for freedom, the freedom to desire. Within this circle, style becomes a compensation for the *substance* that mass produces and markets it.

The phenomenon of style, as marketed by the style industries, achieves its power through the association made between objects and action. This systematic association is a continuous function of advertising; purchasable objects are invested with the connotation of subjectivity. In the kaleidoscope of consumable style, we are confronted by a range of actions and desires which are inhibited by the conventions of everyday life. These objectifications of action and desire, of engagement and self-realization, take a wide variety of forms; together they provide us with a topography of civilization and its discontents.

Pontiac Automobiles

A close-up of a face waits and listens while a voice-over pops the question:

What was the last exciting thing that you did?

An unkempt man answers in monotone:

I won five dollars in the lottery.

A sleek automobile swerves around a mountain curve. The voice-over returns:

Need excitement? . . .

Followed by an inspirational song, men in chorus:

WE BUILD EX-CITE-MENT . . . PON-TI-AAAAC!

Excitement is hard to come by these days. We are reduced to letting the little things count. We will be freed by the machine.

Hathaway Shirts

A magazine page with seven miniature magazine ads for Hathaway shirts: each ad shows a man, accomplished and *known* for his accomplishments. Each wears a Hathaway shirt, and an eye-patch over the right eye. The symbolism of success and the symbolism of the shirt merge. Each man offers a different dream of action:

Ted Turner: "To be bold."
J. W. Marriott, Jr.: "To be a builder."
John Naisbitt: "To be intuitive."
Pete Dawkins: "To be a leader."
Roy Jacuzzi: "To be an inventor."
John Connally: "To be a national presence."
and so on. . . .

At the bottom right, an empty outline of a man, wearing the eye-patch. Underneath, the caption:

To be announced soon

Who will be next? Will it be you? The symbolism of opportunity knocks. Buy it!

To be bold.

To be a builder.

To be intuitive.

To be a leader.

To be dedicated.

To be an inventor.

To be a national presence.

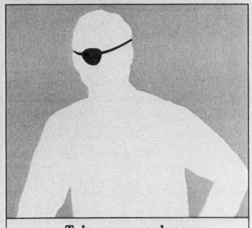

To be announced soon.

Hathaway

Max Weber, the German sociologist, described *charisma* as the extraordinary magnetism that is exerted by a political, military, or religious leader or hero upon his followers. After the hero, or the enthusiasm surrounding him, dies, Weber contended, his charisma is *routinized* into the traditions or bureaucratic structures of the state, or of other social institutions. In the marketplace of style, as depicted in this advertisement, the charisma of great achievers is routinized into *the shirt*. In the space yet to be occupied (*lower right*), one who dons the shirt will inherit the powers of its forewearers. To have is to do.

Candie's Shoes

A young, dark-haired beauty steps out of her sleek, red sportscar. She looks back at those she has left behind. Her mouth opens with a triumphant smile. She wears a pair of Candie's© high-tops. In the traffic jam of life, she lives "LIFE IN THE FAST LANE."

The dream of escape, of triumph, of leaving others behind. The dream of escaping oneself. Place yourself in these shoes. Place yourself in this picture.

Obsession Perfume, Calvin Klein

In a grainy image, a moist veil of haze, five bodies—male and female—explore their nakedness, writhe, become one in an endless moment of unbounded pleasure. Obsession.

A world without rules. Pleasure without anxiety. With this perfume, the id is liberated from the superego. Through a dark glass we rediscover our primordial memory, a time before, or now; desire, dark and wet, and joining many bodies into one throbbing mass. Now available at Bloomingdale's.

In the marketing of style, in its images, surfaces, and scents, the *dream of identity* is paraded before our eye's mind. It is not only a dream of *public identity,* but it also plumbs the wells of *inner identity.* Style, in its images and objects, offers a provocative typology of needs, a symbolic politics of transcendence. In this sense, style provides people with a powerful means of expression.

Insofar as style is a device of the marketplace, however, it is simultaneously a means of containment. By investing purchasable commodities with connotations of action, *having* vies with *doing* in the available lexicon of self-realization. Acting upon the world gives way to the possession of objects/images that suggest the qualities of active personhood.

In Sartre's terms, we are entreated to escape the injuries and anguish of a repressive society by embracing what he called the " 'faith' of bad faith." As a surrogate for action we are invoked to consume the symbols of action. As the joke goes, "When the going gets tough, the tough go shopping."

The style industries, and their marketing strategies, continually substantiate and sustain this transvaluation. As early as 1925, the psychiatrist Thomas Atkinson advised the advertising industry to "Make your reader 'feel himself into' your imagery with a sense of mastery impulse,

When everything you wear knows exactly what it's doing, you can take it easy. —*Alexander Julian*

This empty—but active—suit of clothes embodies the principle of *having* as a surrogate for *doing*.

like that which makes a child want to learn a new game."[43] According to Atkinson, a product should be presented as empowering to the consumer.

J. Gordon Lippincott, the product designer, addressed the problem of *identity* within contemporary society more directly:

> In this era of anonymity of mass production, such qualities of personal appeal are a tangible and specific means of meeting competition. . . . As long as people dislike the anonymity of mass production, there will always be added sales appeal in products that have a personality.[44]

The impact of such thinking is visible throughout commercialized style. Objects take on subjective qualities, or are depicted as fixtures in the lives of people who thrive on a life of total satisfaction. They have status; they are admired; they are potent; they are sexy; they live close to the edge; they step beyond the bounds; they set the bounds; they are self-directing; they are spontaneous. They are spared the limits of everyday life; they are exempt.

In the images of style we see a world where the marketplace becomes its own, closely watched, opposition. That world is utopian: cost is no object; work holds no restrictions; desire has no conscience; each moment is self-governed. A fragile ego is boosted by the surface identity of style.

Style is a realm of being "exceptional" within the constraints of conformity. In a bureaucratic world of rationalized impersonality, style offers the possibility of transcendence. It is style that allows the irrational and the personal to flourish, while its images are meted out in a rationalized and impersonal sort of way. This is its appeal—particularly among those who choose to see themselves as "middle class"—its ability to offer an escape from the routines, routinely.

People, in their lives, continue to seek freedom in *doing,* through self-determined activity. Several aspects of the consumer culture, however, constrict this. The competitive individualism, which is fostered by the contours of work and social life, tends to confine the vision of "self-realization" to atomized and personalistic solutions. Among individuated units, consumption becomes the most *natural* proclivity. Even those self-active opportunities that are available—jogging, computing, cooking, dieting, watching, collecting—are, themselves, easily stylized and "commodified." Whatever the intentions, life is caught between the polarities of *doing* and *having.*

3

Image and Power in a Changing World

CHAPTER SIX

Varnished
Barbarism

THE LOOK OF HISTORY

A 1987 television commercial, for Wendy's fast-food hamburger outlets, offers viewers a tongue-in-cheek, but mean-spirited glimpse of a Soviet fashion show. The setting is predictably dismal, evoking the chill of a penitentiary auditorium. The stage is lit by the artless glare of a searchlight. As each fashion occasion is announced—"evening wear," "beach wear," and so on—an ungainly stereotype of a broad-beamed Russian peasant woman waddles out from behind a drab curtain, onto the runway. Each time she wears exactly the same outfit: a babushka on the head, and a baggy, prison-gray smock, cut just above the knees to accentuate her flabby inner thighs. Each appearance is greeted by an unspontaneous and unenthusiastic round of Politburo-style applause. When all is said and done, the most damning condemnation of Soviet life is that it *lacks style.**

Wendy's, on the other hand, is situated among the lively variety of images that marks life in the *free world*. Democracy delivers glamour; exotic fantasy settings; color; lean mannequins who stride like silken antelopes across the softly lit stretches of the fashion stage; background music that enlists the ears to follow the eyes.

The spoof of Soviet life appeals to the viewing audience's patriotic faith in the multiform surfaces of the image industries. A contest between nations, and between political and economic systems, is reduced to a war of appearances. American capitalism is validated by the sugges-

---

*As Soviet society becomes stylishly *glasnost* (openness, or publicity) in the late 1980s, the U.S. media have become anxious and confused over how to interpret these new developments. So deep was the stereotype of the thick-fingered Russian peasant that the new Soviet style caught the image-watching wing of the Kremlinological establishment off guard.

tive surfaces with which it wraps its products. Within the advertisement, a fast-food chain, which cranks out hamburgers in endless and identical procession, claims the imprimatur of stylistic diversity. Embedded in the Wendy's commercial, and in countless others, is the common assumption that style provides us with ways of understanding societies; our own, and others'. Alongside style's capacity to express personal longings and individual identity is its ability to encode and transmit social values and ideas.

In today's consumer cultures, where style prevails as a dominant form of currency, style presents people with many ways of seeing and comprehending society. As in the Wendy's ad, the proliferation of diverse styles in American life is often cited as tangible evidence of democracy. The extensive choice and variety of images, which enshrine the goods we may purchase, is regularly equated with a choice and variety in ideas and perspectives that we may hold or give voice to.

The ultimate "qualification" for social and political leadership, as well, has increasingly come to reside in the vaporous area of style. As democratic politics moves from an activity engaging the popular participation of its citizens to what David Reisman called "an Object of Consumption," style emerges as its prime mode of presentation. According to Reisman, style addresses the "indifference and apathy" of people whose political lives have devolved to "conditions of passive consumership":

> The mass media act as a kind of barker for the political show. . . . Just as glamor in sex substitutes for both love and the relatively impersonal family ties of the tradition-directed person, and just as glamor in packaging and advertising substitutes for price competition, so glamor in politics, whether as charisma—packaging—of the leader or as the hopped-up media treatment of events by the mass media, substitutes for the types of self-interest that governed the inner directed. In general: *wherever we see glamor in the object of attention, we must suspect a basic apathy in the spectator.* [1]

Social relations of power are also refracted through the prism of style. The global reach of a corporation such as IBM is accentuated and buttressed by a uniformly recognizable, international style that permeates its products, its advertisements and brochures, its corporate offices and display pavilions. Whatever the context, the corporate image is designed to dominate its surroundings. The corporation logo appears to spring out of an overarching idea of efficiency; there is no hint of an individual mind or hand having had any impact on its simple statement of corporate dignity.

For decades, one of the most common ways that Americans compared communism and capitalist democracy was to say that communism encouraged sameness, denied individuality, and lacked style. This advertisement for men's clothing, here using Chinese communism as its foil, plays on this old theme. Today, with *glasnost* and the stylish tone set by Mikhail and Raisa Gorbachev, such comparisons have lost much of their bite. After long years of claiming a monopoly on style, Western democracy faces a moment of crisis.

Along the same lines, the design of an office space, or a university, or a prison, or a factory, is likely to embody the power relations that structure its activity. It will tell us, silently, who is powerful, who is not; who watches, who is watched; who dictates, who takes dictation.

The relationship between style and social power, so evident today, is not a creation of twentieth-century consumer culture in particular. This alliance has a venerable history. Long before the rise of a mass market in style, style was already a visible embodiment of power relations.

In the contexts of European feudalism, for example, style and consumption among the nobility, and the upper clergy, marked their special status within society. Their clothing, for example, set them off, palpably, from the common lot of humanity and demonstrated their power over others. The elaborate cutting and layering of expensive cloth revealed the expanse of precious material that went into constructing their apparel. In certain cases, the clothing of the nobility consumed more than a thousand yards of cloth in a single garment, many times the amount of material necessary to dress an extended family of commoners. The long train, carried by young girls, of the wedding dress worn by Sarah Ferguson in her marriage to Prince Andrew of England is a throwback to an aristocratic age characterized by visible patterns of inequality. In a world where material scarcity and hard work were the common definitions of life, such excessive images connoted a power over others: the employment of enormous forces of long and painstaking labor for the purposes of personal body decoration; the enjoyment of waste and unbroken leisure in a context where the majority of lives were spent in arduous squalor.[2]

Though the material power of feudal relations declined, the power of aristocratic imagery persevered among various parvenus of the new market economy. In the United States, it was adopted and funded by diverse elements of nineteenth-century wealth.

Among the planter class of the slave-owning South, the traditions of feudal Europe supplied them with an iconography of power, a claim within history, legitimating the "peculiar institution" over which they held sway. The elaboration of a mannered, aristocratic style of life, across the antebellum South, masked a deep—and ultimately fatal—contradiction in the structure of the plantation economy. From the eighteenth century onward, Southern elites carefully erected a detailed depiction of themselves as a leisured, landed class, presiding over happy and romantic rural principalities. From courtly manners to the studied consumption of European finery, Southern cavaliers expended enormous energy and wealth to situate themselves in magic kingdoms, ruled—benevolently—by themselves.

If the image to which they aspired was one of landed self-sufficiency, their economic realities were quite different. Southern planters were thoroughly embroiled in the external forces of a burgeoning world market. The development of plantation agriculture in the Americas was decisive in the emergence of a modern global economy. The production of sugar in the Caribbean, and tobacco in the American mainland colonies, provided major sources of New World export. As cash crops these exports became a basic builder of capital for the modern European economy. The cultivation of cotton, which characterized most Southern plantation agriculture into the nineteenth century, was an important producer of capital as well. Not incidentally, cotton was the raw material around which industrial systems of machine production took root both in Britain and the United States. The mass production of textiles, in large measure, signaled the beginnings of modern industrial capitalism.[3]

Southern plantation life placed its economic foundations in one world, and its cultural pretensions in another. Slavery was intertwined with modern, global economic forms, and with industrial patterns of large-scale production, but the stylistic claims of the slave masters suggested the insularity and ostentatious grandeur of feudalism. Unlike early New England merchants, whose "Protestant ethic" was translated into plain aesthetic simplicity, Southern planters were dedicated to aristocratic principles of grand display.

Wealthy planters surrounded themselves with a grandiose if eclectic veil of medieval and classical pretense. Homes, fashioned according to Greek or—to a lesser extent—Georgian motifs, were expansive in scale and design, dramatically situated and landscaped. Often built upon hills, mansions were commonly surrounded by parks or formal gardens, filled with wandering, sandy walkways and marble statues. Tall columns and porticos decorated huge front porches, asserting a genealogical connection to classical taste. Within, an entrance hall provided a frame for a magnificent, sweeping staircase.[4]

The acquisition and display of finely crafted appointments provided visible emblems of venerable power and prestige. A stately architecture was reinforced by

> high ceilinged, spacious rooms, hung with damask or Chinese wallpaper, and furnished with imported pieces. Rooms and halls were paneled, often in rosewood, and the pine or cedar fluted pillars and pilasters were the work of skilled carpenters of the colonial era. The ceilings were frescoed, and gilded settees, silken bellpulls, and quantities of bric-a-brac from France were characteristic of this type of home.[5]

Alongside the systematic maintenance of slavery, and the elaborate litany of racist justifications, the planter class of the South created a style of life in which they occupied the head of the chain of being. If blacks were painted as inherently brutish, the facade of style painted the male Southern aristocrat as inherently noble, a natural leader.

Each element of plantation style spoke for the natural order of hierarchy. "Every group is assigned a place," wrote William Taylor, the historian of American ideas. "At the top is the Cavalier gentleman of English ancestry and unmixed blood and below him are ranked other groups whose subservience to the gentleman is constantly asserted: German and Scotch-Irish 'peasantry,' women and Negroes."[6]

The uses of style in the antebellum South were intended to enthrone the planter class at the summit of an eternal and hereditary corporate order. For planters, the practices of costly display were hardened into a code of etiquette and honor which suggested the abiding continuity of their wealth and social pedigree. Long after the abolition of slavery, the delineation of chivalric precepts continued to emblazon official renditions of the Southern way of life.

In the urban, industrializing North, however, the masks of style were employed in a volatile theater of boom and bust. From mid-nineteenth century to the turn of the twentieth, the growth of industrial enterprise propelled innovative entrepreneurs to new positions of wealth. Through industry, and speculation, these men vied with the scions of *old money* for position in a newly expanded, rapidly shifting elite.

The style of consumption practiced by the old wealth of New England had, by the mid-nineteenth century, solidified into a comfortable but understated dignity. While their material culture evinced an appreciation for quality and craft, their style of presentation tended toward a simplicity of form. As a testament to their breeding and good taste, they shunned the *nouveau riche* practices of ostentation, maintaining a self-image of material restraint.

For the new wealth of the industrial North, however, there was no fortress of established taste to fall back on. As the entrenched, mercantile wealth of the New England Brahmins was challenged by the social and economic mobility of new entrepreneurs, surface display became an increasingly prominent and restless feature of wealth. Unable to rest their reputations on the God-given or timeworn laurels of more entrenched elites, they began to borrow and steal from the diverse traditions and motifs of ruling taste that could be found throughout history, and across cultural boundaries. Conspicuous consumption and the eclectic employment of styles—from wherever—became part of a frantic and ongoing jockeying for position.

The volatile character of class, and the rapid shifts of wealth that accompanied industrialization, made the principle of display all the more important. It was the increased availability of stamped-out goods that made the impulse toward such display all the more realizable. In the city, where the visible ranks of *others* were legion, avenues and institutions of public display began to crop up. Style, in ever-expanding variety, was emerging as an essential tool of emerging elites. "In an effort to establish their positions," writes Lewis Erenberg, "new and old money adopted the behavior patterns described by cynical chronicler Thorstein Veblen":

> They got together to display their monetary power, and hence their industrial might, in such public places as hotels and restaurants, where the circulation of the community and human contact were the greatest. ... Within the city, the hotels and restaurants facilitated social mixing and provided meeting places for the members of an expanded elite.[7]

More than ever before, class position was determined by the *ability to purchase.* Although a rootedness in history was still a feather in the cap, the stuff that allowed a person to put on the cap in the first place was money. Those with money could buy the look of history. The places where the new industrial elites met were encrusted with it. Stylish restaurants, like Delmonico's or Maxim's, provided settings where patrons could imagine themselves as frequenters of the court. "Julius Keller of Maxim's," reports Erenberg, "outfitted his help in the cutaway coats, ruffled shirts, black satin breeches, silk stockings, silver buckled pumps, and powdered wigs that he imagined were part of Louis XIV's livery."[8] At Delmonico's, deferential waiters brought the sophisticated cuisines of Europe to the palates of the newly rich. Grand hotels also provided a luxurious context.

For Erenberg, the development of these palatial restaurants and hotels were part of an emerging public life among the upper classes. The rich went out on the town, to see and to be seen, and tools of display began to multiply as the variety of influences upon upper-class culture became increasingly diverse:

> The huge public hotels represented an attempt by new elites to outdo other wealthy elements in the only way they knew: socially and through social claim to leadership. In this period of flux, the wealthy classes regrouped while they transferred their competitiveness to public spheres, which connoted power, money, and an ability to lead. . . . And once in the public, the lines between the social elect and others continued to blur, especially as the various segments of the wealthy turned to cultivating Broadway figures to increase their now-public notice and reputation.[9]

In the architecture and furnishing of their homes, the captains of industry and finance "buckled history around themselves like moral armor."[10] On New York's Fifth Avenue, where millionaires built mansions to form a visible line between public display and private life, architecture made a dramatic leap from construction to decoration. Becoming "curators of eclectic taste," architects trained in the Ecole des Beaux Arts appealed to the inflated passions of wealth, by housing them within facades drawn from the "fashionable French Renaissance, Italian Romanesque, and Graeco-Roman classical styles."[11] In this era of the wedding cake approach to architectural ornamentation, noted architectural historian Eric Mendelsohn, "the architect . . . degraded himself to be the handiman of wealth, the mere decorator of structural principles invented by different times and civilizations."[12] The unifying principle behind Beaux Arts architecture was excessive display. Its forms and sources varied, but in each case it was designed to convey an impressive message of history and wealth.

The great architects of the period were those who could most effectively quote and innovate from the imageries of patrician culture. Richard Morris Hunt built his reputation as an architect upon his copying of French Renaissance style. Henry Hobson Richardson was the purveyor of the Italian Romanesque. Charles Follen McKim (along with his partner Stanford White) was the pastry chef of Greco-Roman classicism. Although their fortunes were derived from industrial capitalism, the nineteenth-century robber barons surrounded themselves with a grandiloquent display of aristocratic privilege.[13]

The gaudy pretense of these industrial aristocrats was drawn, indiscriminately, from the imagistic reservoirs of past grandeur. In ensemble, these images were little more than a monument to the buck. James Stephens, the Irish nationalist, commented on the mansions along Fifth Avenue, while visiting the United States in 1858: "Most of the houses denote wealth; some of them are sumptuous; but, with few exceptions, they are but the monstrous offspring of barbarizing expenditure." Despite this frantic urge for self-enshrinement, a lack of stylistic coherence was obvious, which, ultimately, compromised the attempt to establish oneself as a "man of taste." Stephens continued,

> But now this display of the almighty dollar, has, like almost everything else in America, something both uppish-sham and cheap about it. I had previously observed that the fronts of stone or marble (dirt-colored stone & . . . streaked marble) were mere *facings* . . . forming an outward coating to the . . . walls of brick! Indeed everything here is done as if no man had any faith in the stability of things—as if each and all were engaged in a rough and tumble scramble, and recklessly grabbed at whatever chance threw in his way. The general taste is barbarous; and the exceptions . . . are but servile imitations, or exact fac-similes, of European dwellings.[14]

A French observer, Paul Bourget, saw the hodgepodge of Europe-inspired mansions on Fifth Avenue as an embodiment of "mad abundance." The contextless parade of opulence, he continued, "has visibly been willed and created by sheer force of millions."[15] With these millions, monuments to industrial power were being built by armies of craftsmen using skills and techniques of the preindustrial age. The "jewel-box" home of William Henry Vanderbilt was but one example of the finely crafted opulence which displayed to "the world how millionaires ought to live":

> Sixty (imported) foreign sculptors and carvers were in employ for two years. . . . Upon the interior decoration were engaged between six hundred and seven hundred men, for a year and a half. . . . The internal wood carving . . . was executed by some two hundred and fifty workmen.[16]

All effort was expended to deny the recent industrial origins of these "castles," to locate the heritage of the owners of these mansions among the nobility of preindustrial history. Skinning the numerous surfaces of "Regal Taste," and applying them indiscriminately around themselves, the flamboyance of millionaires often undermined their attempts to construct a facade of dignity. Contemporary critics perceived the thirst for opulence, and the eclectic display of surface, as a demonstration of crude breeding and tasteless self-promotion. In a poem written by Wallace Irwin, the stylistic discord of Fifth Avenue was the result of outlandish wealth in the hands of uncultured parvenus:

> Senator Copper of Tonapah Ditch
> Made a clean billion in minin' and sich,
> Hiked fer Noo York, where his money he blew
> Buildin' a palace on Fift' Avenoo.
> 'How,' sez the Senator, 'can I look proudest?
> Build me a house that'll holler the loudest—'
>
> ....
>
> Forty-eight architects came to consult,
> Drawin' up plans for a splendid result;
> If the old Senator wanted to pay,
> *They'd* give 'im Art with a capital A,
>
> ....
>
> Pillars Ionic,
>   Eaves Babylonic,
> Doors cut in scallops, resemblin' a shell;
>   Roof wuz Egyptian,
>   Gables caniptian,
> Whole grand effect, when completed, wuz—hell.[17]

As suggested by Irwin's poem, the visions of society that percolated from the surfaces of industrial wealth were rooted in the hierarchical cultures of the European past, with particular obeisance to classical antiquity, medieval feudalism, and the Renaissance. Occasionally, forays into more exotic reservoirs of opulence (Egyptian, Chinese, Persian, Moorish, and so on) were made. Together they provided a self-conscious overlay, applied to the shifting upper crust of a society which had not yet discovered or sanctified its own intrinsic aesthetic of power. For those wishing to situate themselves in a palpable position of privilege, the eclectic symbolism of the old world was a sign both of their uniformed identity and of their desire to establish one by whatever means were available.

THE LOOK OF THE FUTURE

In his fascinating study of the historical significance of sugar, the anthropologist Sidney Mintz maintains that people's use of cultural symbols cannot be understood, simply, as a matter of individual or independent choice. Most of the symbols we employ, he argues, are deeply rooted within historical codes of perception and meaning; part of a legacy, passed on over generations.

> Where does the locus of meaning reside? For most human beings most of the time, the meanings believed to in here in things and in the relationships among things and acts are not given, but rather, learned. Most of us, most of the time, act within plays the lines of which require recognition, not invention. To say this is not to deny individuality or the capacity to add, transform, and reject meanings, but it is to insist that the webs of signification that we as individuals spin are exceedingly small and fine (and mostly trivial); for the most part they reside within other webs of immense scale, surpassing single lives in time and space.[18]

In a society where the interwoven ideologies of individualism and personal style run rampant, and where images are assumed to be continually "new," such a sobering reminder of historical continuity and cultural bonds is welcome. Certainly, the dominant trajectory of bourgeois style, from the late Middle Ages to the turn of the twentieth century, conforms to Mintz's generalization.

The imitative inclinations that motivated the acquisition of style by Southern planters, or the wealthy Northeastern establishment, carried on a tendency established centuries earlier. From the late Middle Ages—when an incipient bourgeoisie attempted to solidify its newly gained position through appropriating established upper-class symbols—the imagistic residues of the past had given shape to the aspirations of the present. As an emerging, late nineteenth-century American "middle class" followed leads set by a style-conscious upper class of industrial parvenus and planters, the same mimetic pattern was in operation. The ornate facades of department stores, movie palaces, and other institutions of middle-class diversion, as well as the kitsch bric-a-brac that began to clutter middle-class parlors, were only popularizations of already established signposts of splendor and privilege.

Yet if the elements of style have most often followed well-trodden pathways, the period embracing the turn of the twentieth century also witnessed dramatic departures from the lines as written. New stylistic directions, propelled by modern power and class, began to leave their imprint on questions of style and taste. Central to this period of stylistic revolution was the increasingly visible tension between new modes of industrial production and the stylistic proclivities of nineteenth-century elite taste.

From the Renaissance in Europe, when knowledge of diverse cultures and different historical eras began to spread, the very notion of *style* implied a coherent, aesthetic expression of a given time, a given place, a given way of seeing. Encyclopedists began to catalog a succession of "period styles," each reflecting what William Morris would term "the needs and aspirations *of its own time.*"[19] "Style," observed Le Corbusier (Charles Jeanneret), a founder of the movement toward a "modern" architecture, "is a unity of principle animating all the work of an epoch, the result of a state of mind which has its own special character."[20]

Against such standards of coherence, the evolution of "style" in the nineteenth century was seen, by an increasingly vocal range of critics, as the absence of style, a significant expression of an age in crisis, confused about its own identity, its own *state of mind.* Behind the indiscriminate multiplicity of images that encrusted the hidden framework of industrialism, "the needs and aspirations" of the present were being submerged, masked. To Egon Friedell, it was a period of "stylessness" more than of style.[21] Writing from the vantage point of 1936, the Swiss historian J. Huizinga reflected that "the nineteenth century never had a style of its own. At most there was a faint afterglow. Its characteristic is lack of style, mixing of styles, imitation of old styles. . . . [a] tendency to imitate."[22]

Alarmed by the stylistic incongruity and discord that surrounded them, many late nineteenth- and early twentieth-century critics—from a wide range of perspectives—began to articulate the need to locate a coherent style, a unifying aesthetic, which would be true to the terms and conditions of the modern age. Their understandings of the problem, and the solutions they put forward, were, themselves, discordant.

Published in 1897—not long after the Columbian Exposition in Chicago had risen as a national monument to pasteboard and stylistic eclecticism—Edith Wharton's *The Decoration of Houses* (written with Ogden Godman, Jr.) addressed the general problem of coherence from a quintessentially bourgeois perspective. For Wharton, bourgeois society had fallen from a "golden age of architecture," when "common sense" approaches and "laws of harmony and proportion" had guided design, to a "gilded age of decoration," where nonsensical clutter ruled. Decrying the "vulgarity" of upper-class taste, she saw it as a reflection of "indifference . . . to architectural fitness."[23]

For Wharton, the past still held important lessons for the present:

> Modern civilization has been called a varnished barbarism: a definition that might well be applied to the superficial graces of much modern decoration. Only a return to architectural principles can raise the decoration of houses to the level of the past.[24]

The architectural principles to which she alluded, and whose rediscovery she championed, were rooted in the Italian Renaissance, a time when merchant capitalists had enshrined themselves in neoclassical monumentation. A "close study of the best models" of ornamentation, "given the requirements of modern life," she contended, would reveal that "these models are chiefly to be found in buildings erected in Italy after the beginning of the sixteenth century, and in other European countries after the full assimilation of the Italian influence."[25] Conforming to the "rational limits" set by neoclassical architecture, was, to Wharton, an act of responsible citizenship, an obligation to society, in an era of confusion. The consumption habits of the wealthy must be reevaluated and reformed, to bring order and dignity to society. The commitment to Renaissance principles was, she wrote, "no more servile than . . . pay[ing] one's taxes or . . . [writing] according to the rules of grammar." Each contributed to a strengthening of the social fabric. A continuity in style would elevate and ennoble conditions of modern life which now stood in jeopardy.[26]

For the English socialist visionary, writer, and craftsman-designer William Morris, the past likewise held answers, but dramatically different answers. Where Wharton's imagistic bromides were concerned with recapturing the nobility of the bourgeois spirit, Morris's concerns were voiced from the perspective of a skilled artisan, whose sense of craft and of materials were threatened by industrial capitalism. For Morris, Renaissance style symbolized the root of the problem. It was then, he argued, that the popular, creative arts were broken, bound in service to the rapacious inclinations of the merchant bourgeoisie:

A few individual artists were great truly; but artists were no longer the masters of art, because the people had ceased to be artists; its masters were pedants. St. Peter's in Rome, St. Paul's in London, were not built to be beautiful, or to be beautiful and convenient. They were not built to be homes of the citizens in their moments of exaltation, their supreme grief or supreme hope, but to be proper, respectable, and therefore to show the due amount of cultivation, and knowledge of the only peoples and times that in the minds of their ignorant builders were not ignorant barbarians.

Morris argued that the embracing of "classical" ideals was a celebration of societies founded on "exclusiveness and aristocratic arrogance." The rejection of late Middle Age motifs as "barbarian" was the rejection of a society in which free craftsmen had worked, cooperatively, to delineate their own principles of design.

The use of labor during the Renaissance, to aggrandize the lives and reputations of merchant wealth, was, to Morris, the beginning of an industrial epoch in which crafts would be systematically devalued and destroyed; in which "the artist-craftsmen" who had conceived and built the coherent beauty of Gothic architecture and design would be transformed "into an enormous stock of human machines, who had little chance of earning a bare livelihood if they lingered over their toil to think of what they were doing." The Renaissance, as a point of departure out of which industrial capitalism sprung, was the product of a workforce that, more and more, was "not asked to think, paid to think, or allowed to think."[27]

The dissociation between work and thought was, for Morris, the root of the modern dilemma. It helped to explain why the "greater part of what we now [1893] call architecture is but an imitation of an imitation of an imitation."[28] The critical issues of modern life could not be approached merely by finding a *proper* style, befitting the modern age. It was necessary to redefine the age itself; style should encourage and promulgate an organic integrity of thought and action, conception and execution, design and materials, among people whose labors created the environments and objects of life. Morris's was a call for a unity of form and content that challenged an age marked by the incremental degradation of labor, and by the expanding consumer market in disembodied images.

For William Morris, the style and spirit of the "Gothic" period— when "guildsmen of the Free Cities" forged an aesthetic that embodied a "freedom of hand and mind subordinated to the cooperative harmony which made the freedom possible"—could help to reeducate the senses. Against the imitative eclecticism of the present, Morris counseled guidance from the Gothic era:

> The style of architecture will have to be historic in the true sense . . . the spirit of it will be in sympathy with the needs and aspirations of its own time, not simulation of needs and aspirations passed away. . : . As to the form of it, I see nothing for it but that the form, as well as the spirit, must be Gothic; an organic style cannot spring out of an eclectic one.

From a rediscovery of the Gothic spirit, Morris argued, nineteenth-century people could acquire a sense of craft, essential in the struggle against "the horrible and restless nightmare of modern engineering."[29]

From radically different viewpoints, both Edith Wharton and William Morris looked, romantically, to the past as they searched for a coherency of meaning. What Wharton looked to, for inspiration in the present, was an idealized "golden age" of the bourgeoisie, when the energies of wealth and power were motivated by a sense of proportion and a harmony of vision. What Morris looked to was an idealized "golden age" of the working class, when craftsmen shaped their world according to precepts of creative freedom and social cooperation.

For many others who sought to move beyond the "varnished barbarism" of nineteenth-century culture, the past offered no such solace. It was seen, primarily, as fetters, to be broken and transcended. It was in the burgeoning structures of industrial society—though often masked by an encrusted facade of ornamentation—that many found the most promising alternative to the stubborn residues of traditional ruling taste. The raw power and unsentimental rationality of industrialism were providing new principles around which a style befitting the modern age could be discovered. Looking more to the future than the past, a modern style would be inspired by precepts of machine production, industrial efficiency, scientific truths, and mathematical principles. Freed from the baggage of sentiment and mystification, style would be ennobled by *reason* and *honesty*. The functional aspect of material culture would no longer be hidden by a shell of diversionary denotation, but would stand by itself as the ruling prescription for form.

At the heart of this prescription lay a new organization of power, the modern industrial corporation. Following decades of fierce economic competition and recurrent social crises, many late nineteenth- and early twentieth-century capitalists—ranging from the financier J. P. Morgan to the department store magnate Edward A. Filene—became increasingly conscious of the need to erect corporate systems of coordination and management. Each desired to establish order and predictability within a volatile social and economic environment. The "search for order," as historian Robert Wiebe described the guiding impulse of the Progressive Era, left its mark across the horizon of early twentieth-century American society. For many, the concept of a finely tuned, smoothly running mechanism provided a common metaphor, one that linked the priorities of corporations and social policy makers with those of architects, artists, and designers interested in delineating a style appropriate to the modern age.

One of the most powerful voices on behalf of a modern style came from the United States, which many saw as a place where the entrenched burdens of European, elite history had been unseated by a fresh and democratic spirit of forward-looking enterprise, where notions of unfettered and irreverent practicality held sway. Louis Sullivan, the Chicago architect who had popularized the dictum that *form should follow function*, saw the dominant approach of architecture—even in the United States—as weighted down by a slavish obeisance to outmoded ideals. This was perpetuated by the Beaux Arts school that had come to prevail over architectural training. Writing in 1901, Sullivan reflected, sadly, "How strange it seems that education, in practice, so often means suppression: that instead of leading the mind outward to the light of day it crowds things in upon it that darken and weary it."[30]

Sullivan, a visionary planner of tall urban buildings, felt that these buildings' style should be derived from their method of construction. Steel frameworks, which stood at the heart of modern urban construction (particularly after the great Chicago fire had provided an impetus for fireproof design, post-1873), should not be hidden by veneers of historical cliché. Rather, the regular grid of steel should be a dramatic element in the building's overall design. Though he was still willing to employ historical quotation as an element in architecture, it was the majesty of the steel latticework that, for Sullivan, provided the decisive component of style.

Sullivan gained his distinction through his passionate willingness to sever the cords—no matter how sacred—that tied architecture to the ornamental practices of the past. The assumption that a building's splendor was derived from its servility to historic decoration, was, he argued, a denial of the "historic power" of the modern age, of the "sensible and practical" temper that had given rise to the "dawning power of democracy." A new age, he proclaimed in 1908, "stands before us now and awaits our awakening. It is now looking at us steadily. When," he asked, "shall we awaken?"[31]

Sullivan was possessed by a near religious vision: a past, ruled by inexorable destiny, finally giving way to a rule by human will, by "Ego." What stood in the way was "graft." Modern man still bowed down to "phantoms" from the past, despite the fact that they threatened to "kill his young!" Slavish historicism sang a "Song of Death" which drowned out the rising potential of "The Ego."

In his book *Democracy*, Sullivan implored all men to embrace the present, and the future:

> O, man in the street. . . .
> Your time has come.
> The cock is crowing the shrillest dawn that the world has known.
> You must declare yourself! . . .
> You must declare for Integrity or against it.
> You must declare for social efficiency or against it. . . .
>
> A new world will open.
> The world of Ego and its dream of power.
> The world of Integrity of man and his works. . . .
>
> The dawn is breaking.
> NOW BEGIN![32]

It was Sullivan's fierce belief in the powers of individual will—its ability to shape the social environment, against all historic odds—which particularly appealed to Ayn Rand as she developed her antisocial, aggressively individualistic philosophy of "Objectivism." Sullivan served as the thinly disguised model for her character Henry Cameron, the iconoclastic mentor of Howard Roark, the hero in her novel *The Fountainhead*. Published in 1943, Rand's novel celebrated the "triumph of the will" as embodied, in this case, by the visionary architect. Although the book focuses on the life of Howard Roark (based loosely on Frank Lloyd Wright), Roark gets his inspiration from Cameron:

> One did not argue with Henry Cameron. Something was growing in him with each new building, struggling, taking shape, rising dangerously to an explosion. The explosion came with the birth of the skyscraper. When structures began to rise not in tier on ponderous tier of masonry, but as arrows of steel shooting upward without weight or limit, Henry Cameron was among the first to understand this new miracle and to give it form. He was among the first and the few who accepted the truth that a tall building must look tall. While architects cursed, wondering how to make a twenty-story building look like an old brick mansion, while they used every horizontal device available in order to cheat it of its height, shrink it down to tradition, hide the shame of its steel, make it small, safe and

ancient—Henry Cameron designed skyscrapers in straight, vertical lines, flaunting their steel and height. While architects drew friezes and pediments, Henry Cameron decided that no building must copy any other.[33]

In many ways, the passage accurately reflects Sullivan's antipathies and visions. Rejecting all of the conventions of the Beaux Arts tradition, Sullivan looked to a dignity born in the simplicity of form. "A building, quite devoid of ornament," he stated simply, "may convey a noble and dignified sentiment by virtue of mass and proportion. It is not evident to me that ornament can intrinsically heighten these elemental qualities."[34]

It was with these considerations in mind, when the Columbian Exposition embraced the ornamental dictates of Beaux Arts architecture, that Sullivan launched into a diatribe against the fair, and against its chief architect, Daniel H. Burnham. The Exposition was to be a glorious tribute to the triumphs of industrial development, a beacon lighting the way into the twentieth century. But it also "expressed the vision of a social and cultural elite eager to recreate society in its own image."[35] This elite, and its vision of social order, was still encumbered by the shadow of customary, parvenu practice. It sought to enshrine itself, and its stucco utopia, in the opulent trappings of the past. To Sullivan this was a crime of historic proportion; a failure of the imagination at a critical juncture. Knowing that the Columbian Exposition would set a tone for future expectations, he felt that this orgy of ornamentation would corrupt industrial society for decades to come: "The damage wrought by the World's Fair will last a half a century from its date, if not longer. It has penetrated deep into the constitution of the American mind, effecting there lesions significant of dementia."[36]

Such vexation, though provoked by particular circumstances was consistent with an international reevaluation of style that was increasingly associating ornamental conventions with depravity and moral decay. In Vienna, the architect Adolf Loos, whose designs were marked by an elegant simplicity, viewed ornament as a sign of "degeneracy," a remnant from a period of cultural underdevelopment.

Following a three-year visit to the United States (1893–96), Loos returned to Vienna under the influence of Sullivan's notion that "it would only benefit us if for a time we were to abandon ornament and concentrate entirely on the erection of buildings that were finely shaped and charming in their sobriety."[37] By 1908, Loos's thoughts on ornamentation had coalesced into a broad theoretical perspective on history and cultural development, set forth in his classic manifesto "Ornament and Crime."

For Loos, the impulse to ornament was an anachronism, a holdover from earlier stages in human cultural evolution. Among primitive people, such as the Papuans, the indiscriminate "urge to ornament one's face and everything within reach" was the result of polymorphous erotic drives, not yet contained by modern civilization.

Loos saw all art, all decoration, as "erotic." This can be seen, he maintained, in the example of the *cross*, "the first ornament to be born." To Loos, the cross was "the first work of art, the first artistic act which the first artist, in order to rid himself of his surplus energy, smeared on the wall. A horizontal dash: the prone woman. A vertical dash: the man penetrating." Given the implicit eroticism of all art, it was necessary for art to be put in its proper place; the sublimation of the erotic drive into useful purposes was, for Loos, the essence of modernity. The continued tendency to eroticize (ornament) the world, promiscuously, meant one of two things. Either it was the practice of people and cultures that were not fully developed, as in the case of the Papuans or young children; or it revealed an individual who was a criminal, a culture that was diseased and degenerate:

> What is natural to the Papuan and the child is a symptom of degeneracy in the modern adult. I have made the following discovery and I pass it on to the world: *The evolution of culture is synonymous with the removal of ornament from utilitarian objects.* [38]

A style for the modern age, Loos argued, could not be found in traditional ornamentation. The modern age had outgrown ornament; its aesthetic task was to move beyond the stylistic practices of a decadent aristocracy, of primitive people, and of children. Functional objects, he asserted, must be understood for what they are: *functional.* The proper place for eroticism, in the lives of modern people, was within the clearly marked confines of the arts.

In Europe, much to Loos's distress, "the ornament disease" was epidemic, "recognized by the state and subsidized with state funds." While ornamentation still stood as the legitimate sign of cultivation for the misguided, yet official cultures of Europe, Loos reviled it as "no longer organically linked with our culture . . . no longer the expression of our culture." In his view, "The ornament that is manufactured today has no connexion with us, has absolutely no human connexions, no connexion with the world order. It is not capable of developing." Beyond being culturally anachronistic, ornamentation was intemperate. It would waste valuable labor, raise costs of production, and encourage irrational consumption, spurred on by ever-changing styles:

Austrian ornamentalists are trying to make the best of this shortcoming. They say: "We prefer a consumer who has a set of furniture that becomes intolerable to him after ten years, and who is consequently forced to refurnish every ten years, to one who buys an object when the old one is worn out. Industry demands this. Millions are employed as a result of the quick change."[39]

Loos's rejection of ornamentation and his ideas of pure, aesthetic simplicity were—in his mind—steps in the direction of a rational and efficient world order. Aspects of his perspective—such as his incisive critique of planned, style obsolescence—show remarkable insight. Yet at the heart of his equation of ornament and crime, stood an evangelical vision of industrial society. Its objective and practical *truths* were posed against those forces which stood in the way of progress: the European aristocracy which continued to encrust Europe with the premodern remnants of their power; primitive cultures, whose backwardness and eroticism made them perfect targets for the missionary ideals of industrial *order* and *progress;* the child, as yet uncivilized, for whom the adult world must lay its plans to control, to educate.

At the heart of this ideology of sublimation and control was a perspective of sexual rigidity, favoring reason over passion, efficiency over *eros,* and social order over personal issues of sexuality. The new aesthetic, the new rational style, would come to the fore as subjective patterns of romantic longing, passion, and erotic expression were effectively suppressed. Modernity required, for Loos, a conquest over those elements of culture which were not consistent with the logic of a new "world order."

The particular concern with unbridled eroticism, and the call for its suppression, was a strong tendency in the modern critique of ornamentation. Specifically, the need to control erotic impulses in style was often posed in terms of an opposition between *male* and *female* styles. Consistent with many aspects of Victorian ideology, it was the feminine impulse that demanded controls. As some critics of nineteenth-century ornamentation articulated their thoughts, they associated the purposeful efficiency of unfettered industrialism with masculinity. It was the depraved, feminine tendency toward kitsch that inhibited forward development. The industrial system of production was being "misused, masked, falsely frilled out with feminine and regal ornament." Its rational potential was being compromised. It was only through a stripping away of these female encrustations that a "virile" aesthetic, appropriate to the machine age, could be found.[40]

Reinforcing the metaphor, it was customary in late nineteenth- and early twentieth-century industry to create a sexual division of labor along these same lines. Men were employed to perform the pure work of production, while women were regularly employed to do decorative work, often at a lower wage. They did lace-work and embroidery, and also operated the "fret saws" which were used to do the scroll work in the mass production of ornamental products.[41]

In their call for a simple, functionalist, modern aesthetic, advocates saw themselves as champions of an orderly masculinity, as cultural saviors from the feminized depravity marked by ornamentation. Admiring a warehouse of the Marshall Field Company, Louis Sullivan expressed this sexual bias unabashedly. Describing the building, he exclaimed, "Here is a man for you to look at. A man that walks on two legs instead of four, has active muscles . . . lives and breathes. . . . in a world of barren pettiness, a male."[42]

Well into the twentieth century the tension between the spare inclinations of modern design and the ornamental aspects of traditional style continued to maintain the sexual metaphor. Writing in 1930, Emily Post described modern design as "well suited to men. . . . Empty spaces, the absence of ruffles and curtains, and beautifully polished surfaces of wood and metal were masculine."[43]

Yet the fierce attack on "depravity," marked by a desire to purge eros and femininity from the public arenas of daily life, was not the only trajectory of a nascent modernism. Its alter ego was visible as well. As historian Carl Schorske has pointed out, while the "common hell" of historic style provided various modernists with a common enemy, "it soon became clear that the critics had very different heavens."[44] If one powerful, modernist tendency was drawn from the stark, functional logic of the industrial machine, another drew its inspiration from the murky waters of an increasingly acknowledged subjectivity, against which the rules of order had pitched themselves.

Contemporaneous to the emergence of rational modernism in the latter decades of the nineteenth century, another morphology—Art Nouveau—was being promulgated as a significant break from the stylistic conventions of the past. Not convinced by the notion that hard edges and plane geometry were the components of an elemental and "honest" vision, the various contributors to the Art Nouveau delved, instead, into the polymorphous sensuality of some imagined, primordial life. It was as if Sigmund Freud had laid out the conflicted terrain of the visual arts, charging some with the job of designing the symmetrical and systematic prohibitions of the super ego, and enjoining others to explore, without fear, the lawless and pulsating realm of the id.

Rational modernism was an appeal to the cold and distant eye. It was the product of deliberate calculation. Art Nouveau, on the other hand, evoked the more intimate and provocative senses of taste, touch, and smell. Rational modernism pointed toward a mathematically synchronized social order; Art Nouveau spoke to the impetuous hungers of an inner, private realm. Rational modernism drew its inspirations from the metallic and uniform properties of the machine; Art Nouveau drew its visual metaphors from a precivilized conception of nature.

Art Nouveau was really an umbrella term, linking various arts and crafts that emerged—primarily in Europe—in the late 1880s and enjoyed influence into the early years of the twentieth century. It included *Jugendstil* in Germany; *style moderne* in France; *stile Liberty* or *stile nuovo* in Italy; *modernismo,* and, later, *estilo Gaudi* in Spain; and *Sezessionstil* in Vienna. In the United States, where the movement was less prominent, Art Nouveau was limited, in large measure, to the Tiffany style.[45]

The term Art Nouveau has been applied to the works of various artists, architects, and craftsmen; not all conform to a singular vision. Yet across much of its tableau, "a feeling of sensual weirdness and exoticism" prevails.[46] Images and objects merge into an environment where diaphanous surfaces strain against thin, plantlike veins. Against the predictable symmetry of rational modernism, the netherworld of Art Nouveau was irregular, tantalizing, protoplasmic. If rational modernism represented the arenas of work and production, Art Nouveau was languid, sensual, organically reproductive. Its sense of motion did not mimic the forward-driving pistons of the locomotive, but of an uncanny, damp respiration, a reverie of postorgasmic repose. Its sexuality was not masculine, but neither was it clearly feminine; rather, it evoked an erotic totality, polymorphous, undifferentiated, unrestrained.

In representative examples from the Art Nouveau period, we are carried into some strange, second life, where a mix of oriental exoticism and primeval organicism transform iron and stone, glass and glazed tile, into a pulsing, multiform carnality. Antonio Gaudi's Casa Mila, for example, constructed in Barcelona (1905–7), offers viewers a mass of undulating, sinuous ectoplasm. Overwhelming the static clichés of the ornamental past, here is a building characterized by heaving waves of metamorphosis and growth.

An interior entrance hall in the Coilliot House in Lille, designed by Hector Guimard (1898–1900), provides visitors with a swirling passageway, a birth canal, a stage set for a fantastic journey to the origins of life. All matter is in the simultaneous process of occupying, and then withdrawing, from space.

Entrance hall of Coilliot House, designed by Hector Guimard.

Even Peter Behrens, who would later take the lead as an industrial designer and a prime mover toward a geometric, machine aesthetic, prefaced this overcommitment to corporate order with a youthful journey through the personal valley of desire. His woodcut *The Kiss* (1898) conveys a conspicuous sexual ambiguity, an androgynous vision in which two faces merge amid the serpentine frame of their hair.

In a discussion of Art Nouveau jewelry, critic Robert Melville points to Edvard Munch's *Madonna* as a prime example of the Art Nouveau sensibility. The lithograph, he maintains, combines "ecstasy and pain in the act of love," and is framed by a "decorative border . . . composed of sperms trailing long wriggly filaments which meander round three sides of the image and end in a foetus-like pendant."[47] Here are the forbidden realms, the unity of "ecstasy and pain" that reside in the deep wells of inner life, ordinarily covered up by the orderly building blocks of reason. Against the rationalistic order of the machine age, Art Nouveau posed a "biomorphic" disorder, filled with "eels, noodles, and tapeworms," primal spores, and strangely familiar, plantlike genitalia. Here was a representation of all-consuming passion, in which "the curve . . . becomes a twisting, living thing, enclosing or even swallowing up whatever is nearby. . . . each line in the border seems to loop in upon itself, and then move out to entangle a neighboring form."[48]

Although Art Nouveau has enjoyed some revivals in the marketplace of style, its particular influence, as a strain of modernism, ended by about 1905. In the articulation of modernity, geometric rationalism was to emerge as the predominant force, shaping our conception of "the future" up to the current time. Yet the coterminous emergence of rational modernism and Art Nouveau, during the closing years of the nineteenth century, offers us a glimpse of the powerful forces, tensions, and visions that have permeated the modern age. Although the dominant themes of modernity would be expressed by the visual representation of mechanical production, standardization, and lean abstraction, the early, uneasy companionship with Art Nouveau reveals the duality of life in the epoch of the machine. At first glance the two tendencies appear opposed, irreconcilable, unrelated. Together, however, they illuminate the fragmentation and contradiction of twentieth-century life. The triumph of machine civilization, and mass production, generated two concurrent themes. On one side, the rise of mechanical production led to a visual idealization of the machine and its principles: rationalized order, geometric progression, and a methodically controlled social and material environment. On the other hand, Art Nouveau explored the churning reservoirs of an awakened and restless subjectivity: disordered, instinctive, driven by primordial nature.

Both rational modernism and Art Nouveau posed alternatives to the "varnished barbarism" of Victorian culture. The machine aesthetic provided an idealization of efficiency and control which rejected the puffed-up excesses of Victorian gentility. Art Nouveau brought the publicly denied eroticism of Victorianism out in the open, placing the importance of instinctual, sensual gratification squarely within the purview of an emerging consumer culture.

This coexistence of early rational modernism and Art Nouveau was historically specific to the fin de siècle, yet it embodied a visual dialogue that illuminates the more general paths of style throughout the twentieth century. Together, these two tendencies of style may be said to constitute an aestheticization of the modern psyche: the concurrent tensions between conscience and desire, standardization and individual autonomy, mass society and human freedom. In advertising, in fashion, in much of the ubiquitous imagery of the marketplace, the encroaching disciplines of the industrial era are mediated by a continuing appeal to the fantasies, provocations, and frustrations of a turbulent and hungry inner life.

The impulse to discover a modern style was fed by many streams.

Each defined itself, in one way or another, in opposition to kitsch, against nineteenth-century eclecticism. Each sought a fitting alternative. Most rejected the past as a guideline. "Architecture," wrote Le Corbusier, "is stifled by custom. The 'styles' are a lie." The tension between the evolving terms of modern life and the imagistic obedience to an ornamental past was—unless checked—going to fulminate a social explosion:

> The man of today is conscious, on the one hand, of a new world which is forming itself regularly, logically and clearly, which produces in a straightforward way things which are useful and usable, and on the other hand he finds himself, to his surprise, living in an old and hostile environment. . . .
>
> Society is filled with a violent desire for something which it may obtain or may not. Everything lies in that: everything depends on the effort made and the attention paid to these alarming symptoms.[49]

People living and working in the machine age, for Le Corbusier, were developing a consciousness, a way of understanding, with which the purveyors of style (architectural and so on) were out of touch. Peter Behrens, the industrial designer and architect, echoed the concern: "Our eyes fall everywhere on disharmony. . . . chaos."[50] Both, in their work, sought to delineate a style animated by the "special character," the particular *truths* of industrial society. The style would not spring, unaided, from their heads. It would not come from the tradition-based education they had received. It would only come from observing the world unfolding around them: "Our own epoch is determining, day by day, its own style. Our eyes, unhappily, are unable to discern it."[51]

While they, and others, looked to the industrial world, particularly America, for inspiration, certain elements of the modern style began to fall into place. For many, it was the factory, the machine, tools of measurement (geometry, mathematics), and regimentation that provided a visual grammar for the future.

CHAPTER SEVEN

Mechanical Sentiments

In his novel *A Rebours* (1880), J. K. Huysmans announced the ascendancy of a sleek, new order:

> Does there exist, anywhere on this earth, a being conceived in the joys of fornication and born in the throes of motherhood who is more dazzling, and more outstandingly beautiful than the two locomotives recently put into service on the Northern Railroad? . . . Nature . . . has had her day.[1]

"Slowly, through a mixture of morality, practicality and the disgust at bourgeois taste," remarks Brent Brolin, the historian of architectural styles, "the aesthetic of precise machine forms gained prestige." Foreshadowing Adolf Loos's argument in "Ornament and Crime," the social Darwinist Herbert Spencer saw the development of a machine aesthetic as a sign of advancing civilization, an emblem of a higher order.[2] Previously seen as artless and utilitarian, factories and power plants began to assume a "classical" status, as models of "structural simplicity and harmonious proportion."[3]

To many Europeans, the United States served as a beacon, illuminating the aesthetic future. Europe still carried the burden of its feudal past. Its imagery was still directly influenced by a powerful if "degenerate" aristocracy. The United States, however, offered a more progressive connection to history, one that looked more to the future than the past. While parvenu Americans tried to surround themselves with the accoutrements of European "high" culture, their lineage was in question. Their links to traditions of elegance and luxury were tentative, and unconvincing. On the other hand, America's separation from Europe allowed it to develop a utilitarian culture of its own, without having to stand, continuously, on ceremony.

Writing in 1864, an English visitor to the United States saw the unintended seeds of a new aesthetic being planted in the regular furrows of industrial technology:

> The American, while adhering to his utilitarian and economic principles, has unwittingly, in some objects to which his heart equally with his hand has been devoted, developed a degree of beauty in them that no other nation equals. . . . [an] equilibrium of lines, proportions, and masses, which is among the fundamental causes of abstract beauty.[4]

The great industrial expositions of the late nineteenth century provided Europeans with further reasons for excitement. Despite the pretentious ornamentalism of the exhibition halls themselves, the halls were filled with simple implements—even farm tools—which Europeans understood to be a singularly American aesthetic. Unlike the decorative motifs that paid homage to hierarchy on even the most humble of European surfaces, the unfettered simplicity that graced American tools suggested not only modernity, but *democracy:* freedom from the inequities of the past.

Visiting the Centennial Exposition in Philadelphia, in 1876, a German witness was stunned by the unpremeditated simplicity of utilitarian product design. For him it portended the future. "American industry in its progress," he reported, "breaks with all tradition and takes new paths which seem to us fantastic."[5]

Clearly, European history had also offered prototypes for the delineation of a modern aesthetic. Historians of architecture and design repeatedly point to the Crystal Palace, at the 1851 London Exposition, as an early "functionalist" structure, designed by Joseph Paxton out of prefabricated parts of cast iron, wrought iron, and glass.[6] Others point to a cotton mill of seven stories, erected at Manchester in 1801, or to the designs of Claude Nicholas LeDoux, the architect of the "saltworks project," an industrial city—built, by commission, for Louis XVI—in eighteenth-century France.[7] Some historians have delved even further back to locate the progenitors of modern design.[8]

Yet because the search for a modern style in the late nineteenth and early twentieth centuries was so ideologically charged, so committed to a severance from the past, the distant, "youthful," and "uncultured" United States provided many Europeans with a more powerful symbol of redirection and recommitment. The innovation that was fomenting within the cracks of European ornamentalism might be significant, but the zealous search for the future found greater comfort in the "virgin land" of the United States.

Laszlo Moholy-Nagy, the Hungarian Constructivist designer and Bauhaus teacher, for example, located the roots of his modernist vision in his early glimpses of the Manhattan skyline in travel magazines, brought to him in Hungary by his uncle, Gusti Bacsi. "It seemed to me then," he recalled in a letter to his wife Sibyl (8 July 1937), "that the skyscrapers of New York were the destination of my life."[9] Many Americans agreed on this location of destiny. New buildings, like the "Flatiron," on Twenty-third Street and Fifth Avenue in Manhattan, were seen as a collective monument to the new age. Writing of the Flatiron Building, a sharp, projecting wedge that still overlooks James Madison Park, Edgar Saltus described this early skyscraper as a visible, dramatic, historical benchmark: "Its front is lifted to the future. On the past its back is turned."[10]

Whatever the source of inspiration, the first decades of the new century witnessed an acceleration in the depiction of *the modern* in both Europe and the United States. Peter Behrens, in his design work for the Allgemeine Elektricitäts-Gesellschaft, attempted to invest all elements of corporate design with the naked, if aestheticized, principles of mass production. Even the advertising work he did (posters, logos, brochures, and so on) was imbued with an industrial sensibility. His typeface designs and his poster layouts deliberately suggested "mathematical harmony . . . absolute precision of all the elements . . . unity of all the assembled parts."[11] Behrens's workshop, an archetype for that of the modern (corporate) industrial designer, had an immediate impact on the codification of a modern style. Working as Behrens's assistant, Le Corbusier developed ideas about form that would, over decades, give shape to the way in which twentieth-century people visualize *progress.*

In his manifesto *Towards a New Architecture,* Le Corbusier summarized his thinking on the necessity for a modern style. "Modern life," he asserted, "demands, and is waiting for, a new kind of plan." Architectural thinking offered little in the way of advice. To Le Corbusier, the architect was mired in "an unhappy state of retrogression," one that imprisoned the whole of the decorative arts.[12]

The unwitting prophet of the new style, the hero of the modern age, he asserted, was the engineer. He was the person whose cold, mathematical eye was constructing a new world order upon the decaying shell of the old. The engineer places "us in accord with universal law," he stated. "He achieves harmony."[13] In a world encrusted by stylistic lies, the engineer was the herald of a universal, transhistoric truth. His vision was not chained to a particular sensibility of a time or a place. It transcended specificity; its glory rested upon the timeless "pleasure of geometric forms."[14]

Yet against the clean geometry that the engineer applied to machinery, or to the factory, the cloak of the old world still dominated the realms of social and private life. To Le Corbusier, the tension between the material structures of industrialism and the images of the past that still clung to the home and much of the public sphere constituted a dangerous mix:

> Bewilderment seizes us . . . if we bring our eyes to bear on the old and rotting buildings that form our snail-shell, our habitation, which crush us in our daily contact with them—putrid and useless and unproductive. Everywhere can be seen machines which serve to produce something and produce it admirably, in a clean sort of way. . . . There is no real link between our daily activities at the factory, the office or the bank, which are healthy and useful and productive, and our activities within the bosom of the family which are handicapped at every turn. The family is everywhere being killed and men's minds demoralized in servitude to anachronisms.[15]

For Le Corbusier, the visual sphere of everyday life needed to be reconciled with the realities of the factory, reconstituted around the aesthetic principles that derived from the priorities of corporate engineering. "Inspired by the law of economy and governed by mathematical calculation," the engineer was the fortuitous avant-garde of a new, and increasingly "universal," social order. His unvarnished mission—to coordinate disparate elements of production into a well-oiled, glitch-free apparatus—was generating devices and structures suited to the achievement of social harmony. Understanding modern style as an expedient to well-regulated socialization, he proposed that it was essential to "create the mass production spirit" in the daily lives of the industrial population.[16] "If we challenge the past, we shall learn that 'styles' no longer exist for us, that a style belonging to our own period has come about; and there has been a Revolution." The modern home, he contended, must be synchronized with the order of the day. Not only should it be "made in the factory"; it must be a "machine for living."[17]

Le Corbusier's belief in the stylistic synchronization of work and life coincided with a more general appreciation of modern style as a medium of social integration. The growth of industrialism since the nineteenth century had exponentially expanded society's ability to produce, but its rhythms had also engendered the development of an increasingly militant and organized working class. In the first decades of the twentieth century, Europe and the United States were rocked by explosions of labor violence, by the rise of a largely socialist labor movement. As the factory attempted to bring a calculable order to the realm of production, some reasoned that its motifs could inspire order and harmony in the volatile theater of everyday life. A social world, reinforcing industrial values at home and at work, was seen as a complement and reiteration of the promise of industrial progress. If the continued tension between old shells and new realities would, unchecked, eventuate revolutionary destruction, a style reflecting the principles of the factory could tame the increasingly dangerous masses. As Le Corbusier proclaimed, again and again throughout the pages of his impassioned manifesto:

> Architecture or Revolution.
> Revolution can be avoided.[18]

The utilitarian guidelines governing engineering, rooted in the ascendency of the modern, industrial corporation, were giving rise to a new aesthetic of power: calibrated, plainly geometric, unadorned, predicated on the synchronicity of moving parts. Against the ossified remains of the ornamental past, it projected an aura of vitality and motion. Particularly in Europe, where the baggage of history had elevated aristocratic styles to a sacred pedestal, this new visual universe promised to bestow honor upon the present, glorify corporate claims to the future. From the early twentieth century onward, corporations in Europe and the United States followed a lead set by Peter Behrens and Walter Rathenau of the AEG, embracing and promulgating the aesthetics of the *bottom line*. Once demeaned as the parvenu imitator of grandeurs to which he had no rightful claim, the capitalist had come into his own. Corporate values and priorities no longer had to hide themselves behind an ill-fitting cloak of respectability, but had begun to assume their own iconography, one that enshrined the modern contours of economic life.

Yet it was not corporate designers alone who understood the machine aesthetic as the style for the future, the style for all time. As in most revolutionary movements, the forces that combined to attack the old regime were composed of an odd and uneasy alliance. If the new aesthetic lionized the structures of the industrial corporation, it also spoke to many others who sought to liberate the future from the burdens of the past.

For some people, the allure of the machine aesthetic was in its straightforward assault on the imagery of social inequality, its celebration of an industrial apparatus that could produce, as never before, the wherewithal of universal, material well-being. Within the modern apparatus of production—despite its many oppressive implications in the present—they saw the structural foundations of a new, egalitarian society in which new standards of quality would emerge.

The Bauhaus school of design, founded in Dessau, Germany, by Walter Gropius (1919), was motivated by such visions. A school "to train young students both for hand work, and for machine work, and as designers at the same time," Bauhaus was influenced by a conjuncture of forces.[19] The simple geometry and efficiency that became the emblem of its products bespoke a relationship to large-scale industrial design. As in the case of Le Corbusier, Gropius's training with Peter Behrens (commencing in 1908) provided a strong link to the principles of engineering and economy. "It was Behrens," Gropius would recall in 1965, "who first introduced me to logical and systematical coordination" in design projects.[20]

Yet alongside the lessons he drew from AEG, Gropius and his associates were deeply affected by the socialist "arts and crafts" ideas of William Morris. They sought to contribute to the development of a society in which creativity would be fostered, and in which human needs would motivate the forces of production. Rejecting the elitism and decay of academic, or "salon," art, the Bauhaus was interested in reinvigorating "the spontaneous traditional art that had permeated the life of the whole people" within the vernacular traditions of handcraft, before the nineteenth century. Claiming to carry on the spirit of William Morris (and John Ruskin), the Bauhaus sought "to find a means of reuniting the world of art with the world of work." In their estimation, however, Morris was hopelessly tethered to the past. By 1919 it was clear to Gropius that Morris's unswerving animosity to the machine, and affinity for preindustrial handcraft, relegated his proposed alternatives to oblivion. "Morris's opposition against the machine," he noted with a hint of resignation, "could not stem the waters." The world of the mass-production machine was here to stay.[21]

If Bauhaus accepted the industrial mode of production as its inevitable context, its project was to humanize the world of the machine. Training in design and construction, Gropius argued, must commence with an understanding of the human being. Only in "his natural readiness to grasp life as a whole" would the designer be able to give positive direction to the industrial process. True to the overarching spirit of the machine aesthetic, however, Gropius's own grasp on "life as a whole" was defined, essentially, by cold tools of measurement. Whereas Morris's ideas assumed a working class that would guide its own future, Gropius held to a managerial perspective. Urban populations and their needs were things to be measured sociologically, to arrive at the minimum dwelling conditions they required. Morris's visionary was the creative craftsman, recuperated from the "horrible and restless nightmare of modern engineering"; Gropius's craftsman was the enlightened social engineer, the policymaker, the technocrat, dispensing the rationalized necessities of life to a mass of modern consumers. Gropius spoke of the Bauhaus as a return "to honesty of thought and feeling," but his ideas were inextricably wedded to an underpinning of rational calculation and industrial efficiency.[22] In accepting an economistic approach to human needs, Gropius, and much of what Bauhaus produced, remained closely linked to the underlying premises of modern corporate ideology.

For others associated with Bauhaus, the aesthetic of the machine could help bring about socialism. Early in his career, the Hungarian designer Laszlo Moholy-Nagy participated in the Constructivist movement, an avant-garde group that saw in machine images the suggestion and possibility of social transformation. In her biography of Moholy-Nagy, his wife Sibyl spoke of their common "faith in man's salvation through image-making." The image of the machine, Laszlo Moholy-Nagy contended, reflected the spiritual force of the modern era: "The reality of our century is technology: the invention, construction, and maintenance of machines. To be a user of machines is to be of the spirit of this century. It has replaced the transcendental spiritualism of past eras." He saw the machine as a force of democratization. In its overwhelming power, "everyone is equal before the machine."[23] It sweeps away the old structures of the past, he felt, having no intrinsic allegiance to any tradition, or any class.

For Moholy-Nagy, the "constructivist idea" represented the thinking of an artistic vanguard, a beacon for the proletariat. As corporations embraced the machine aesthetic as an embodiment of corporate ideals, many tendencies within the leftist avant-garde saw the machine as creating the historic conditions for socialism, for the proletarian revolution. In his 1922 article "Constructivism and the Proletariat," Laszlo Moholy-Nagy spoke of the machine, and its imagery, as an inexorable force for change:

> This is the root of Socialism, the final liquidation of feudalism. It is the machine that woke up the proletariat. We have to eliminate the machine if we want to eliminate Socialism. But we know there is no such thing as turning back evolution. This is our century: technology, machine, Socialism. Make your peace with it; shoulder its task.[24]

If the machine had created the inevitable conditions for socialism, Constructivist art could awaken a new, communal consciousness among the proletariat. Forshadowing ideas later popularized by Marshall MacLuhan, Moholy argued that the age of the printed word was at an end. "Words are heavy, obscure," he asserted. "Their meaning is evasive to the untrained mind." Visual imagery, on the other hand, speaks "the language of the senses." Constructivism, as the visual expression of the machine era, speaks the unfettered language of essential truths.

> Constructivism is neither proletarian nor capitalistic. Constructivism is primordial, without class or ancestor. It expresses the pure form of nature, the direct color, the spatial rhythm, the equilibrium of form.
> The new world of the masses needs Constructivism because it needs fundamentals that are without deceit. Only the basic natural element, accessible to all senses, is revolutionary.
> In Constructivism, form and substance are one . . . Constructivism is pure substance. . . . Constructivism is the socialism of vision.[25]

Though his youthful works and thought were identified with socialist ideals, Moholy-Nagy's later career only reminds us of the affinity between corporate and radical modernisms. The very images which in his early life stripped away the facades of the past, to reveal the inevitability of socialism, became essential to the visions of the future that were promulgated, from the 1920s onward, by huge industrial corporations, and by their attendant image industries.

The machine, its plain, angular lines and its seemingly perpetual forward motion, provided the most palpable metaphor for the force and progress of the machine age. As a "transcendental" symbol, it could be employed—simultaneously—by a variety of contending interests.

Diego Rivera, the Mexican muralist, saw the machine as an essential component within a new, revolutionary, working-class iconography. A Communist, Rivera placed workers and machinery arm in arm in his murals; they constituted a modern "collective hero, man-and-machine," that, in his mind, replaced "the old traditional heroes of art and legend." They comprised "the new race of the age of steel." Despite his intentions, the power of his work reached across the class lines of capitalist society. Brought to Detroit in 1932, by Henry Ford, to decorate the Detroit Institute of Arts' glass-roofed Garden Court, Rivera painted a "wonderful symphony" that reconciled the enormous productive forces of capitalism with the visionary ideals of Marxism. "Marx made theory," he said, "Lenin applied it with his sense of large-scale social organization. . . . And Henry Ford made the work of the socialist state possible."[26] The machine imagery, which for a Communist artist depicted the coming to power of the working class, was, at the same time, funded by American capitalists to glorify the industrial colossus over which they ruled. True inheritors of a nineteenth-century wisdom, these skinners of the visual world did not hesitate to appropriate any image—regardless of its origins—in order to represent themselves to a world at large.

Consistent with Oliver Wendell Holmes's modern prognostications regarding the autonomy, and interchangeability, of images, the "primordial" truth of the machine was adaptable to a number of uses. Perhaps it should not surprise us that Moholy-Nagy, who in his youth had delineated a modern vision of proletarian revolt, ended up employing that vision as a corporate advertising and display designer. Moholy-Nagy, and others, had assumed that their art had stripped the modern reality down to its substance, yet they helped to invent a vision of the *future* that, itself, was to become a facade, a surface for conveying a *feeling* of transcendent possibility, and technological achievement.

By the middle of the 1920s, the interplay of radical and commercial modernism was institutionalized. Seizing upon "the power of the artist to say things which could not be said in words," advertising, industrial design, and the fashion industry all began to draw upon the futuristic imagery of the modern art movement. Speaking of the potential commercial uses of modern art, Earnest Elmo Calkins spoke of "the innate appropriateness of the new forms to express the spirit of modern industrialism."[27] In trying to "shake off bonds of tradition and strike out in new and unknown worlds of imagination," he reasoned, modernism in the arts had provided advertising and industrial design with a compelling grammar of suggestion, a grammar that could provide a silent, but persuasive, link between products to be sold and popular aspirations. In the lean and geometric lines that asserted themselves in women's fashion, in the simple abstractions that began to grace packaging, in the sharp clarity of the shop window, the influence of the machine aesthetic could be seen. It was shaping the visible contours of daily life. Writing in 1927, Calkins noted that the influence of the "new art" was becoming nearly universal, even being employed by manufacturers "whose goods are remote from those ordinarily influenced by style":

> Modern color and design are styling not only products hitherto in the style class—silks, prints, fabrics, textiles, gowns, hats, shoes, and sports clothes—but social stationery, foods, motor cars, building materials, house furnishings, book bindings, interior decoration, furniture, and bric-a-brac.[28]

The functional angularity of the power plant, of the factory, of the profit and loss column, was becoming a sign of the times. With the rise of the now familiar "International style" of architecture—from the early 1930s—this modern outlook took on a global reach. Corporate headquarters around the world began to project a devotional commitment to the principles of economic efficiency and instrumental rationality. As architect Philip Johnson has described the International style,

"steel and concrete skeletons at last became the essence of a new style."
Carrying the invocations of Louis Sullivan to their logical outcome,
"ornament was completely rejected, roofs were flat, columns exposed.
. . . The machine became an object of worship—grain elevators the
rage."[29] As Talbot Hamlin, a critic of the International school, wrote in
1933, this was an architecture motivated by purely "sociological and
economic" considerations, "interested primarily in economy, efficiency, and bareness . . . a complete surrender to the industrial machine."[30]

Between the early 1920s and the late 1930s, the machine aesthetic
underwent a significant metamorphosis. Born in the imaginative minds
of Futurists, Constructivists, Dadaists, and other tendencies of modernism, the early conception of the machine bore a sharply political edge.
In its hyperkinetic motions, its projecting geometric lines, it unified the
look of the machine with an aggressive assault on the inequalities,
decadence, and deceit of the old order. It was, self-consciously, an art
of conflict and turmoil. This can be seen in the gagged constructions of
El Lissitzky, or heard in the twelve-tone dissonance of Schoenberg or
Bartók. Even Le Corbusier's engineered "harmony" could only be realized through the overthrow of an old and putrefying past. The look of
things to come, as conceived by Moholy-Nagy and others, conveyed a
sense of defiance, of contradiction, of critical alternatives. Even as capitalists patronized the muralist Diego Rivera, his murals were filled with
"hammers and sickles, red stars, and unflattering portraits of Henry
Ford, John D. Rockefeller, J. P. Morgan, and other robber barons."[31] A
rapidly changing, sometimes chaotic, presentation of modern social life
was, in their work, transformed into imagistic typeforms. The jagged
edge marked a highly contested borderline between the energies of the
present and the utopian promises of the future.

With the 1930s, much of this changed. The first throes of modernistic
style erupted in Europe but were dramatically influenced by the United
States; its cities, its vernacular designs, its democratic ethos. The next
wave of modernism took hold in the United States, as commercial
enterprises began to draw upon the artistic developments from Europe.
Ironically, American industrial society was being presented with visions
of its own modern vitality, its own teeming energy, mediated through
the eyes of European architects, artists, and designers who were searching for an idiom of the future. The first such confrontation came in 1913,
with the Seventh Regiment Armory Show, where New Yorkers got a
shocking first glimpse at the trajectory of modern art. By the 1920s the
shock had worn off. As part of the rise of "consumer engineering,"
modernist conceptions of structure and order, of elemental form rela-

tionships, were becoming integrated into the commercial imagery of advertising, packaging, and product design.

In the realm of style, the United States had looked toward Europe for its cues. Now, driven by the logic of the marketplace, the United States began to take an active part in the stylistic delineation of modernity, leaving an imprint on nearly every aspect of daily life. As modernism became a marketing device, however, its affinities changed. As the voice of resistance against the encrusted imagery of the old order, modernism had represented a search for elemental truths, for an "honesty of expression" appropriate to the new age. As an overlay of the consumer market, its intentions became increasingly quiescent; its radical political content became muted. The primary form of change it encouraged was that circumscribed by planned "style obsolescence." "Modernizing" had been shorn of much of its social imperative and had become defined as a "new quality or character given to a product."[32]

The transvaluation of the modern became tangible as industrial designers went back to their drawing boards during the 1930s. With the Depression, the machine had broken down; its luster had tarnished. People were out of work; the buoyant consumer ethos of the 1920s was drying up. In an attempt to stimulate markets, American consumer industries became increasingly committed to the lure of industrial design.[33] Within this context, the sharp and jagged lines of resistance gave way to the smooth, lubricated look of *streamlining*.

Streamlining became the look of the future, the "first new and uniquely American approach to form."[34] As it inherited the mantle of the modern, it was also a rejection of much that had, to that time, defined modernism. Although it drew its reference points from machines (particularly airplanes), it represented a dramatic break with the prior commitments of the machine aesthetic. Already by the late 1920s, Calkins had noted the limits that the machine aesthetic placed on the priorities of marketing. "Efficiency," he declared, "was not enough. The machine did not satisfy the soul."[35] With streamlining, the machine was invested with a soul. Its surfaces were decidedly metallic, but its forms were seamless and rounded, organic. In a period of industrial crisis, when confidence in the progressive capacities of the machine had waned, this was a vision of a machine that was more spherical, softened, humanized; purged of its mechanical complexities and its threatening angularity.

If the initial mission of modernism was to strip the object world of its deceptions, to reveal and aestheticize its inner workings, streamlining was a return to the cover-up. The connection between engineering and design, which had been so essential to the faith of the modern

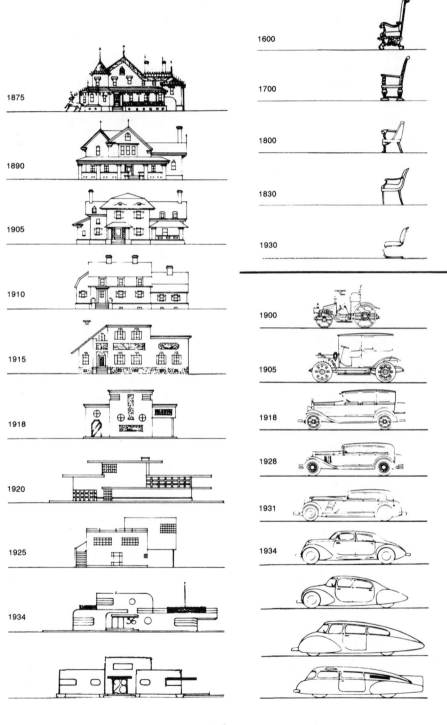

1875

1890

1905

1910

1915

1918

1920

1925

1934

1600

1700

1800

1830

1930

1900

1905

1918

1928

1931

1934

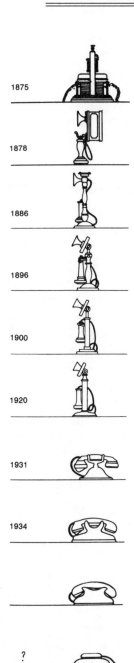

1875

1878

1886

1896

1900

1920

1931

1934

?

Progress

As market priorities call for the continual implementation of "style obsolescence," the sequence of changing styles has given rise to the visual representation of an ever-improving standard of living: of **progress.**

In these Evolution Charts, from a series designed by Raymond Loewy in the 1930s, we see a peculiar variation on Darwinism, one which encapsulates and canonizes the styling process as one of natural selection. Continually presented with such visions of yearly incremental improvement, we begin to internalize their logic, to associate the idea of social advancement with visual changes in the look of things. With U.S. consumer industries dependent on a perpetual, competitive, often frantic process of styling change, American capitalism can claim an affinity for progress unmatched by any other society, nation, or system of government in the world.

Appealing to us on an aesthetic level, such depictions of advancement are extraordinarily persuasive. It is only when we begin to employ other yardsticks—access to proper nutrition, housing, education, employment, human camaraderie, the preservation of the environment and its resources—that such claims begin to lose some of their credibility.

Billboards of the Future

Raymond Loewy,
pencil sharpener, 1933.

movement, had been broken. "When engineering directs styling," J. Gordon Lippincott asserted, "designers lose a great deal of their creativeness."[36] Modernism had once called for a unity of form and substance, now it had become a fluidly suggestive shell, wrapped around an inner mechanism that was hidden and mystified. By 1940, the designer Harold Van Doren reported that "the tendency today is definitely towards 'covering things up,' making them look less and less mechanical—'streamlining' them. . . . We are wrapping everything in packages—metal packages."[37]

Designers and other industrial stage directors continued to employ the catch-phrase "functional design" to impress their products with the modern faith, but the function was becoming less and less connected to utility, more and more ideological. Refrigerators, toasters, radios, water heaters, and pencil sharpeners were all imprinted with a modern look. The aerodynamic capacities of each were irrelevant to their use, but relevant to their image of being up to date, relevant to their sales. Henry Dreyfuss, a leading player in the theater of the modern, readily admitted that the "teardrop form," which graced many streamlined products, had nothing to do with aerodynamic realities.[38] "True streamlining," concurred Van Doren, "is not nearly so important, nor so frequently met with in problems of industrial design, as the general public thinks. But it is a phenomenon no designer can ignore."[39] The main form of resistance that the streamlined product was designed to cut through was sales resistance on the part of the customer. While the battle cry of "form follows function" would continue to be heard—

primarily as an advertising slogan—the priorities of the market assured that the actual guiding imperative would be one of *form following profit*.

A century that had begun with a heady vision of moving beyond the ornament and uncovering the beauty of essential truth had rediscovered the lie. Out of the excrescences of the *modern* movement, the machinery of consumer engineering had created a fast-paced display of ever-evolving surfaces, each committed to the future, each destined to become the past.

With the development of streamlining (and that which followed), the twentieth century had committed itself to a new, abstract form of ornamentation, reflecting, in large measure, the structures, power relations, and notions of value intrinsic to a world market society. As retail economics requires concepts of value that are inherently mobile and abstract, as corporations and bureaucracies strive to envision the world as a comprehensible and controllable mechanism, as the consumer market demands the perpetual destruction of goods and images in order to keep going, each of these priorities became embedded within the dominant aesthetic. While revivals of traditional style would continue to march in the ongoing parade of soon-to-be obsolescent dreams, new contours of vision had emerged as well, ones that derived their power not from associations with an elite past, but from a bold claim of ownership to the future. As the aristocratic traditions of ornamentation had underwritten the hierocratic prerogatives of the society that generated them, the modern trajectory of style aestheticized the modern contours of power. It is to those contours that we now must turn.

4

The Politics
of Style
in Contemporary
Culture

CHAPTER EIGHT

Form Follows Value

O that this too, too solid flesh should melt. . . .
—SHAKESPEARE, *Hamlet*

ROMA, 1948

Antonio Ricci, a thin, drawn figure, a man of about thirty, has been without a job for over two years. He and his family—his wife Maria, his young son Bruno, and a baby girl whose name we do not know—are destitute, living from hand to mouth. Like countless others living in the rubble of postwar Italy, none of their possessions are their own. Their bicycle is in hock, pawned for money to put food in their mouths. Soon the bedsheets will be hocked, to retrieve the bicycle. Their small apartment is gray and dim, its walls are bare, mottled by soot. Though these are people of faith, there appears to be little hope for the future. In a world dominated by the cruel logic of the market, their lives have become cheap.

Each day Antonio joins the other unemployed men in the piazza, where job openings are announced though jobs remain scarce. Antonio and the other men mill around. This daily ritual has taught them to expect little. Though they are willing to sell themselves, there are few takers. In war-torn Italy the cash value of muscle has declined precipitously.

Today Antonio shuffles aimlessly at the far edge of the crowd of jobless men, while a small, neatly dressed man with spectacles announces a few available jobs. "Ricci! Ricci!" calls the man. A friend of Ricci's signals to him, "Antonio, your name has been called." Ricci runs to the front of the crowd. Finally, a job. He will need a bicycle—a small problem, given the circumstances—but finally, a job. Having reclaimed the bicycle, at the price of his family's bedsheets, Antonio resumes the life of a working man. Holding his bicycle dearly, he goes to the employment office to get assigned.

Antonio is the worker-protagonist in the film *The Bicycle Thief* (*Ladri di Biciclette*, 1948), directed by Vittorio De Sica, written by Cesare Zavattini. A classic of Italian neorealism, the film makes a stylistic assault on the technically enhanced world of the "superspectacle," the dominant aesthetic of fascist cinema, and of Hollywood. For De Sica and Zavattini, the allure of the superspectacle conformed to Walter Benjamin's assessment of the fascist cinema. Within the culture of fascism, Benjamin argued, the masses were mobilized for war around a glorious rendition of their own demise. Mankind's "self-alienation has reached such a degree," he wrote in the early 1930s, "that it can experience its own destruction as an aesthetic pleasure of the first order. This," he concluded, "is the situation of politics which fascism is rendering aesthetic."[1]

Neorealism rejected this aestheticization of politics. Technically crude, and making no use of professional actors (Antonio is played by a factory worker from Breda) or elaborate sets (most of the film was shot in the streets, by sunlight), *The Bicycle Thief* presents life as a product of social circumstances, to reveal what it means to be a worker in a society where the means to survival are alienated, degraded, and elusive. This is not simply the story of one individual, nor is it larger than life. Here is a life shaped by the conditions of an impoverished reality.[2]

For Zavattini, the neorealist cinema was inspired by an "overwhelming desire to see, to analyse, its hunger for reality." Neorealism was "an act of concrete homage towards other people, towards what is happening and existing in the world." This, for Zavattini, was "what distinguishes 'neo-realism' from the American cinema. . . . reality in American films is unnaturally filtered, 'purified,' and comes out at one or two removes."[3] It was the purpose of neorealism, he argued, to recover "the reality buried under the myths."[4]

It is ironic, then, that the job that Antonio finally obtains requires him to ride around Rome on his bicycle, stopping to put up movie posters. Antonio, the neorealist hero, is employed pasting up pictures of Rita Hayworth, the monumental star of the Hollywood spectacle. Somewhat ineptly, he tries to smooth out the crinkles on the surface of the statuesque Hayworth. His hands are rough and dirty; her entire body is a seamless porcelain shell. His eyes have been hollowed by hunger and humiliation; her breasts are swollen with a promise of infinite bounty.

Ricci contemplating the bust of Hayworth.

In his unfinished novel *The Man Without Qualities,* Robert Musil reflected that "if there is such a thing as a sense of reality, there must also be a sense of possibility."[5] It may be that for Ricci, it is Rita Hayworth who embodies his "sense of possibility." Following months upon months of unemployment, she has provided him with a job. Perhaps she also denotes a vision of plenty, a counterpoint, an alternative to his own meager circumstances.

Here, on the street, there is a resounding clash of film aesthetics; *neorealismo* meets the Hollywood dream factory. Two worlds collide, head on. Each denies the outlook of the other.

Yet at another level, when Ricci meets Rita he is also, oddly, face to face with a sylphlike depiction of himself. In an unforgiving labor market, he has become a commodity, an object whose value has been set by the cold rationality of the marketplace. Rita Hayworth is also a commodity, a "face," a "body," whose considerable worth has likewise been calculated by market forces. As she reclines languorously across the placard—her arms stretched back behind her opulent head; her magnificent body displayed with shopkeeper's pride; her soft eyes fetching—her status as an object can not be denied. In Rita Hayworth,

Antonio Ricci confronts his own condition, his own circumstances of work and survival, aestheticized. As in Benjamin's critique of fascist culture, the human object, the human commodity, is made into a thing of beauty, an aspiration. Meaning flees. In this moment of silent interaction, in Rita Hayworth's ravishing promise of hope, the significance of Ricci's place within the world becomes all the more incomprehensible.

This kind of mystifying, unconsidered confrontation—between the concrete world of human relations and its aestheticized reinterpretation—is a perpetual occurrence in a world permeated by the manufactured imagery of style. We often find ourselves, so to speak, in Ricci's shoes.

We are constantly addressed by alluring images; they speak the universal language of the eye. Each is the product of deliberate creation. Each has been selected for its particular appeal, its particular purpose. Each offers a point of view. Yet as we look, we rarely reflect upon what Kenneth Burke called a "rhetoric of motives." We are educated, from infancy, to *look,* we are not encouraged to see and interpret simultaneously. Our eyes imbibe images, with little critical resistance, as if they offer an ordained glimpse of some distant, yet accessible *reality.* It rarely occurs to us, as we pass through the perpetual corridors of visual representation, that (to borrow a phrase from Helen Merrell Lynd) "every way of seeing is also a way of not seeing."[6]

In capitalist societies, where the power of commercial images has become ubiquitous, the tendency toward aestheticization may be among the most profound arenas for what Georg Lukacs described as the "phenomenon of reification." For Lukacs, reification was the process by which the social relations of a modern exchange society assume the apparent status of universal truth, stamping their "imprint upon the whole consciousness of man." As relations among people are drawn, more and more, into a web of commodity exchange, "the reduction of all objects for the gratification of human needs to commodities" takes on a "ghostly objectivity," establishing a common discourse for survival, and for aspiration.[7] Within the selectively seductive frame of the commercial image, the dominant power relations of contemporary society are transmitted, not as a set of arbitrary rules by which the exploitation of labor and resources is enforced, but as a natural, even beautiful, rendering of things. The secrets of power remain protected.

As a panorama of apparently random images, the implicit language of style offers a way of seeing, and of not seeing, the world we inhabit, and our places within it. It affects our understanding of *value,* of *social power,* and of *social change.* At the same time, it may restrain the horizons of critical thought. It is to these three important arenas of confrontation—between image and substance—that we must now address ourselves.

THE VAPORIZATION
OF VALUES

Not long before Antonio Ricci's search for work had begun, H. L. Hunt, the billionaire Dallas oilman, had made his fortune by parlaying poker winnings and borrowed funds into a hold on one of the richest oil fields in Texas. From there he spread out into real estate, silver, sugar, cattle, horses, and electronics. At his death in 1974, he was worth an estimated $4 billion.

Hunt had mastered the risky game of speculation and had won big. In passing his diversified empire on to his sons, he warned them to steer clear of "free floating paper." People will always have material needs, he reasoned, and he counseled that they limit their investments to "physical goods—oil, land, livestock," and, as a hedge against an economy gone bad, "precious metals." The sons, Bunker, Herbert, and Lamar, followed their father's advice to a T. They sank their fortune into tangible goods, "real estate, oil, collectibles, and, most prominently . . . silver." By 1986, however, this strategy had soured. In the aftermath of an attempt to corner the world market in silver (at one time they held "about half of the world's deliverable supply"), the silver market collapsed, leaving the sons, and their companies, Placid Oil and Penrod Drilling, at the edge of bankruptcy. The rule of thumb which had spelled *billions* for the father had come up with *zeroes* for the sons. According to Hunt family biographer, Harry Hurt III, this represented "the most monumental financial reversal in modern American business history."[8]

What the Hunt progeny had failed to realize was that in today's economy, the preeminence of *hard goods* has given way to that of abstract value, immateriality, and the ephemeral. As Oliver Wendell Holmes had predicted in the middle of the nineteenth century, the modern world would come to value disembodied form over palpable substance. For predaceous speculators in the current epoch, Holmes's observation offers sound advice; the *big money* is being made in the evanescent markets in information, imagery, "junk bonds," "service," and in money—or other, even more delicate forms of *floating paper*—itself. Some get rich betting on crop "futures," or building endless stockpiles for future wars. The material requirements of the present seem to weigh little in the volatile world of speculative gain.

This increasingly abstract conception of economic value can be heard in an October 1986 advertisement from United Technologies, heralding new directions for "Industry in the Info Era":

> Enter the information age. Information is the raw material for many of the business activities shaping this new era, just as iron and steel were the basic commodities in the dawning of the industrial age.

The composition of the workforce—increasingly unprotected by union organization—already embodies these changes. "The need to collect, analyze, and communicate great quantities of information," continues the United Technologies ad, "is spawning new products and services, creating jobs, and widening career opportunities." The *New York Times* "1987 National Employment Report" underwrites this claim:

> The new worker is not an auto worker, coal miner or steel worker. ... He or she is more likely to be an executive, an office or financial-house worker sitting at a computer terminal, a consultant, fast-food worker, warming freeze-dried hamburgers, or a pizza deliverer.[9]

In the wake of these recent social trends, a perceptual schizophrenia has become normalized in thinking about the economy. On 8 January 1987, the Dow Jones Industrial Average Index closed—for the first time in its history—above the 2,000 mark. Along Wall Street, as reported in the *New York Times* this was seen as a forceful sign of confidence among stock investors.[10] Televised news reports depicted joyous after-hours partying all throughout New York's financial district. Yet, as business editor Leonard Silk noted in the same issue of the *Times,* "the frenetic trading in the financial markets has . . . very little to do with the production of real goods and services."[11] His assertion was dramatized when, on the following Sunday, the *Times* quoted management professor Bela Gold, who offered the following estimation of the US economy. "Bit by bit," Gold ventured, "the economic bowels of America are being ripped apart."[12] The precipitous decline of the United States as a manufacturer of material goods had prompted this grim evaluation.

This stark duality of consciousness is rooted in what some observers describe as a "basic change in the world economy." According to Peter Drucker, one of the most distinguished business thinkers in the United States, "the 'real' economy of goods and services and the 'symbolic' economy of money, credit and capital are no longer bound tightly to each other . . . and 'are moving further and further apart.' "[13]

Survival, of course, continues to be rooted in the availability of material goods, but economic wealth is derived, more than ever, in the circulation of detached and imponderable representations of value, with an occasional freeze-dried hamburger thrown in as a stabilizer. At a time when the United States' once prodigious industrial capacities are "rusting" away, and when the legendary fruitfulness of US agriculture is likewise in decline, there are constant reports of "economic health" in those industries which specialize in the production and peddling of thin air. Advertising, public relations, and other industries of image and hype are consolidating into global megacorporations; their prime role is to envelop a jerry-built material world with provocative, tenuous meanings, suggesting fathomable value, but occupying no clear time or space. And ambitious college graduates anxiously scramble for places on the lucrative playgrounds of investment banking, an industry whose prime product appears to be self-indulgent twenty-four-year-old millionaires.

The utter triumph of abstract value can only be fully appreciated when we listen to the ongoing celebrations of the "new prosperity," while bearing witness—in our lives—to industrial breakdown, widespread "hunger" and "homelessness" (new age terminology for poverty), and the sacrificing of concrete social priorities upon an altar of economic exigency, mammon. It is upon this increasingly fragile foundation that more and more people rest their hopes for the future.

Amid an economy made of empty air, hope and anxiety are never too far apart. Even in those arenas where the giddy celebration of prosperity is most raucous, the reality principle occasionally makes an unwelcome incursion. This was the case in October of 1987, when many investors' hopes were suddenly and precipitously dashed by a dramatic stock market crash, itself—in large part—a by-product of the economy of abstraction.

To some extent, this valorization of thin air can not be separated from the rise of a money economy as the predominant arena of subsistence and exchange. The elevation of the money economy has occurred over a span of centuries; representative and transmittable value was an essential device of incipient mercantile capitalism, permitting mobility in trade. For most people, however, the dissociation of value from materiality began to make inroads with industrial capitalism, when wages and salaries replaced traditional systems of localized self-sufficiency and barter.

If money dissociated people from a direct apprehension of material worth, today's financial transactions have moved far beyond the scope of money. Since the 1920s, *credit* has become a prime mode of everyday existence. Cash has taken on an aura of substantiality. Compared to the ever more vaporous hierarchy of exchange, money, itself, has been devalued as too *weighty.*

Prior to the credit society, conceptions of wealth were measured in dollars, the absence of dollars was equated with material deprivation. Now, the *use of money* has become the most evident indicator of poverty, or at least illegitimacy (street peddlers, drug dealers, dispensers of bribes, and so on). The signs of solvency have become increasingly invisible. If the rich of the nineteenth and early twentieth centuries could be depicted as toting bags full of money and flashing thick wads of bills, today, the burdens of wealth have been considerably lightened. The credit card—an abstraction of an abstraction—is now the most acceptable sign of solvency, a public statement of living above the margin. For the "middle class," the anxiety of payment has been relegated to the privacy of the home.

This pecking order of economic viability becomes evident when one attempts to rent an automobile. It has become virtually impossible to secure a rental with cash.

The hierarchy of credit cards, itself, reveals the devalued status of money. The card that bears the abstract representation of money *(green)* is low card on the totem pole. Those which bear a synthetic facade of precious metals (the *gold* card, or better yet, the *platinum* card) increase the abstracted value (status) of the bearer. Among some credit card companies it is the *black* card, paying no homage to any material source, which stands at the apex.

The negligible worth of the "raw" plastic contained in each card is beside the point. The appreciation of value has become more and more symbolic. The more vaporous and transmittable the symbol, the greater its value.

While for common consumers thin plastic reigns as the lingua franca of abundance, the higher echelons of wealth and power have moved beyond. For them, plastic is *passé,* too weighty, too massive, a sign of depleting wealth, increasing debt. The highest stratum of value has now, literally, become thin air. Those who can mobilize abstractions to the third power, to the formlessness of electronic blips, the record of which is kept in the evanescence of a magnetic charge, are the ones who, today, inhabit the upper stratum of net worth. The concrete and tangible holdings of the landowner have given way to the chimerical belongings of the speculator. Within the shift, to paraphrase Mies van der Rohe, less has, *indeed,* become more.

Alongside this shift, of course, the parameters of parvenu behavior have also changed. Whereas earlier emulators were content to surround themselves with the ornamental accoutrements of landedness, today's parvenus surround themselves with the implements of abstraction. A central purchase within this evolving mode of conspicuous consumption is the PC, the personal computer. More and more, the consumer economy is providing *middle-class* arrivals with this most recent variant of the cultural wage, so that they, too, may emulate the abstract negotiations of those who really rule.

With the shifting conception of value, from concrete tangibility to the mobile immateriality of the abstract, the aesthetic dimension of style has shifted as well. If more traditional incarnations paid tribute to the weighty, and stationary, tangibility of landed wealth, modern style is imprinted with the valued quality of transient, unembodied worth.

LESS IS MORE

Writing in 1920, Le Corbusier offered readers the following definition of style. "Style," he declared, "is a unity of principle animating all the work of an epoch, the result of a state of mind which has its own special character."[14]

The eclectic and fickle terrain of contemporary style, drawing inspiration from nearly every conceivable source, seems to fly in the face of single-minded vision. Some conservative critics have suggested that this eclecticism reflects a crisis of modernity: a lack of guiding ideas, a lack of mind, the end of style.[15] They long for a past in which meanings were secure.

Yet surrounding the confusion of surfaces, there have been certain motivating forces which have shaped the physiognomy of style in modern, capitalist societies. One of the most conspicuous of these has been the ever-increasing prominence of abstract conceptions of value, conceptions that celebrate representation divorced from matter. Foreshadowings of this influence can be dated from the rise of merchant capitalism in Europe, when feudalism was in decline, and when "the market was no longer tied to the marketplace but was progressively becoming a placeless, timeless phenomenon coextensive with society itself."[16] From that period, the frequency of exchange relations, and the use of mobile representations of value (money, notes of credit, and so on) began, slowly at first, to cast an ever-lengthening shadow across the paths of everyday life.

By 1900, the modern landscape of style increasingly reflected the triumph of abstract representation over an aesthetic that had been rooted in the landed hierarchies of feudalism. Within the traditions of landed wealth, value was extracted from the concrete permanence of the land. Wealth and power were defined by ownership of land, by its fecundity and by its ability—if one owned enough—to generate an agricultural surplus. This tangible notion of value was inherent in societies in which both wealth and poverty were determined by power over land and access to its fruits.

In European cultures of ecclesiastical and secular nobility, style was imprinted with this concrete definition of worth. Lavish ornamentation, and the excessive use of materials of construction, affirmed the privileges of a caste that derived its wealth directly from the palpable bounty of the land. Like the earthen floor of some mythical garden, the decorative surfaces of upper-class life were conspicuously covered with weighty riches, overrun by representations of lush vines and cornucopian fruits. While the culture of peasants was, in many ways, distinct from the hierocratic outlook of the nobility, peasant imagery was also infused by a landed sensibility, the aestheticization of "fertility, growth, and a brimming-over abundance." Carnival and other customary rituals were permeated by the idiom of natural life-cycles, seasonal transformations, and other familiar aspects of self-sufficient, agrarian life.[17] Within the confines of a self-sufficient, localized, agrarian society, there was not yet an appreciation, or understanding, of a wealth which could occupy no space, which was divorced from the natural rhythms of life, and which could be transported, like light, across the immeasurable expanse of thin air.

An embryonic aesthetic of abstract value can be uncovered among the creations of a developing merchant capitalism, but it was only in the nineteenth and twentieth centuries—when an economy of money, credit, and speculation became hegemonic—that an aesthetic of weightless abstraction began to be deliberately pursued. With the rise of mercantile wealth, an appreciation of abstract wealth became increasingly conceivable. Even as parvenu burghers emulated the lifestyles of hereditary nobility, they were unwittingly forging an admixture of feudal pomp and mercantile values. The very fact that these *nouveaux riches* employed the emblems of entrenched hierarchy as a currency of social mobility revealed a proclivity for the disembodied image, divorced from its historic source, transported to a new and volatile context.

More important, even within this early mercantile period, imagery itself began to suggest the ascent of a mobile and abstract concept of value. Comparing the cathedrals of Europe which were built on feudal lands, under the aegis of monasteries, with those constructed during the subsequent period of emergent commercial town life, the beginnings of a transvaluation of values can be recognized. The Romanesque cathedrals, products of the monasteries, were massive and weighty in appearance, committed to a sense of abundant materiality. Their stout, barrel-vaulted arches hugged the ground, motionless, as if asserting a permanent claim to the land below. This was an expression of a feudal conception of value.

On the other hand, the Gothic cathedrals, erected by mercantile wealth in the towns, reflected an ambivalence. Arnold Hauser notes that while the Gothic style paid tribute to a hierarchical Kingdom of God, it also revealed nascent aspects of a bourgeois outlook.[18] The bourgeois concept of value was intrinsically more abstract and mobile, and it is significant that the Gothic cathedral broke with the enunciation of massiveness. Relative to the Romanesque, argues Christian Norberg-Schulz, the walls were thin, nearly "diaphanous" shells of stone and glass. Whereas, the central compositional element of the Romanesque style was stone, the principal component of the Gothic was light. The kinetic play of radiance, the apparent weightlessness of structure, joined to suggest an emerging ideal of mobile immateriality. These stylistic features, along with the upwardly reaching (aspiring!) sweep of pointed vaults and spires, formed the early prints of a newly emerging, if not self-conscious, bourgeois sensibility.[19]

Other examples of early mercantile imagery reflect this increasingly abstract trajectory. Within the framework of colonial American merchant culture, for example, the Puritan notion of the "plain style" represents a dramatic break from the landed traditions of Europe.

With the global dominance of finance capital, a "state of mind" which could comprehend wealth independent of matter began to be monumentalized in style. The iconography of Western cultures was shifting, reflecting the glory of intangibility, evanescence, and uninhibited motion. If the aesthetics of feudalism were rooted in a tactile appreciation of nature, the new capitalist aesthetic began to explore a conception of value and desire that transcended nature, which operated by its own immaterial laws of physics.

The synchronicity of style and value, a feature of all cultures, was conforming to an emergent economy of thin air. Holmes's notion that "matter in large masses" was "always fixed and dear," while disembodied form offered the advantage of being "cheap and transportable," revealed an uncanny appreciation of both the stylistic and economic dimensions of the modern age. Both were based on the autonomous power of representation, freed from the conditions and burdens of material reality.

By mid-nineteenth century, new industrial methods of construction, combined with a modern imagination, were giving form to the archetypes of an abstract, dematerialized style. In the field of architecture, the most celebrated of the early monuments to evanescence was Joseph Paxton's Crystal Palace, built in London for the Exposition of

1851. The floor plan was still wedded to the ecclesiastical past, in a "traditional cruciform with its naves and transepts"; nevertheless, its innovative construction employed what were to become the essential expedients of modern architecture: glass and iron (later steel). The stone ribs of the Gothic cathedral had appeared "weightless" relative to the Romanesque style; now the Crystal Palace's iron "balloon frame" provided an ethereal strength that stretched the imagination, reducing the structure to a latticework of attenuated lines. Encased in a glimmering sheath of glass, the palace suggested a new structuring of meaning. "Light, airy, and almost fairy-like in its proportions," the building appeared to be held up by the force of an idea.[20]

For those visiting the Exposition, the effect was mesmerizing. Writing to her father in the spring of 1851, Charlotte Brontë spoke of the Crystal Palace as a place that transcended earthly physics, and exerted a new and intangible force upon any who entered it:

> Yesterday I went for the second time to the Crystal Palace. . . . It is a wonderful place—vast, strange, new and impossible to describe. . . . The multitude filling the great aisles seems ruled and subdued by some invisible influence. Amongst the thirty thousand souls that peopled it the day I was there not one loud noise was to be heard, not one irregular movement seen; the living tide rolls on quietly, with a deep hum like the sea heard from the distance.[21]

Seemingly without mass, the visual power of the Crystal Palace was a resonating break with a system of value rooted in concrete materiality, a forceful statement representing a culture that measured worth, more and more, in the imaginary and transmissible idiom of exchange and speculation. It also addressed another concern of capitalism, one that will be discussed shortly. While seemingly *without* mass, its appearance, its structuring of space, could, according to Brontë, *tame* the masses.

By the end of the nineteenth century, the rule of abstraction, and of the autonomy of image, had enveloped the palette of bourgeois style. "Everything earthly," said Egon Friedell, "is intended to be sublimated, as well as concentrated, in mind. Only then," he argued, "does it in the higher sense become real."[22]

Insofar as architecture addresses the organization of social space, it provides an illuminating arena for observing the aestheticization of abstract value. Among innovators of modern architecture and design, from 1900 onward, the fascination for the insubstantial emerged as a defining purpose of their work. In their designs, and often in their words, the impulse to liberate form from substance provided a common *telos*.

Peter Behrens, who at AEG had initiated the twentieth-century field of corporate image management, sought to design buildings and objects that evoked an immaterial idea of transcendence. As an architect he plainly understood the problems and contradictions that one faced in attempting to objectify the new terms of beauty and desire. One was forced to use materials. "Architecture," he related, "strives toward infinity; but more than any other art" it "remains bound to tangible materials. For this reason, it cannot carry itself off into the spheres of a transcendental world in which it metamorphoses into an idea. It remains," he concluded, "tied to the earth."[23]

Yet despite these limits, Behrens felt that industrial society had generated a new kind of materials which, if properly used, could translate the socioeconomic principle of transcendent abstraction into a new style of visual representation in architecture.

> The success of structural design [he advised] lies in establishing the minimum amount of material for a given construction, and the beauty of iron and steel lies partly in their rigidity without volume. In a certain way they have a *dematerializing character*. This character [he added] . . . is only revealed when the iron and steel are openly exposed.[24]

As the arts and crafts of an earlier time had internalized a sense of value which was wedded to the notion of a palpable, renewable surplus, the new society of money, credit, and capital speculation was leaving its indelible mark on the imaginations of its inhabitants. A new way of seeing was leaving its imprint on the minds of those architects, designers, and image peddlers whose work would come to comprise much of what we understand to be "modern" style.

Le Corbusier, in his manifesto for modern architecture, voiced an unqualified affection for the tools of pure abstraction. By employing simple, unadorned elements of construction (cubes, cylinders, spheres, cones, and so forth) architectural space would become conceptual. "Civilized man," he asserted, could objectify "the imponderable, the relationships which create the imponderable. . . . This," he continued, "is genius, inventive genius, plastic genius, mathematical genius, this capacity for achieving order and unity by measurement."[25] Frank Lloyd Wright proposed a different modernity from that of Le Corbusier, but he, too, heralded "the new reality that is space instead of matter."[26] Similar thoughts were voiced by Walter Gropius, of the Bauhaus, who praised the qualities of glass as a material for construction: "Glass is assuming an ever greater structural importance." Its most appealing feature, he continued, was "its sparkling insubstantiality." With it, one could achieve what he admiringly termed "the growing preponderance of voids over solids."[27]

In the 1930s, when the material economy was in a state of collapse, the dream world of imagistic abstraction took over, as many people tried to envision a future "world of plenty." In 1935, when the British film producer Alexander Korda requested that Laszlo Moholy-Nagy design a set for a utopian city for his film *Things to Come*, the most important characteristic of Moholy's vision was its insubstantiality. As related by his biographer and wife Sibyl Moholy-Nagy,

> Alexander Korda . . . commissioned him to create special effects for *Things to Come*, a film based on a story by H. G. Wells which told of a future society, half technologists, half robots.
> . . . The fantastic technology of the Utopian city of the future would, so Moholy dreamed, *eliminate solid form.* Houses were no longer obstacles to, but receptacles of, man's natural life force, light.*
> There were no walls, but skeletons of steel screened with glass and plastic sheets.

Consistent with a world view that was coming to elevate abstract value above, and apart from, material circumstances, she adds, "The accent was on perforation and contour, an indication of *a new reality rather than reality itself.*"[28]

Even before he ever reached New York, Moholy-Nagy's "new reality" had been inspired by photographs and descriptions of the Manhattan skyline. When he finally came to New York, in 1937, he found his vision confirmed. The skyline, he wrote in a letter to his wife, provided a dramatization of a transmigration from materiality to evanescence, a stunning epiphany in light. "Dearest Sibyl," he began on 8 July 1937,

> This then is New York. . . . This is what made it so fantastic—these buildings, the skyscrapers of New York. Obelisks, menhirs, megaliths— every shape, historic and prehistoric—straightly perpendicular, or terraced like a pyramid; in solid formations, or single-pointing. . . . There was no detail. Night came and even the sharp-edged contours melted. A million lights perforated the huge masses—switching, flickering—a light modulation dissolving the solid form. . . . I got drunk—from seeing. . . .[29]

Interestingly, the source of his conversion, the escalating skyline of Manhattan, was itself an outcome of the "symbolic" economy. It grew to its modern proportions during a period of runaway real estate speculation during the 1920s which, notwithstanding its comely dazzle, played its part in contributing to the economic breakdown of the 1930s.

---

*It should be noted that, in the film, the city is entirely enclosed, hermetically sealed from the natural world.

Both of these buildings were designed to express the promise of the industrial future. However, the Administration Building from Chicago's Columbian Exposition of 1893 (*above*) still holds to the aesthetic dictates of landed power. Weightily encrusted with ornamental foliage and reaching horizon-

tally outward, this vision of the future assumed that industrialism would make the style of landed wealth accessible to more and more people.

Less than forty years later, Moholy-Nagy's "city of the future" (*right*) forswore horizontal mass for vertical light and cavernous volume. In the film *Things To Come*, this futuristic city was totally enclosed and separated from the natural world. No longer emulating the stylistic conventions of landed society, its vision expressed an affinity for the speculative airiness of abstract value.

The pioneers of modern architecture and design spoke of their work as the cutting edge of universal truth, slicing its way through the lies and the kitsch that had compromised the integrity of nineteenth-century taste. Yet despite their claims to transhistoric universality, the "truths" of their vision—like the ruling "truths" of the past—were embedded in the particularities of history, in the emergence of a market economy where the "symbolic" was taking precedence over the "real."

The unspoken *rapport* between modern forms of representation and modern incarnations of value is nowhere more entrenched than in the rise of the skyscraper as an ultimate symbol of contemporaneity. In popular culture, the skyscraper is most often filled with powerful ideological connotations: progress, a reaching for the beyond, the freedom of the creative human spirit, and so forth. It is one of the foremost monuments of progressive capitalist development from the early twentieth century onward, the embodiment of a commercialized interpretation of modernism. For small to medium-sized towns, across the American landscape, the erection of at least one "tall building" is a fundamental requirement for membership in the "modern age."

But the skyscraper is a form that embodies a particular social and historical outlook. Its grandeur is founded in a society where abstract financial speculation was overwhelming a system of value founded in the concreteness and resourcefulness of the land.

The vertical reach of the skyscraper contrasts, powerfully, with the horizontal reach of monuments in societies where land and its resources have been the most commonly understood index of wealth. Where the primacy of agriculture, or of the earth's material resources, hold sway over the imagination, power asserts itself by reaching outward, attempting to enclose more and more land within its grasp. A given piece of land, in this context, is limited by material and ecological conditions. Used to its highest efficiency, an acre of land can produce just so many calories of nutrition; can support the grazing of just so many head of cattle; can yield just so many tons of mineral ore, and so on. In order to preserve this value for the future, the land's resources must not be plundered to the point of exhaustion. Given such an understanding of value, where wealth is directly related to the productiveness of the earth, accumulation asserts itself horizontally. As a terrain's ability to yield wealth is bounded by natural conditions, the only way to multiply wealth is by multiplying acreage.

The sensuous proximity of land left a recognizable mark on the monumental styles that evolved before the late nineteenth century. The aesthetics of the chateau, the palace, even the grand boulevards of cities, was marked by a scale of latitude. Versailles, and the formal gardens that surrounded it, proclaimed its extensive dominion over land. The landed sensibility of Russia created a Kremlin which, according to architect Allesandra Latour, expresses its strength and majesty in an idiom of expansiveness more than height.[30]

If architecture may be viewed as a visual rhetoric, expressing changes in the meaning of wealth and value, the skyscraper signaled the ascendency of a new, more speculative society, less grounded in the conditions of nature. With the growth of finance capital from the mid-nineteenth century onward, the intrinsic resources of land seemed to decline in importance. Fortunes could be built within the framework of a market no longer constricted by the spatial dimensions of the past. If wealth was once measured by the ability to claim vast expanses of the earth's surface, now the value of land—like other provinces of modern value—could spiral upward toward the sky, seemingly unencumbered by the economics of nature.

As an approach to building, the skyscraper embodied the essence of *form following profit*. With no increase in land area, the value of real estate now escalated to levels as high as greed and engineering would allow.

The appearance of tall buildings provoked the transcendent imaginations of nearly all who saw, or heard, of them. A writer for *Munsey's Magazine* (July 1905) praised the emerging skyline of New York as a sight that would elevate the intellectual capacities of everyone who witnessed it. "It will be demonstrable," he predicted, "that as buildings ascend so do ideas. It is mental progress," he concluded, "that skyscrapers engender."

Yet in the architectural community itself, numerous voices took exception to such unqualified tribute. Behind the gleam of its visionary symbolism, a broad number of critics saw the skyscraper as the excrescence of speculation run amok. Writing in *American Architect* in January 1926, Harvey Wiley Corbett described "the birth and development of the tall building" as the outcome of "speculative interests . . . keen to realize the income bearing possibilities of tall buildings." From the last decades of the nineteenth century, he argued,

> the enhancement of [urban] real estate values made the cost of an ordinary site mount to high figures. There was a commercial insistence for more revenue, which meant added stories, as lateral extension was not possible and like in a poker game "the blue sky was the limit." So capital said to art, which is an old fashioned term for architecture, "Go higher up." And art . . . said to science, "Hear that? Hear what capital says?"[31]

Another writer in *American Architect,* Egerton Swartwout, described the process more simply. Arguing that it was "greed" that made "the high building possible," he explained that "it is commercially a good thing for the owner of a valuable plot to erect a building which will house ten times as many tenants as the ground should hold."[32] A way of seeing grounded in an ecological conception of land was giving way to a perspective rooted in nothing more than the exigencies of gain.

The resulting congestion, according to Lewis Mumford, was an inescapable effect of a system driven by speculation in land rents and mortgages. Because of this, he noted, "almost every bank, every insurance company, every individual land owner, ultimately every savings bank depositor has . . . a *stake in congestion.* The whole structure of our present pecuniary values and prestige values," he predicted in 1938, "assumes the indefinite continuance of this metropolitan pattern."[33]

The accord between architectural aesthetics and speculative value was the target of many architects' criticisms as well. It was the architect, after all, whose job it was to aestheticize the gains of the real estate speculator or the corporate giant. Speaking at Princeton in 1930, Frank Lloyd Wright contended that "the skyscraper of today is only the prostitute semblance of the architecture it professes to be." Showing remarkable understanding of the machinery of modern style, he continued,

> The usual service of the doctor-of-appearances has here again been rendered to modern society. . . . New York, so far as material wealth goes, piled high and piling higher into the air, is a commercial machine falsely qualified by a thin disguise. . . .
>
> The skyscraper envelope is not ethical, beautiful, or permanent. It is a commercial exploit or a mere expedient. It has no higher ideal of unity than commercial success.[34]

Another architect of the 1930s, Frederick Ackerman, saw the development of tall buildings as a process that responded to market mechanisms, independent of social concerns. "During the last decade," he wrote in 1932, "need and effective demand played little or no part in the promotion of structures representing in total an investment of billions of dollars." The "utter uselessness" of much of this construction, he noted, "had to be dramatized by such events as followed October 1929," when real estate as well as other markets collapsed. An advocate of human-scale communities, Ackerman was particularly irked by the way in which many skyscrapers were represented as products of modern, "functional" principles of design. Though the rhetoric of "functionalism" was imbued with connotations of human usefulness, these buildings, he argued, functioned for one purpose in particular:

> The tremendous surge of activity surrounding the erection of these structures was utterly unrelated to consideration of use; and strange as it may

seem, it was during this period that the theory of utility and functional expression revived and burst into flower. . . .

The bulk of this excess *functional* architecture was in truth functional only in a most peculiar and limited sense. The structures served the end of floating some billions of real estate bonds and of jeopardizing the utility of and the investment in a very large amount of property adjacent to these new creations.

Despite all the endless talk about the planning of communities they continue to grow in response to the exigencies of speculation.[35]

Regarding such criticisms from the vantage point of the late 1980s, little has changed. The correspondence between tall building development and an economic ethos of boundless speculation continues. In terms of the argument that skyscraper construction proceeds in the absence of serious social evaluation, current circumstances concur. In New York City, the recent ascent of corporate buildings and luxury dwellings corresponds directly to an increase in homelessness and the decimation of neighborhoods.

Yet if the critics of the skyscraper, in the architectural community of the 1920s and 1930s, provide us with an incisive intellectual grasp of the implicit motives of form, somehow their perspective seems elusive. In those districts where the vertical grandeur of the modern spectacle still casts its shadows and light, the visual intoxication described by Moholy-Nagy somehow seems more palpable. In the presence of a skyscraper, it is difficult not to be overwhelmed by a sense of majesty that is conveyed.

From the deep canyons of the street, a succession of skyscrapers provides a kinetic vista of upward-thrusting motion. True to the aesthetic of evanescence, the walls of each building converge far above our heads, dissolving—at the zenith—into a *vanishing point.* Materiality—be it stone and mortar or steel and glass—is vaporized by the raw, aspiring power. Even ornamentation, where it has been applied, loses its historic grounding, participating, now, in a spectacular defiance of gravity.

From below, the pedestrian is overcome by awe. For some this is exaltation. For others, an uneasy sense of threatened or diminished humanity. In either case, it is but a feeling. The aestheticization of value leaves little space for the exercise of critical reason or socioeconomic analysis. Power resides above the canyons, but for most it is incomprehensible.

From the top-floor office, or from observation decks, the skyscraper can afford an individual an unparalleled experience of power. Looking

Vanishing point, 1988. An office tower on Fifty-third Street in Manhattan, viewed from the canyon below.

down from above, the chief executive officer (or the interloping tourist) sees the mass of humanity through the eyes of God. The matters of humanity below are reduced to amusing insignificance, while the spectator from above is afforded the conceit of endless vision.

Amid this sublime theater of transcendental mythification, there is little opening for an "overview" such as that posed by Ackerman, Mumford, or Frank Lloyd Wright. Here, the "commercial machinery" of speculation in abstract financial value, has been transformed into a statement of *philosophical* speculation, of "pondering the imponderable," as Le Corbusier would have put it. Operating on the aesthetic plane, ruling patterns of social and economic power are transmuted into standards of beauty and, perhaps, into standards of *truth*. Working furtively on the senses and on the emotions, these underlying patterns of power become, in essential ways, invisible.

Even though the social groundwork is not always obvious, the aesthetic is ubiquitous. By the 1920s, the jurisdiction of an increasingly abstract and weightless theory of value was moving beyond the confines of architecture. Stimulated by the growing economic importance of consumer engineering, these new aesthetic principles left their mark on style. The motif of immateriality, the principle that *less is more,* was repeated again and again.

Women's fashion was one of the first and most significant spheres to be consumed by this modern propensity. For a society that had customarily designated women as the "decorative" sex, the adornment of the female body offers a particularly illuminating lens through which one may observe changing cultural patterns. Though a mass market in ready-to-wear clothing had begun to develop by the 1880s, the contours of these fashions followed entrenched European ideals. Produced in sweatshops by cheap, immigrant labor, early mass-market fashions imitated those of traditional, aristocratic elites and bourgeois parvenus. Generous folds of layered cloth, intricately decorated by embroidery and lace, became available to women who, according to previous custom, could never have hoped for such palpable signs of privilege.

By the 1920s, however, the influence of modernism was altering the silhouette of fashion. Economic and social priorities propelled this transfiguration. With the entry of the United States into World War I, key materials were conscripted into the war effort. Cloth and other goods, which had contributed to the shapely and "sumptuous" infancy of mass fashion, became scarce in the domestic consumer market. For fashion to survive, it became necessary to evolve a sparer, less wasteful use of materials.

Simultaneously, the changing social role of women encouraged new standards of fashion. As women began to enter the urban marketplace in larger numbers, the restrictive conventions of Victorian fashion lost much of their allure. For women moving beyond the confines of the home, corsets and excessive layerings of cloth were revealed as devices of incapacitation. The reform of clothing was an essential component of women's liberation. As women gained a more legitimate social identity, the efficacy of a newly mobile approach to dress became manifest.

By the 1920s, the avenues of fashion had responded to the redeployment of materials and the social aspirations of women. The abstract ideal, which had found its most articulate ideologues in the realm of architecture, was applied to the female body. Dresses were shorter, revealing more of the body. The layering of cloth had given way to the flapper's shift. Where earlier fashion ideals were predicated on the stationary display of wares, the geometric angularity and simple, energetic lines of the new fashion conveyed frenetic motion.

With few exceptions, substance and texture were persistent characteristics of women's fashion through the early years of the twentieth century. This was true of visual representations of fashion as well. Late nineteenth-century fashion plates—consistent with the clothes they depicted—were imprinted with a clear appreciation for detail. Each fold of cloth, every flounce or rosette, was rendered with deliberate precision. The minute particulars of a garment's construction were realistically conveyed. According to an outlook that stressed the primacy of substance, engravings and lithographs exuded a sense of indissolvable materiality. The epistemological power of the *touchable* was stated in full.

This material quality was even more evident in the "fashion babies" that circulated as an important medium of fashion in the late nineteenth century. Mainly for women whose dresses were handsewn by seamstresses, these pasteboard dolls were shipped from France, wearing miniature versions of the latest in *haute couture*. Here, again, the depiction of fashion was marked by a tribute to tangibility.

By the 1920s, however, a more modern aspect was taking hold. It suggested the transmigration of matter, the freeing of form from substance, the flight of an autonomous idea. Increasingly, fashion designs were transmitted by airy sketches, mere suggestions of lines or contours. Whereas earlier depictions were presented in full, the modern fashion plate was a mere trace, the suggestion of a bodily attitude or gesture. Here was a presentation of fashion, not as a palpable sign of station or of material consumption, but as a highly volatile idea, transforming matter into energy and action.

The clothing itself followed the spirit of the sketch. Promulgated by sophisticated techniques of marketing and merchandising, and highlighted by the translucent flicker of the movies, the fashions of the 1920s suggested the dissolution of bodily mass. Whereas traditional women's fashions depended upon a solid body, the new fashions displaced the earthbound idiom of horizontal expanse with that of unfettered, vertical ascendency. Not only was the "flapper" lithe and lean, she appeared as if—at any point—she might transcend the force of gravity, dissolving into the weightless ecstasy of some modernistic frenzy. Silk stockings rolled at the knees, body wrapped to eradicate all evidence of secondary sexual characteristics, she was, if nothing else, streamlined.

Consistent with the general trajectory of architecture, fashion helped to reform the visual world according to the principle of form in motion. Anne Hollander, a historian of fashion images, has pointed out,

> After about 1920 the fact that women's clothes showed such a reduction in overall volume was undoubtedly partly due to the visual need for the completely clothed body to be satisfactorily seen *in motion.*
>
> The still body that is nevertheless perceived as ideally in motion seems to present a blurred image—a perpetual suggestion of all the other possi-

This American fashion sketch from the 1840s is committed to an aesthetic of tangibility and mass. Mass, texture, and ornament are rendered in great detail.

This 1930s fashion sketch accentuates body line over mass.

In this 1980s sketch, all suggestion of mass has disappeared. The elevation of abstract value is complete.

Drawing by Derek May for Linda Dresner Inc.

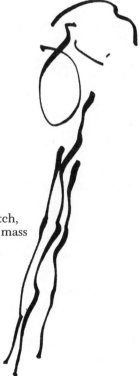

ble moments at which it might be seen. It seems to have a dynamic, expanding outline.[36]

The ebbs and flows of fashion since the 1920s have drawn upon a wide range of imagistic traditions, but it is the abstract, the sparse, and the ephemeral that have continued to prevail as the ruling standards of modernity. The incandescent conception of style and value is so preponderant that even when more *weighty* traditions of dress are revived, they ineluctably take on the characteristics of the modern. As disembodied skins, historically divided from the apparent permanence of landed value, their ephemeral quality necessarily overwhelms their ostensible tangibility. As "current" manifestations within a continuously volatile market in style, their most promising characteristic is that they, like the thin air that fuels their appearance, will soon disappear from view.

Advertising reinforces this transitory and vaporous quality. Even weighty items are wrapped in a seductive patter of evanescence. A 1984 newspaper ad for a broad-shouldered autumn coat suggests, in a flow of provocative non sequiturs, the evaporation of matter:

VIEWPOINT NOW: THE GREATCOAT
Instantly, you see the difference. Where once you thought coat . . . now you'll think a toss of covering. Where shape is more a fling of texture and color . . . the silhouette, merely a launching point to a new level of contour and line. These are the greatcoats. Where movement is all! . . . The greatcoats . . . a serious, all-desirable evolution in the great cover-up!

THE BODY POLITIC

Over the course of the twentieth century, the aesthetic of abstract value has left its mark on architecture, product design, fashion, packaging; even language has been affected by a certain sparseness. Above all else, however, its imprint on ideals of the human body is particularly striking.

Nowhere can the aestheticization of value be more profoundly witnessed than in the evolution of body ideals since the beginning of the twentieth century. It is here, in the complex tissues of biology, ideology, and consciousness, that the modern commodity aesthetic, and the incarnations of personal identity, uncomfortably—at times pathologically—mesh.

Inasmuch as weightless evanescence has emerged as a paramount quality of value, it is little wonder that the *body of woman* has served as the prime locus, the palaestra, for its corporeal representation. In patriarchal cultures it has been custom for women to be looked upon as objects of value; to be traded between families in the consolidation of wealth and power; to be coveted and secreted away like precious gems; to be displayed, as conspicuous signs of masculine achievement; cloistered, to maintain the purity of the male line. The association between women and exchange value is an age-old, if repressive, tradition. Yet if the traffic in women is an ancient curse, the delineation of feminine worth has undergone, in the twentieth century, a radical transfiguration.

Into the early years of the twentieth century, idealized representations of the body still reflected the tangible biases of landed value. Consistent with the same priorities that shaped weighty, ornamental goods, a well-fed, corpulent body was visible evidence of material prosperity. Even among those Protestant merchants who attended the Constitutional Convention in 1787, notes historian Forrest McDonald, "obesity was the norm. . . . John Adams," he adds, "weighed in at 270."[37]

Among wealthy Americans of the late nineteenth century, plumpness still bespoke a life of self-satisfied abundance. Although a money economy had taken hold, and was part and parcel of their accruing wealth, the middle class was as yet psychologically unprepared to embrace an aesthetic of unfettered abstraction. Revealing a historic insecurity characteristic of *nouveaux riches,* the average bourgeois still sought prestige in weighty visions of monumentality. In the excess of their lives, and in the weight of their bodies, they revealed an affinity to the privileges of aristocracy. In photographic portraits, jowled men and ample women proudly displayed a plenitude of flesh. For women— whose object-value was intimately tied to their reproductive capacities—a heavy bosom and stout hips were conspicuous elements of beauty. The abstract calculations of finance capital had not yet left their disintegrating mark on the female form.

Among poor people, whose sensibilities were shaped by recurrent periods of scarcity and famine, the vision of a well-fed body also held an obvious appeal. In the folk traditions of carnival, Mikhail Bakhtin reminds us, the symbol of the overflowing body, which perpetually "outgrows itself, transgresses its own limits," depicted the contours of popular aspiration, providing a utopian vision of a fecund Mother Earth, ever giving birth, ever replenishing herself.[38] For the millions of immigrants who arrived in the United States in the years girdling 1900, eating well was inextricably linked to their notion of *doing well.*

Even in the surging modernity of a blossoming urban nightlife, the voluminous aesthetic persisted. "In the 1880s," historian Lewis Erenberg relates, "May Howard, the first burlesque queen, employed no one under 150 pounds." The same standard of beauty ruled the selection of chorus girls for the aptly named "Billy Watson Beef Trust."[39]

Into the early years of the twentieth century, most women in the United States were still evaluated in relation to a land-based sense of patrimony, appraised for the role they played in the timeworn confines of a home economy. Courtship was structured—for the most part—by patterns of arranged marriage, and a stout wife possessed a palpable aura of fruitfulness. For a time the influx of old-world immigrants from southern Italy and Eastern Europe reinforced the prevalence of this disposition. "Eat, eat!" was a familiar maternal command.

The lure of being thin and mobile had not yet arrived. Weight had not yet arisen as a "problem to be solved." Dieting for weight loss had not yet shown its face as a twentieth-century obsession. A spare body, especially in women, was a symptom of nervous exhaustion, of life out of balance.[40]

By the end of the First World War, however, the female body principle had broken away from the notions of fertility and material abundance. Within the burgeoning urban, industrial society, women increasingly ventured beyond the confines of the home. The teeming anonymity of metropolitan life drew women into the social sphere, as they became part of a broad wage-labor market, and also as they entered a freer market of sexuality. Courtship, formerly regulated by arrangements of family and community, became—more and more—an outcome of individual negotiation and choice. In the process, a woman's *worth* shifted from the landed idiom of materiality to one more suited to the mobility of modern social and economic life. Once a bountiful repository of agrarian values, a new ideal of the female body began to emerge, taking on the volatile characteristics of abstract, market value. As the dominant system of profitability was coming to rest on a foundation of thin air, the female body—along with other icons of the new order—followed suit. While the predominant masculine body ideal followed patterns set by modern work discipline and the machine, the female body ideal began to mimic the immateriality of a floating currency.

From the mid-1910s, bodily substance became identified with cumbersome excess, an outward sign of outmoded, old-world proclivities. The "new woman," as she was often called in the mass magazines of the day, was "slim, long, sinewy, panther-like."[41]

To be sure, people schooled by centuries of custom were alarmed by the rise of this new, *flatter*-ing ideal. The "straight up and down" contour that was emerging flew in the face of more voluptuous standards.[42]

Yet against the habits of the old culture, the ubiquitous voices of the new culture—especially the mass media—touted the virtues of slimness. On the eve of the First World War, women's magazines had begun to take aim against the "fat walk," "waddling gait," and the "clumsy bulk" which had, not long before, been seen as the constituents of beauty.[43] In April of 1914, the *Delineator* magazine posed a rhetorical question in the title of one of its articles: "Don't You Want to Be Thin?" "This is the age of the figure," the magazine counseled. "The face alone, no matter how pretty, counts for nothing unless the body is as straight and yielding as every young girl's."[44]

A mania for thinness was taking hold. Its grip would tighten in the decades to follow, capturing the eye and the imagination; embedding itself within an often troubled, modern subjectivity. From the 1920s onward, the image of a spare and fleshless body was projected everywhere by the newly prominent agencies of mass impression. As the Hollywood fantasy factory provided audiences with a steady flow of images to emulate; as standardized mannequins became a basic ingredient of advertising, selling everything from cars to cigarettes, the notion that "less is more" increasingly came to dominate the signposts of the commercial landscape. Although periods of economic depression, war, and recovery have made some imagistic concessions to the idea of a bountiful physique, the general trajectory of twentieth-century life reveals a continuous trend toward ever-decreasing substance.

Raymond Loewy noted this tendency when, in 1979, he wrote an account of his fifty-year career as one of the world's premier industrial designers. Describing his commission to redesign the Studebaker automobile, he utilized an idiom that revealed a fateful link between bodies and things. Prior to the appearance of his "Starliner" design, Loewy argued, automotive styling had failed to capture the true spirit of the age. "Up to this time," he wrote, "body 'character lines' were raised panels that gave a car a heavy look." The bulbous quality characterized the so-called streamlined cars of the 1930s. In arriving at an alternative approach to design, Loewy introduced "an intaglio [depressed] surface." The result achieved his goal, "to give Starliner its hungry and slenderized look."[45]

Loewy's facelift for the world famous Coca-Cola bottle utilized the same anthropomorphic idiom. The familiar "hobble-skirt" Coke bottle, which was first introduced in 1916, was a tribute in glass to the bounteous ideals of Victorian womanhood. Its indented waist separated a full bosom from broad hips. When, nearly fifty years later, Loewy was commissioned to bring the familiar trademark up to date, he merely drew upon the changed silhouette of *femininity*. Elongating the fluid glass, he put the bottle on a diet, achieving—once again—a "slenderized look."[46]

This association between product design and (particularly female) body ideal is, today, commonplace. The cigarette industry has turned the process into a cultural cliché with Virginia Slims. The narrow, neutrally hued cigarette pack, striding beside a narrow, neutrally hued woman, is an essential feature of an advertising campaign that endlessly compares the "liberated" status of today's thin woman, with the "oppressed" status of her predictably rounder foremother.

A 1987 television commercial for LESS diet bread furthers the association, but from the opposite direction. Here the threadbare slogan of modern architecture and design is employed as a precept of nutrition. As the jingle intones:

> Less is more,
> Less is best,
> When your body says more,
> Say LESS!

Perhaps it is in the frothy instructions of this commercial for diet bread that the morbid contradictions of abstract value, and its embodiment as a physical ideal, are most clearly revealed. Surely, it may be argued that the concern for dieting and weight loss, which has gathered momentum since the 1920s and has reached its zenith in the current craze over "fitness," is a health-conscious response to the more sedentary quality of life that has accompanied the historic shift from manual to mechanized modes of survival. Likewise, the more emaciated body type prescribed for the *modern woman* may be interpreted in light of her gradual emancipation from the customary enclosures of a patriarchal hearth and home. Although such explanations deserve serious historical consideration, it must be added that the unrequited quest for thinness that besieges so many today offers them little in the way of either health or emancipation. The insatiable passion for thinness is, at bottom, antagonistic to the body's natural need to be fed.

If customary conceptions of beauty were consistent with the human need for nourishment, the haunted desire to conform to the modern contour is at war with the physical and emotional hungers of the individual. This ever-widening fissure between body aesthetics and vitality is synchronous with the more generally alienated world view that has seen the ascendency of abstract value as an independent, disembodied conception of worth. In the realm of the human body, however, the search for immateriality can yield pathological results. The very existence of body flesh comes to symbolize a barrier to perfection and satisfaction.

The implosive contradictions of this ideal can, at times, be seen within the very media that promote it. A 1984 survey of 33,000 women readers, published in *Glamour* magazine, reveals a madness that resides just beneath the surface of media images.

Glamour, a beauty and "lifestyle" magazine aimed at a young, fashion-conscious readership, is permeated by countless images of ageless, porcelain beauty, totally immune to the changes of life. Advertisements and editorial content merge, proffering a parade of "come hither" glances from the sultry eyes of standard-issue models. Articles offer four-step road maps from *before* to *after,* from *don't!* to *do!,* from inadequacy to perfection. Poring over the magazine, the reader is invited, over and over again, to measure herself—in her life—against the svelte, satisfied, photogenic sirens who call out to her. Messy hair can become "sleeker." A "make-over" can provide "a new look for a new job."

Prominent are articles offering counsel on weight loss. A "diet and exercise blitz" must be waged against the body at all times. Self-monitoring and eternal vigilance are a must, as the body's tendency is to "creep" back across the line separating desirability from desire.

Yet underneath (perhaps *fueling*) this perpetual program for perfection, the women who read *Glamour,* and other such magazines, experience and express feelings of doubt and self-revulsion. The survey of readers (entitled "Feeling Fat in a Thin Society: 33,000 Women Tell How They Feel About Their Bodies," *Glamour,* February 1984), reveals women tormented by the images they consume.

Some 73 to 75 percent of the women who responded to the survey feel they are "too fat." These far outnumber the 15 percent who believe they are "just right," or the 3 percent who see themselves as "too thin."

The epidemic feelings of negative self-consciousness reveal themselves in behavioral patterns that have begun to appear earlier and earlier in life. Dr. William Feldman, a medical professor at the University of Ottawa, reports, "I've been seeing 5- and 6-year-old girls who were preoccupied with their weight. . . . One young girl broke into tears when her mother asked her to go for a swim. The girl said she'd look fat in a swimsuit, when in fact her weight was normal for her height."[47] *Ms.* magazine (February 1987) reports that "half of all fourth-grade girls diet," while *Vogue* (May 1986) contends that "*70 percent of fourth-grade girls* are concerned enough about their weight to start the battle against unwanted pounds." *Vogue* continues that "80 percent of women have been on a diet by age eighteen . . . and more than half of U.S. adult women are currently on a weight-loss regimen."

The details of these regimens deserve an accounting. According to the *Glamour* survey, 50 percent of respondents "sometimes" or "often" use diet pills; 27 percent use liquid formula diets; 18 percent use diuretics (water reduction pills); 45 percent use fasting or "starving." Purging the body (often after bouts of binge eating) is also surprisingly common: 18 percent use laxatives for rapid weight elimination; 15 percent engage in "self-induced vomiting."

1890

Perhaps the most telling statistics to come out of the survey concern those women who are clinically "underweight." These women, also, feel "overweight": 45 percent believe they are too fat, 66 percent of them often contemplate dieting. Even those who are decisively thin share the feelings of anxiety, depression, and repulsion that permeate a growing testimony on body image.

1900

J. Kevin Thompson, writing in *Psychology Today* (April 1986), reports that "many women see themselves as roundfaced and pudgy, even when no one else does." Women's "distorted images of their bodies" are fairly common:

1905

> Liz stands in front of the mirror each morning, trying various combinations of make-up to get her cheeks to look less puffy. She is satisfied with her waist, hips, and thighs, but she keeps trying to get those cheeks to look smaller. . . .
>
> Cathy also stands in front of the mirror each morning, but she tries various combinations of skirts and blouses to reduce the apparent size of her stomach. Although no one agrees with her, she can't get over the feeling that her paunch protrudes, making her look three months pregnant. Her mid-section continues to haunt her.

1910

1915

Therese Bertherat, the French physical therapist and author, reports on a woman, H., who arrived at one of her physical awareness classes, complaining, "I eat chocolate . . . too much chocolate."

"Why do you want to come to this class?" inquired Bertherat.

"To get rid of my belly," answered H.

1920

What Bertherat saw, however, was not a woman who was too fat, but one who was, in essence, uncomfortable living in her own skin, in her own body. "She doesn't have any belly," Bertherat reports; "she doesn't have any fat anywhere. A former model, her neck and legs are extraordinarily long. And," she adds, "extraordinarily stiff." As a postscript to this story of H., Bertherat notes that "the dissociation not only of the limbs but of all the parts of the body is very common and considered normal."[48] Even H., who has made her living as an admired model of perfection, is haunted by her own image, unable to find comfort within her self.

1925

1930

1935

For Kim Chernin, who has written extensively of her obsession with slenderness, "the sense of fulness and swelling, of curves and softness,

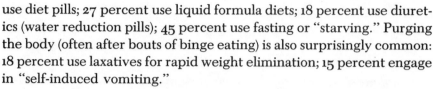

the awareness of plenitude and abundance . . . filled me with disgust."
"Hunger," she relates, "filled me with despair."[49]

Such feelings are most common among women, but men also may be possessed by a sense of bodily "excess." Steven G——, a nice-looking man in his mid-thirties, speaks of his daily encounter with his own body:

> My body and I are at war. I awaken each morning and before anything
> I stand in front of the mirror. Almost like a reflex I grab and pinch the
> fleshy part of my stomach. It's still there . . . and I feel like it's a reminder
> of work unfinished, undone. My dream, if you can call it that, is that
> someday I'll reach for it, and it won't be there.[50]

This craving for disappearance is not dissimilar from that of Ellen West. A young psychiatric patient whose "obsession with eating and losing weight" is discussed at length by Chernin, West speaks reflectively of her problem. "I must now be able to look at my ideal," she says, "this ideal of being thin, of being without a body."[51]

Here we begin to see that anorexia or bulimia, which are marginalized and diagnosed as "eating disorders," are not anomalous, but logical extensions of the norm. In describing her anorexia as "a feeling of profound humiliation that the body exists at all," one woman merely indicates her profound, if self-destructive, commitment to the more general aesthetic of abstraction.[52]

In these people's words, and in the undocumented lives of countless others, we come to the socio-somatic heart of the matter. Whatever elements of personal guilt and self-punishment may afflict an individual's biography, the external, *social* ideal of thinness is a by-product of modernity. It speaks for a life that claims to live beyond the consequences of nature. It reflects the pure logic of abstract value—the economy of thin air—transported and implanted within the inner realm of the human subject. Conforming to ideals that have informed developments in architecture, design, advertising imagery, and fashion, the ideal body is one that no longer materially exists, one that has been reduced to an abstract representation of a person: a line, a contour, an attitude, skinned from its biological imperatives. Regardless of the shape one's body takes, whatever flesh remains is *too much;* image must be freed from the liabilities of substance.

In anorectic body ideals, in architectural ideals that claim to transcend structural physics, in the social world we inhabit, this displacement of priorities reveals a fateful corruption. The problem has been stated succinctly by architectural critics Kent Bloomer and Charles Moore, in their book *Body, Memory and Architecture.* Speaking of the need to bring architectural space and human life into greater harmony, they note that

> one of the most hazardous consequences of suppressing bodily experiences and themes in adult life may be a diminished ability to remember who and what we are. The expansion of our actual identity requires greater recognition of our sense of internal space as well as of the space around our bodies. Certainly if we continue to focus on external and novel experiences and on the sights and sounds delivered to us from the environment to the exclusion of renewing and expanding our primordial haptic* experiences, we risk diminishing our access to a wealth of sensual detail developed within ourselves—our feelings of rhythm, of hard and soft edges, of huge and tiny elements, of openings and closures, and a myriad of landmarks and directions which, if taken together, form the core of our human identity.[53]

*The phrase *haptic sense* is taken from James J. Gibson, *The Senses Considered as a Perceptual System* (Boston: Houghton Mifflin, 1966). According to Bloomer and Moore, it means "*the means of touch* reconsidered to include the entire body rather than merely the instruments of touch, such as the hands. . . . It includes all those aspects of sensual detection which involve physical contact both inside and outside the body" (*Body, Memory and Architecture*, p. 34).

CHAPTER NINE

Form
Follows Power

What a piece of work is a man.
—SHAKESPEARE, *Hamlet*

HARD BODIES

We no longer trust the human hand,' said the engineer, and waved his roll of blueprints." Thus begins "Men of Iron," Guy Endore's unsettling fable of industrial regimentation and its human toll. The engineer is a familiar villain of modern life, the thief of individual initiative, the creator of plans in which the creativity of others will be systematically and methodically squelched. His prime victim is Anton, an old and sickly worker who has spent more than fifty loyal years with The Crescent Manufacturing Company, selecting his materials, making calibrations by hand, loading pins into the chuck of his lathe. Now, under the direction of the engineer, the lathes are to be automated into a centrally controlled, "automatic and foolproof" system in which "the attendant's skill is beside the point." The master of his tools becomes an extension of the machine.

Against the backdrop of the new, smoothly humming machinery, Anton cuts an increasingly pathetic figure. At night he covers the machine with a tarp, and trudges back to the "gray, wooden shack" that he and his wife call home. As he enters the bedroom, his wife half-dozes and listens:

She did not stir when Anton entered. She lay resting on the bed, not so much from the labor of the day as from that of years. She heard his shuffling, noisy walk, heard his groans, his coughing, his whistling breath, and smelled, too, the pungent odor of machine oil. She was satisfied that it was he, and allowed herself to fall into a light sleep, through which she could still hear him moving around in the room and feel him when he dropped into bed beside her and settled himself against her for warmth and comfort.

The next day, the encroachments of the engineer and his system prove too much for Anton. As the directors of the factory celebrate the arrival of a new era, Anton retreats to a shadowy corner near the now automated lathe and, with a sigh, dies.

That evening, when the factory shuts down, the self-regulated lathe awakens itself and, one by one, detaches its legs from the factory floor. Rising up on its haunches, the machine walks over to Anton's lifeless form and covers it with a tarpaulin. A protean force, the machine has bypassed the organic in the great chain of being:

> Out of the hall it stalked on sturdy legs. Its electron eyes saw distinctly through the dark, its iron limbs responded instantly to its every need. No noise racked its interior, where its organs functioned smoothly and without a single tremor. To the watchman, who grunted his usual greeting without looking up, it answered not a word but strode on rapidly, confidently, through the windy streets of night—to Anton's house.

For Anton's wife, "waiting, half sleeping on the bed" as usual, the door, as it opened, ushered in a pleasing surprise. Anton's machine oil odor was familiar, but the man had been reborn. "It seemed to her that a marvel happened: her Anton come back to her in all the pride and folly of his youth, his breath like wind soughing through treetops, the muscles of his arms like steel."[1]

In ironic and uncanny terms, the story of Anton expresses one of the fundamental contradictions of modern life. If the engineer is the author of a smoothly running, controllable system, that system is predicated on the destruction of the skilled worker, and on the replacement of the human by the machine.

Some of the human implications of modern, corporate technology have been raised by an unusually candid study of the "Microelectronics Revolution," sponsored by the National Institute of Research Advancement (NIRA), in Tokyo. Although much of the study favorably analyzes the contribution of microelectronics to industrial and social efficiency, a remarkable section of the report examines the "negative impacts of the microelectronic revolution" with stunning clarity. Within these pages of the *NIRA Report,* the metaphorical world of "Men of Iron" is elaborated upon and updated.

The "rapid progress of microelectronics technology," the 1985 study contends, "is bringing . . . the computerization of society ever closer." It is in the arena of work that some of the most dire "effects on human nature" are projected:

The advance of microelectronics . . . has the potential of increasing the number of people who withdraw into their own world and become functionally autistic.

Computers are machines where speed is vital; they demand one instantaneous decision after another. Thus it is necessary to be able to respond constantly to incessant stimulation. Conversation with computers is very quick, brief, to the point, and functional. . . . Furthermore, since computers require instantaneous responses of the YES or NO variety, computer users may fall into a mechanical way of thinking in their daily life, dividing every topic up into black or white, accepting everything on face value and jumping to hasty conclusions.

On an individual level, the report suggests, the emerging conditions of labor will give rise to new job-related pathologies. In those industries where "a new type of employment called 'VDT [Visual Display Terminal] Labor' has appeared. . . . a large number of health and other problems are coming to light":

A survey by the All Japan Federation of Electric Machine Workers' Unions showed that 65.2 percent of all word processor and personal computer operators complained of "tired eyes," 66.2 percent of "neck, back or shoulder stiffness," and 65.0 percent of "mental strain." Compared to conventional office and factory workers, a relatively large number of VDT workers complained of "mental strain or the inability to maintain concentration," indicating the tension that the VDT operators are under since they are not allowed to make mistakes.

Among employees in general, the demoralization that overtook Anton, in the face of a new machine, has become a regular occurrence. The automated workplace has, for many who must march to the digital beat, led to a failing sense of self:

A large number of production plants have introduced robots and other automated systems. As the use of such systems increases, however, they have raised a number of problems. First is the problem of a sense of purpose to life. For many people . . . their self-esteem is supported by a sense of confidence and pride in their skills and abilities. As these skills and abilities are rendered meaningless by automation, workers may experience increased feelings of inadequacy and alienation.

Second is the problem of isolation. In conventional Japanese factories, an essential part of the job has been the formation of harmonious interpersonal relations and close cooperation. On the automatic production line, however, cooperative labor has disappeared, and employees are forced to function in solitude.

The NIRA, a think tank funded by the Japanese government, and by large Japanese corporations, concludes this grim report with a warning that the unchecked continuation of these problems may, ultimately, undermine the profitability of these industries. "Feelings of inadequacy, alienation and isolation intensify psychological disease and have the potential to cause serious damage to labor morale."[2]

The particular venue for the NIRA study was Japan, and the historic specificity of these developments varies from place to place; nevertheless, the issues raised are transnational in scope. The deployment of high-efficiency, high-profit technologies is in conflict with an integrated sense of human identity.

The story of Anton is, in many ways, a prophetic fable. It underlines a particularly modern malaise. While the story speaks to the dilapidation and demoralization of the worker, it also raises the specter of a new aesthetic ideal, one inspired by the interlocking principles of instrumental reason, engineering, and technological regimentation. The machine, with its indefatigable "arms of steel," emerges as the prototype for virility, the mold from which the *new man* will be cast. If the idealized conception of the female body has provided a locus for the articulation of modern structures of value, the "masculine physique" has been the tablet on which modern conditions of work, and of work discipline, have been inscribed.*

Writing in 1934, the sociologists George A. Lundberg, Mirra Komarovsky, and Mary Alice McInerny addressed the question of "leisure" in the context of an emerging consumer society. Understanding the symbiotic relationship between mass-production industries and a consumerized definition of leisure, they wrote of the need for society to achieve a compatibility between the worlds of work and daily life. "The ideal to be sought," they proposed, "is undoubtedly the gradual obliteration of the psychological barrier which today distinguishes work from leisure."[3]

That ideal has been realized in the daily routine of Raymond H——, a thirty-four-year-old middle-management employee of a large New York City investment firm. He is a living cog in what Felix Rohatyn has termed the new "money culture," one in which "making things" no

---

*The split between female and male archetypes, following patriarchal patterns of gender, represents a general trend rather than an absolute. Clearly, as more and more women have entered the corporate workforce, and as patriarchal structures unravel, there is a good deal of crossing over, of women into "male" ideals, of men into "female" ideals.

longer counts; "making money," as an end in itself, is the driving force.[4] His days are spent at a computer terminal, monitoring an endless flow of numerical data.

When his workday is done, he heads toward a local health club for the relaxation of a "workout." Three times a week this means a visit to the Nautilus room, with its high, mirrored walls, and its imposing assembly line of large, specialized "machines." The workout consists of exercises for his lower body and for his upper body, twelve "stations" in all. As he moves from Nautilus machine to Nautilus machine, he works on his hips, buttocks, thighs, calves, back, shoulders, chest, upper arms, forearms, abdomen, and neck, body part by body part.

At the first station, Raymond lies on the "hip and back machine," making sure to align his hip joints with the large, polished, kidney-shaped cams which offer resistance as he extends each leg downward over the padded roller under each knee. Twelve repetitions of this, and he moves on to the "hip abduction machine," where he spreads his legs outward against the padded restraints that hold them closed. Then leg extensions on the "compound leg machine" are followed by leg curls on the "leg curl machine." From here, Raymond H—— proceeds to the "pullover/torso arm machine," where he begins to address each piece of his upper body. After a precise series of repetitions on the "double chest machine," he completes his workout on the "four-way neck machine."

While he alternates between different sequential workouts, and different machines, each session is pursued with deliberate precision, following exact instructions.

Raymond H—— has been working on his body for the past three years, ever since he got his last promotion. He is hoping to achieve the body he always wanted. Perhaps it is fitting that this quintessential, single, young, urban professional—whose life has become a circle of work, money culture, and the cultivation of an image—has turned himself, literally, into a piece of work. If the body ideal he seeks is *lean*, devoid of fatty tissue, it is also *hard*. "Soft flesh," once a standard phrase in the American erotic lexicon, is now—within the competitive, upscale world he inhabits—a sign of failure and sloth. The hard shell is now a sign of achievement, visible proof of success in the "rat race." The goal he seeks is more about *looking* than *touching*.

To achieve his goal, he approaches his body piece by piece; with each machine he performs a discrete task. Along the way he also assumes the job of inspector, surveying the results of each task in the mirrors that surround him. The division of labor, the fragmentation of the work process, and the regulating function of continual measurement and observation—all fundamental to the principles of "scientific management"—are intrinsic to this form of recreation. Like any assembly line worker, H—— needs no overall knowledge of the process he is engaged in, only the specific tasks that comprise that process. "You don't have to understand *why* Nautilus equipment works," writes bodybuilder Mike Mentzer in the forward to one of the most widely read Nautilus manuals. "With a tape measure in hand," he promises, "you will see what happens."[5]

The body ideal Raymond H—— covets is, itself, an aestheticized tribute to the broken-down work processes of the assembly line. "I'm trying to get better definition," H—— says. "I'm into Nautilus because it lets me do the necessary touch-up work. Free weights [barbells] are good for building up mass, but Nautilus is great for definition."[6] By "definition," H—— is employing the lingo of the gym, a reference to a body surface upon which each muscle, each muscle group, appears segmented and distinct. The perfect body is one that ratifies the fragmentary process of its construction, one that mimics—in flesh—the illustrative qualities of a schematic drawing, or an anatomy chart.

Surveying his work in the mirror, H—— admires the job he has done on his broad, high pectorals, but is quick to note that his quadriceps "could use some work." This ambivalence, this mix of emotions, pursues him each time he comes for a workout, and the times in between. He is never quite satisfied with the results. The excesses of the weekend-past invariably leave their blemish. An incorrectly struck pose reveals an overmeasure of loose skin, a sign of weakness in the shell. Despite all efforts, photogenic majesty is elusive.

The power of the photographic idiom, in his mind's eye, is reinforced, again and again, by the advertisements and other media of style visible everywhere. The ideal of the perfectly posed machine—the cold, hard body in response—is paraded, perpetually, before his eyes and ours. We see him, or her, at every glance.

An advertisement for home gym equipment promises a "Body By Soloflex." Above is the silent, chiaroscuro portrait of a muscular youth, his torso bare, his elbows reaching high, pulling a thin-ribbed undershirt up over his head, which is faceless, covered by shadow. His identity is situated below the neck, an instrumentally achieved study in brawn. The powerful expanse of his chest and back is illuminated from the right side. A carefully cast shadow accentuates the paired muscle formations of his abdominal wall. The airbrush has done its work as well, effecting a smooth, standardized, molded quality, what John Berger has termed "the skin without a biography." A silent, brooding hulk of a man, he is the unified product of pure engineering. His image is a product of expensive photographic technology, and expensive technical expertise.

The desolate loner,
by Calvin Klein.

Photographer: Bruce Weber
Creative Director: Sam Shahid

His body—so we are informed—is also a technical achievement. He has reached this captured moment of perpetual perfection on a "machine that fits in the corner" of his home. The machine, itself, resembles a stamping machine, one used to shape standardized, industrial products. Upon this machine, he has routinely followed instructions for "twenty-four traditional iron pumping exercises, each correct in form and balance." The privileged guidance of industrial engineering, and the mindless obedience of work discipline, have become legible upon his body; yet as it is displayed, it is nothing less than a thing of beauty, a transcendent aspiration.

This machine-man is one of a generation of desolate, finely tuned loners who have cropped up as icons of American style. Their bodies, often lightly oiled to accentuate definition, reveal their inner mechanisms like costly, open-faced watches, where one can see the wheels and gears moving inside, revealing—as it were—the magic of time itself. If this is eroticism, it is one tuned more to the mysteries of technology than to those of the flesh.

In another magazine advertisement, for Evian spring water from France, six similarly anatomized figures stand across a black and white

"Revival of the Fittest"

two-page spread. From the look of things, each figure (three men and three women) has just completed a grueling workout, and four of them are partaking of Evian water as part of their recovery. The six are displayed in a lineup, each one displaying a particularly well-developed anatomical region. These are the new icons of beauty, precisely defined, powerful machines. Below, on the left, is the simple caption: "Revival of the Fittest." Though part of a group, each figure is conspicuously alone.

Once again, the modern contours of power, and the structures of work discipline, are imprinted upon the body. In a world of rampant careerism, self-absorption is a rule of thumb. If the division of labor sets each worker in competition with every other, here that fragmentation is aestheticized into the narcissism of mind and body.

Within this depiction, sexual equality is presented as the meeting point between the anorectic and the "nautilized." True to gender distinctions between evanescent value and industrial work discipline, the three women are defined primarily by contour, by the thin lines that their willowy bodies etch upon the page. Although their muscles are toned, they strike poses that suggest pure, disembodied form. Each of the men, situated alternately between the women, gives testimony on behalf of a particular fraction of segmented flesh: abdomen, shoulders and upper arms, upper back. In keeping with the assembly line approach to muscle building, each man's body symbolizes a particular station within the labor process.

Another ad, for a health and fitness magazine, contains an alarmingly discordant statement: "Today's women workers are back in the sweat shop." There is a basis to this claim. In today's world, powerful, transnational corporations search the globe looking for the cheapest labor they can find. Within this global economy, more and more women—from Chinatown to Taiwan—are employed at tedious, low-paying jobs, producing everything from designer jeans to computer parts.

Yet this is not the kind of sweatshop the ad has in mind. The photographic illustration makes this clear. Above the text, across the two-page color spread, is the glistening, heavily muscled back of a woman hoisting a chrome barbell. Her sweat is self-induced, part of a "new woman" life-style being promoted in *Sport* magazine, "the magazine of the new vitality." Although this woman bears the feminine trademark of blonde, braided hair, her body is decidedly masculine, a new body aesthetic in the making. Her muscles are not the cramped, biographically induced muscles of menial labor. Hers is the brawn of the purely symbolic, the guise of the middle-class "working woman."

While the text of the advertisement seems to allude to the real conditions of female labor, the image transforms that truth into beauty, rendering it meaningless. Real conditions are copywritten into catchy and humorous phrases. The harsh physical demands of women's work are reinterpreted as regimented, leisure-time workouts at a "health club." Real sweat is reborn as photogenic body oil.

The migration of women into the social structures of industrial discipline is similarly aestheticized in an ad for Jack LaLanne Fitness Centers. A black and white close-up of a young woman wrestling with a fitness "machine" is complemented by the eroticized grimace on her face. Once again, the chiaroscuro technique accentuates the straining muscles of her arms. The high-contrast, black and white motif may also suggest the "night and day" metamorphosis that will occur when one commits to this particular brand of physical discipline.

In large white letters, superimposed across the shadowy bottom of the photograph, are the words: "Be taut by experts." With a clever play on words the goal of education moves from the mind to the body. Muscle power is offered as an equivalent substitute for brain power. No problem. In the search for the perfectly regulated self, it is implicit that others will do the thinking. This woman, like the Soloflex man, is the product of pure engineering, of technical expertise:

> We were building bodies back when you were building blocks. . . . We know how to perfectly balance your workout between swimming, jogging, aerobics and weight training on hundreds of the most advanced machines available. . . . Sure it may hurt a little. But remember. *You only hurt the one you love* [emphasis added].

These advertisements, like Raymond H——'s regular visits to the Nautilus room, are part of the middle-class bodily rhetoric of the 1980s. Together they mark a culture in which self-absorbed careerism, conspicuous consumption, and a conception of *self* as an object of competitive display have fused to become the preponderant symbols of achievement. The regulated body is the nexus where a cynical ethos of social Darwinism, and the eroticism of raw power, meet. Yet despite the currency of this body ideal, the roots of the regulated body have been deeply implanted in the terrain of Western culture since the Enlightenment.

Within the dialectic of Enlightenment thinking, two different but interwoven conceptions of human perfectionism emerged. The first stood at the emancipatory heart of democratic movements and ideals. It held that with Reason, and through scientific, secular education ("improvement"), people could dismantle the repressive, unenlightened hierarchies of the past and become the masters of their own lives. Such thinking spurred ideas of cooperative commonwealth and individual liberty.

Yet the rise of commercial power in the Age of Reason also fueled more instrumental notions of human transformation. While likewise making reference to the touchstones of Reason and Science, these ideas suggested that the rational perfection of an individual could be engineered by another, armed with a knowledge of scientific law, and employing modern techniques of social management. Whereas the bodies within the egalitarian tradition of perfection were those of free individuals, this latter tradition gave rise to the notion of malleable bodies, trainable or teachable for whatever purpose. If the first tradition sparked ideas of liberation among the underclasses, the dark side of Enlightenment was possessed by ideas of controlling and shaping them.

From the mid-eighteenth century on, the rise of this managerial sensibility began to be imprinted on more and more bourgeois social institutions. Particularly where the social organization of power was essential, Michel Foucault has argued, "a policy of coercions that act upon the body, a calculated manipulation of its elements, its gestures, its behaviour," began to be employed.[7]

An example of this, discussed by Foucault, may be found in the military, in the body of the soldier. In the early seventeenth century, he relates, the "ideal figure of the soldier" was still conceived in reference to a great chain of being. His military bearing was understood to be inborn, inseparable from his identity as a person within the social order:

To begin with, the soldier was someone who could be recognized from afar; he bore certain signs: the natural signs of his strength and his courage, the marks, too, of his pride; his body was the blazon of his strength and valour; and although it is true that he had to learn the profession of arms little by little—generally in actual fighting—movements like marching and attitudes like the bearing of the head belonged for the most part to a bodily rhetoric of honour; "The signs for recognizing those most suited to this profession are a lively, alert manner, an erect head, a taut stomach, broad shoulders, long arms, strong fingers, a small belly, thick thighs, slender legs and dry feet, because a man of such a figure could not fail to be agile and strong."[8]

The body of this soldier bore the marks of muscular strength, but it was also implicit that this strength was intrinsic to the man. He was motivated, from within, by natural courage and pride, not by the techniques of externally imposed discipline. His "strength and valour" were signs of his elite status among men.

By the end of the eighteenth century this had changed. With the consolidation of national sovereignty, the development of a world market, and the spread of colonialism, the military requirements of Europe escalated. The recruitment of armies from among the "masses" necessitated a technique for producing soldiers. Under the rubric of this priority, Foucault argues, the human body entered "a machinery of power that explores it, breaks it down and rearranges it." The notion of the born soldier gave way to that of *basic training:*

By the late eighteenth century, the soldier has become something that can be made; out of a formless clay, an inapt body, the machine required can be constructed; posture is gradually corrected; a calculated constraint runs slowly through each part of the body, mastering it, making it pliable, ready at all times, turning silently into the automatism of habit; in short, one has "got rid of the peasant" and given him "the air of a soldier" (ordinance of 20 March 1764). Recruits become accustomed to "holding their heads high and erect; to standing upright, without bending the back, to sticking out the belly, throwing out the chest and throwing back the shoulders; and, to help them acquire the habit, they are given this position while standing against a wall in such a way that the heels, the thighs, the waist and the shoulders touch it, as also do the backs of the hands, as one turns the arms outwards, without moving them away from the body. . . . Likewise, they will be taught never to fix their eyes on the ground, but to look straight at those they pass . . . to remain motionless until the order is given, without moving the head, the hands or the feet . . . lastly to march with a bold step, with knee and ham taut, on the points of the feet, which should face outwards" (ordinance of 20 March 1764).[9]

Foucault's discussion, here, focuses on the changing conception of the soldier, but the implications of this discussion shed light on changes within an ever-widening sphere of social activities from the eighteenth century onward. In the routinization of labor, in the rote teaching of schoolchildren, in the measured strides of fashion models, even in the detailed positional instructions of exercise tapes or sex manuals, Foucault's "well-trained regiments" can be heard marching in the distance.

Against this historical panorama, the monitored, regulated and segmented body ideal goes against its own claims for itself. On the aesthetic plane of the commercial culture this bodily motif suggests self-motivated, individual power. But its historic roots and its method of construction ("bodybuilding") reveal a person who is, to quote Foucault, the "object and target of power."[10] In their aestheticization, the modern structures of power are turned on their heads, posed as symbols of a *free individual.* In the world of style, where images seem to float, disconnected from the world that produces them, mastery can be confused with obedience.

The strange intersection of the calculated body with the broader realm of style finds no better expression than the *persons* of "Joe" and "Josephine." Not actually people, these two were, in fact, "austere line drawings of a man and a woman. . . . staring coldly at the world, with figures and measurements buzzing around them like flies."[11] They were created, and so described, by Henry Dreyfuss, one of the premier industrial designers in the United States.

"Joe" and "Josephine," Dreyfuss explained, "are very dear to us." They were, in his own words, the "hero" and "heroine" of a career spent "designing for people." Yet the *people* they stood for were divested of all subjectivity, all self-determined action, all irrational impulses; they conformed totally to plan. "Anthropometric" models, they were people reduced wholly to specifications, icons of total administration.

Such models were not new. The anthropometric categorization of people was a product of late nineteenth-century science, initially an effort to develop a system of human typologies which would allow various authorities (religious, police, medical, educational) to identify *inborn* predilections toward "virtue and vice." Historian James B. Gilbert argues that anthropometrics allowed a society, still marked by vast chasms of inequity, to give inequality a rational, scientific justification:

> To an age that worried desperately that the old social order and its familiar signs of stations, quality, and hierarchy were disappearing, anthropo-

metrics, the identification of syndromes of physical and mental characteristics, was enormously welcome. The possibility of reclassifying a citizenry on the basis of physical qualities offered scientific confirmation of what many people assumed to be true. The criminal had a low and vulgar aspect; the lower classes were weaker and smaller physically than the upper classes; blacks and immigrants were racially, intellectually, and morally inferior to native whites; genius was a variety of mental disease just as epilepsy was a physical disease.[12]

Within the more democratic ethos of twentieth-century consumer capitalism, however, the uses of this science underwent a change. With the development of mass-production techniques, and of an increasingly inclusive mass consumer market, the science of *difference* became one of *sameness*. Anthropometrics began producing a more generic concept of humanity, one that would be responsive to the mechanical demands of the productive process, as well as to the visual or tactile appeal of a given product. Joe and Josephine, then, were children of standardization, and they were designed to include all men and women simultaneously.

Embracing an abstract, measurable, and predictable notion of humanity, Dreyfuss's creations were, for him, people stripped to the bottom line, "common denominators."[13] For marketing purposes, goods could be designed so as to elicit automatic response. "Color," for example, "can make Joe and Josephine gay or sad; aid their digestion or make them ill; relax them or produce fatigue. It can suggest youth or age. . . . Color has become increasingly important to the industrial designer in recent years," Dreyfuss continued. "A dark 'heavy' color in an airplane can give a sense of security, and a light color can suggest lack of weight in a vacuum cleaner and help sell it."[14]

Like the "man of steel" who laid to rest the outdated worker Anton, Joe and Josephine were vibration-free, smoothly running machines, fit for integration into a totally automated system. A creation of the conceit of power, they were totally controllable people, adjustable to the economic exigencies that affected corporate planning on the shop floor, or in the marketplace. "Our job," Dreyfuss explained in 1955, "is to make Joe and Josephine compatable with their environment. The process is known as human engineering." Anatomy could be calculated, psychic motivations could be specified, and the gap could be filled "between human behavior and machine design."[15]

Prototypical humans for the age of mechanical reproduction, Joe and Josephine were the missing links between style and social control. Although they were created, according to Dreyfuss, for the purpose of

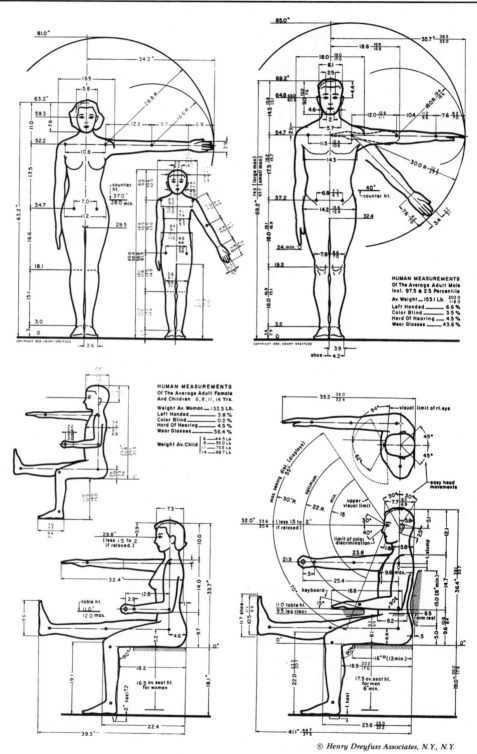

© Henry Dreyfuss Associates, N.Y., N.Y.

The New Family: Joe, Josephine, and Joe, Jr. (1955)

designing a comfortable and attractive machine-made environment, it is little wonder that their figures were soon adopted, by industrial time-motion experts, as textbook models for the perfect worker.[16]

REGULATING
LINES

In February of 1948, speaking before a symposium held at New York's Museum of Modern Art, the Hungarian-born architect and designer Marcel Breuer responded to those critics who rejected modern design as *cold, mechanical,* and *dehumanizing.* A member of the Bauhaus school and a leading figure in the elaboration of a modern, rational, "International" aesthetic, Breuer saw the clean and regular geometry of modern architecture as a mark of order and progress in civilization. A proponent of the idea that a house should be a "machine for living," Breuer was one of a group of "Functionalists" who believed that "participation in the modern world calls for individuals who have become free of preconceived ideas and sentimental attachments."[17] "If human . . . is considered identical with imperfection and imprecision," he retorted unabashedly, "I'm against it."[18]

Some twenty-five years earlier, and in a different context, Elton Mayo, the pioneer of industrial sociology and psychology, had expressed similar sentiments. Addressing the serious dilemma of unrest in the workplace, Mayo attributed this recurrent problem to the "Night-Mind" in workers, their primitive predilection toward "revery and unreason."[19] "The human mind and the social organism," he explained, "are still very largely uncivilized. The domain of reason and understanding is extended but slowly; primitive passions still obscure and go far to determine every social issue."[20]

For industrial management, interested in attaining profitable efficiency and order in the workplace, Mayo counseled the need to study and respond to these "animistic" psychological tendencies. They were, he claimed, underlying forces within "unrest, dissatisfaction, agitation, reduced production, personal friction, strikes and the like." According to Mayo, labor troubles were a "symptom of mental disorganization," and he encouraged managers to establish a corrective psychological environment, one that would cultivate and appeal to the "Day-Mind" of workers, their capacities for "concentration and reason."[21]

For Marcel Breuer (a master technician of space) and Elton Mayo (a master technician of mind), the idea that an orderly, rationally structured environment would help to inculcate an orderly population was a commonly held faith. In the work of these two men, and others like them, an imminent, twentieth-century link between modernist aesthetics and social management can be readily perceived.

The idea of orderly, functional space has been a characteristic trend in twentieth-century aesthetics. Yet the roots of this idea were essentially sociopolitical, part of the modern instrumentation of power as it developed in Europe in the late seventeenth and eighteenth centuries. The Cartesian notion of a measured, calculable environment, which would exert a predictable effect upon those inhabiting it, was not developed by architects. Formal architecture, though affected by classical, Enlightenment conceptions of order, was still imbued with ornamental references to the great, historic styles. The calculated environment was, in large measure, the creation of those concerned with keeping the public peace, with maintaining control over an often rebellious popular culture, and with delineating the parameters of crime and punishment. It is ironic that at a time when the call of *Reason* was inspiring the poor to revolt against the rules of the established social order, this same *Reason* (in the form of instrumental rationality) was being called upon to sustain those rules.

The notion that a rationally deployed physical and/or visual environment could impress order upon a population was a conception fed by new ways of seeing.

The orderly symmetry and stark economy that we, in the twentieth century, associate with modern architecture and industrial design, finds an influential precursor in the rise of *panoptic institutions* and *panopticism* from the turn of the nineteenth century onward. Literally meaning "all seeing," the panoptic organization of space has left its imprint upon a broad range of modern institutions, including prisons, asylums, hospitals, schools, offices, and factories.

The term *panopticism,* coined by Foucault, derives from Jeremy Bentham's innovative design for a prison, as set forth in his book *Panopticon* (1791–92). It was a building, an apparatus, designed to serve, above all else, as a machinery of power. Built into the structure were the inequities of power it sought to uphold.

As described by Bentham, the Panopticon was "circular—an iron cage, glazed. . . . The Prisoners in their Cells occupying the Circumference—The Officers (Governor, Chaplain, Surgeon, &c.) the Centre." This arrangement consolidated the power of the prison officials within central observation posts, from which they were able to observe all that went on at the circumference. Conversely, the prisoners—in cells situated around the perimeter of the circle—were isolated from one another, unable to see other inmates, or even those who kept watch:

By Blinds and other contrivances, the Inspectors concealed (except in so far as they think fit to show themselves) from the observation of the Prisoners: hence the sentiment of a sort of invisible omnipresence—The whole circuit reviewable with little, or, if necessary, without any, change of place.

One Station in the Inspection-Part affording the most perfect view of every Cell, and every part of every Cell, unless where a screen is thought fit occasionally and purposely to be interposed.

A relatively small number of guards were thus afforded a position of power over a large number of inmates; meanwhile the potential danger of the inmates was to be undermined by keeping them in a perpetual condition of "Solitude, or limited Seclusion. . . . The degree of Seclusion fixed upon may be preserved in all places, and at all times, inviolate." The ability to consolidate power at the top, while enforcing fragmentation among the general population, was key to the workings of the Panopticon. According to Bentham, this individuated application of power would ward off the breakdowns of order that were endemic within institutions where unstructured, "occasional associations" among prisoners could not be prevented.[22]

Summarizing the panoptic doctrine, Foucault notes that using no other instruments save "architecture and geometry," panopticism "acts directly on individuals; it gives 'power of mind over mind.' The panoptic schema makes any apparatus of power more intense."[23]

The panoptic principle went beyond mere physical restraint. Within the confines of the "iron cage," reasoned penologists and other theorists, inmates would begin to internalize the systemic priority of discipline, would become, in a sense, their own keepers. Elucidating panopticism as a social principle, J. Servan, a late eighteenth-century French military theorist, advised that "when you have thus formed the chain of ideas in your citizens, you will then be able to pride yourselves on guiding them and being their masters. A stupid despot," he continued, "may constrain his slaves with iron chains; but a true politician binds them even more strongly by the chain of their own ideas."[24]

Making novel use of backlighting, central observation posts, and spatial unity, panoptic architecture offered an imagistic rendering of an unequal social relation; in its individuation and symmetrical regulation of space, it embodied the priorities of observation, surveillance, and discipline. Its intended result—whether applied to a prison, a factory, or a school—was the rationalization of social control; it diminished the ability of an individual (prisoner, worker, student) to act unseen.

If the desolate, regimented loner provides an aesthetic body ideal for

Two examples of the panoptic organization of space are seen in these illustrations.

Above, a photograph of twentieth-century Stateville Penitentiary in the United States: the isolation and regimental ordering of cells along with bright skylight illumination provide total visibility from the central guard tower. The picture on the left depicts a nineteenth-century prison auditorium in France where the prisoners were brought for lectures on morality. Here, too, social relations of power are embedded in the organization and design of space. To twentieth-century folk, this picture provides a grim metaphor for the contemporary structuring of the television audience. Those who speak have access to a mass of people, while those within the mass watch in relative isolation from each other.

the late twentieth century, it is also in keeping with the managerial ideal that took hold in the nineteenth. The new wealth and power of industrial capitalism was based in an economic system that could mass produce and standardize goods as never before. By the latter decades of the nineteenth century, a vision of a *social* system of power had emerged which sought to mass produce and standardize behavior. At the heart of this social vision lay the idea that a properly controlled environment could regulate the lives and spirits of people contained within that environment.

Throughout most of the nineteenth century, the unadorned, regulatory lines of the Panopticon were not visible across the facades of formal architecture. Nonetheless, the "panoptic schema" spread, visibly, throughout the urban, industrializing world. Factory capitalism presented its overseers with many of the same issues facing prison officials. How could work discipline be maintained? How could a relatively small number of managers maintain control over masses of laborers? How could potentially dangerous associations among workers be restrained or discouraged? Each of these questions helped to structure factories along functional, panoptic lines. The same set of questions shaped public schools, hospitals, asylums, and—with the growth of clerical labor—office settings. Yet, according to the official cultural standards, these institutions were not appreciated as *architecture.* They represented some other genre of space, defined by raw, instrumental purpose, with little thought for pleasing the eye.

By the latter part of the nineteenth century, however, even formal architects found themselves face to face with issues of social control. In the United States, where industrial development had been fed by a low-paid, largely immigrant working class, cities had become volatile centers of popular misery and unrest. Strikes and other incarnations of industrial turbulence shook the urban landscape, as an extended period of economic depression provoked concern—among economic and social elites—over an impending social crisis. Under the banner of "moral reform," the need to establish a pervasive aura of authority, to educate the masses to the standards of "good citizenship," began to enter the purview of urban planners and captains of commerce.

This controlling impulse was the same that had inspired the Panopticon, but whereas the Panopticon was a stark, unembellished machinery of power, these planners clothed their motives in the aesthetic trappings of a glorified, European past. Hoping to invest the grim industrial cityscape with a sense of imposing, historical perpetuity, architects and commercial ideologues borrowed from the ornamental grandeur of the Beaux Arts school, in order to dignify their panopticism with a venerable iconography of power. The aestheticization of power still relied on the visual clichés of aristocracy.

Mounting an eclectic facade of pseudoclassical motifs, the world's fairs of the late nineteenth and early twentieth centuries were prime examples of the attempt to create visual environments that would "exercise political power in cultural terms." The motifs of these fairs, historian Robert Rydell convincingly argues, were intended to "confirm ... and extend ... the authority of the country's corporate, political and scientific leadership."[25] It was an attempt to erect a self-consciously ideological tableau, a theater of modern power.

Writing of the Columbian Exposition in Chicago (1893), G. Browne Goode, assistant secretary of the Smithsonian Institution, and an architectural advisor to various expositions, was deeply aware of the ways in which visual representation constituted a far-reaching vehicle of power, a potent conveyor of ideas. "To see is to know," he said, and the impact of images on people must be considered in the planning of public expositions:

> The exhibition of the future will be an exhibition of ideas rather than objects, and nothing will be deemed worthy of admission to its halls which has not some living, inspiring thought behind it, and which is not capable of teaching some valuable lesson.[26]

Many middle-class observers of the Columbian Exposition—with its imposing "White City"—ratified the idea that the fair was a lesson in social harmony. Historian Paul Boyer shows that for many visitors to the Chicago exposition, the "moral significance" of the experience, "outweighed even its aesthetic satisfactions":

> A more orderly and uplifting urban environment *could* be achieved, with impressive effects upon human behavior. The moral destiny of a city *could* be influenced by its physical character! "Order reigned everywhere," William Rainsford went on; ". . . no boisterousness, no unseemly merriment. It seemed as though the beauty of the place brought gentleness, happiness, and self-respect to its visitors."
>
> This note was sounded over and over again in contemporary accounts of the fair. "No great multitude of people ever . . . showed more love of order," marveled John C. Adams in the *New England Magazine.* "The restraint and discipline were remarkable," agreed another observer. "Courtiers in . . . Versailles or Fontainebleau could not have been more deferential and observant of the decorum of the place and occasion than these obscure and myriads of unknown laborers. . . . In the presence of the ignorance, vice, poverty, misery, and folly of modern society, . . . pessimism seems the only creed; but doubt is banished here."[27]

Such enthusiasm mirrors that of Charlotte Brontë, upon the occasion of her visit to the Crystal Palace in London. There, at the London Exhibition of 1851, she had marveled that "the multitude . . . seems ruled and subdued by some invisible influence."[28]

Following the dismantling of the Columbian Exposition, the same writer for the *New England Magazine* noted that although "the great White City has disappeared," its moral impact would be felt in the design of future American cities. "We shall yet see springing into being throughout the land," he predicted, "cities which shall embody in permanent form [the exposition's] dignified municipal ideals."[29] Sentiments such as these motivated the "City Beautiful" movement among urban planners in the years following the Chicago fair.

Even before the fair, however, urban vistas were beginning to be consciously designed to establish a "cohesive and orderly urban environment" and to "stimulate public spirit and morality." Art historian Martha Buskirk writes of Stanford White's Washington Memorial Arch, in New York's Washington Square Park, as an early example of a movement toward an "architectural environment" which "would offer the aesthetic and moral standards necessary to the inhabitants of America's urban centers." Situated at the foot of Fifth Avenue, the arch was, in Stanford White's words, "a structure intended to stand for all time and to outlast any local or passing fashions."[30]

Using an eclectic, Beaux Arts interpretation of European, historical grandeur as its ornamental reference point, the arch was part of a movement to establish an "architectural . . . hierarchy . . . by means of symmetry, vista, and an orderly progression of forms and spaces within which shifts in axis are clearly indicated. . . . Standing as it did at a key transitional point in traffic," Buskirk contends, the arch was consistent with the general desire "to structure the experience of the urban environment." Employing European, Beaux Arts ideals "to create the appearance of a shared tradition," structures such as this, and others of the City Beautiful movement, can be seen as an imagistic response to the heterogeneous, increasingly volatile population that was coming to inhabit the metropolis:

> The influx of new residents, combined with the economic fluctuations of the period, created the need for some sort of unifying force. The response to this need for unity can be seen both in the formation of a mythology of early American virtues, which, it was hoped, would provide a model for contemporary life, and in the developing City Beautiful movement to provide some sort of externalized urban structure.[31]

Buskirk's conclusions are borne out by Daniel Burnham, chief architect for the Columbian Exposition, and the author of the *Plan of Chi-*

cago, published in 1909 as "the quintessential expression of the social vision underlying the Progressive city-planning movement."[32] The disorderly jumble of the contemporary city, he felt, inspired nothing but social, moral, and physical decay. In developing his plan for the future, Burnham argued that the city must encourage the "love of good order" among its inhabitants. "The city has a dignity to be maintained and good order is essential to material advancement." This order would be enforced by monumental groups of public buildings which would capture the eyes of inhabitants, inspiring "the feeling of loyalty to and pride in the city." Old neighborhoods would be dislodged, or broken up by wide boulevards, imprinting the grand plan upon the terrain of daily life. "Good citizenship is the prime object of good city planning," Burnham argued, and his symmetrical architectural symphony would uplift "the intellectual, social, moral, and aesthetic conditions" within which Chicago's residents would dwell.[33]

Burnham's plan, like the Washington Memorial Arch, and other Beaux Arts shrines of the City Beautiful movement, represented a marriage between discordant sensibilities. While the overarching conception reflected a modern, panoptic commitment to the principle of a rational and controllable social apparatus, it looked toward the ornamental detritus of European history for its aesthetic instruction. While an emerging industrial society was looking for new mechanisms of social management, the aesthetic imagination was unable to look beyond the past to find meaningful symbols of command.

After 1900, a regular, geometric visual idiom had begun to assert itself, first within the embattled arenas of European style, and later in the United States. The principle of panopticism, which was midwife to the concept of a standardizable, regulated social order, was now beginning to affect aesthetic considerations. Since the exigencies of industrial discipline stood at the core of a more general call for order, it is little wonder that these modern priorities of mass production would begin to yield a visual idiom of expression.

Early on in the twentieth century, as architects and designers began to contrive a representation of the modern, they repeatedly looked toward the machine as "the modern vehicle of form." For Walter Gropius, this direction was "simply the inevitable logical product of the intellectual, social and technical conditions of our age."[34] It was in the image of the machine that the modern system of production and the desire for a smoothly running society were iconographically joined.

From the first decade of the twentieth century, when assembly line production began to be instituted in an ever-increasing number of industries, the issue of social control was accentuated. The factory was,

Time

While a consumer society expands the details of life, it also tends to divert our gaze from the whole. An example of this is mirrored in the evolution of **time perception** that has accompanied the historic rise of a consumer culture.

Within traditional **agrarian** societies, people's sense of time related to the tasks to be done each day, or to the seasonal variations that announced a time for planting, or for harvest. One's place or activity at any given moment was understood in relation to the whole of life. The height of the Sun at midday was intimately connected to the dawn and the dusk, as were the tasks and rituals which filled the day.

With the rise of wage labor and factory production, the natural cycles gave way to the rhythms of the machine. Where factory production disciplined the day, the clock emerged as a mechanical tool for dividing and measuring time. Yet, on the face of the clock, a process similar to the movement of the Sun was taking place. While propelled by a spring, the hands—like the Sun—made their journey across the day, and the telling of time itself required the ability to relate the moment to the whole of the day. The **analog** clock or watch cannot be read, except by seeing a given moment in relation to all other possible moments. Perhaps this connectedness between part and whole was the imprint of a society in which skilled crafts and industrial processes were still widely known among mechanics and other working people.

Against this brief historic tableau, the rise of **digital** time takes on a new significance. While as a consumer item the digital watch, or clock, provides its owner with the most "up-to-date" technology or time—dividing hours and minutes into a blinding whirr of tenths of seconds—it also is a technology of time that is in step with the modern day. Telling time has become unskilled labor, it no longer requires a sense of whole. In a "live for the moment" environment, each moment lives only for itself, then is consumed, with no trace left, only to be replaced by a new moment.

Billboards of the Future

in Raymond Williams's words, "a complex apparatus of interrelated and moving parts" which, as directed by issues of profit, set the rhythm of work to be done.[35] As the Panopticon was designed to reduce inmates into controllable cogs within a vast social machinery, the modern factory required a similar ambience of individuated submission. Ironically, while the underlying premise of this system assumed a well-oiled, unthinking human machine, much of the labor strife that surrounded large-scale mechanization during the period was a response to this incremental nullification of workers' skills and control over the work process.

In this increasingly turbulent context, many influential prophets of rational modernism proposed an aesthetic that would acclimate and train workers' minds to the rhythms and realities of the new machinery. In 1910, Franz Mannheimer, a close associate of Peter Behrens, had noted that Behrens's approach to industrial design expressed an appreciation of the modern inclination for calculation and control. "The Behrens style," he observed, seeks to mold the object and is much more responsive to mathematical and constructional ideas. It is a style of *"exact fantasy,* appropriate to a machine *artist."*[36]

One of Behrens's students, Le Corbusier, took the idea of the *exact fantasy* and located it squarely within the boundaries of social discipline. Traditional, ornamental buildings were monuments to the social inequities of the past. With the rise of machine civilization, and popular aspirations for a better life, such architecture constituted an environment that invited class hostility and revolution. For revolution to be "avoided"—a constant theme in his modernist manifesto—a "spirit of order, a unity of intention" must be instilled within the architectural environment. This unifying spirit could be found, he argued, in the context of the factory. For Le Corbusier, the factory is the modern locus of satisfaction:

> Specialization ties man to his machine; an absolute precision is demanded of every worker, for the article passed on to the next man . . . must be exact in order that it may . . . fit automatically into the assembling of the whole. The father no longer teaches his son the various secrets of his little trade; a strange foreman directs . . . the restrained and circumscribed tasks. The worker makes one tiny detail, always the same one, during the months of work, perhaps during years of work, perhaps for the rest of his life. He only sees his task reach its finality in the finished work at the moment when it is passed, in its bright and shining purity, into the factory yard to be placed in a delivery-van. The spirit of the worker's booth no longer exists, but certainly there does exist a more collective spirit. If the

workman is intelligent he will understand the final end of his labour, and this will fill him with a legitimate pride.[37]

The centrally imposed collectivity, made up of individuated units, is the panoptic goal of factory organization, and for Le Corbusier it represented the apotheosis of the modern age. Yet given these necessary conditions of labor, he argued, it is essential that the remaining portion of a worker's life be consistent with the modern state of affairs that govern industry. The current state of architecture, the homes in which workers lived, would, he argued, only produce demoralization: "There is no real link between our daily activities at the factory, the office or the bank, which are healthy and useful and productive, and our activities in the bosom of the family which are handicapped at every turn."[38]

The aesthetic solution provided by Le Corbusier was to bring that realm in which workers spend their "hours of liberty" in tune with the precise discipline required in the realm of work. Architecture, he advised, must embrace "the necessity for order." The simple exactitude of geometric forms, introduced into the environment of everyday life, would bring people to "a modern state of mind." Following the disciplinary precepts of industrial engineering and scientific management, Le Corbusier maintained that "the regulating line is a guarantee against wilfulness."[39]

The priority of restraining individual willfulness, of inhibiting independent activity on behalf of an overarching plan, was intrinsic to the power relations of the factory. In drawing upon the smooth, repetitive geometry of the factory for inspiration, Le Corbusier aestheticized those relations of power, elevating them to the position of universal beauty. As a physical space, the factory was functionally designed to submit all that went on within it to the common production "plan." Its calculated regularity was an expression of pure, instrumental rationality. Its product was the outcome of a tightly coordinated social mechanism which left no room for imprecision. In delineating a style befitting the machine age, Le Corbusier looked toward "the healthy and moral organism . . . [of] big business" for guidance; he was attempting to do for the eye and mind, what the factory had done for the body.

THE AURA OF TECHNICAL PERFECTION

Le Corbusier, Walter Gropius, Marcel Breuer, and other exponents of a rational, modern style, pursued their vision behind the rallying cry of "form follows function." In a mass-production world, where more goods were being produced with rhythmic, mechanical regularity, these men argued for an orderly aesthetic that would incorporate and elevate the industrial principle of smooth, standardized precision. An appropriate style for the machine age, they maintained, must approximate the economical efficiency of the machine.

The plane geometry that characterized their vision was a simultaneous assault against two diverse traditions of design. Explicitly, they attacked the accumulating clutter of nineteenth-century kitsch, the shoddy and eclectic mass-produced imitations of handcrafted, ornamental grandeur. Yet underlying the assault on kitsch, there was a general prejudice against all forms that eschewed the idea of a grand plan. Implicitly, the spare and orderly symmetry of their conception was also a critique of anonymous traditions of vernacular design which contained little sense of imposed order, but tended to develop, organically and incrementally, out of the immediate needs and available resources of common people. Apparently haphazard, these vernacular designs could only be understood in relation to the lives and outlooks of the people who created them. Against the counterfeit grandeur of kitsch, and the asymmetrical autonomy of vernacular styles, the oracles of the *modern* sought to build an ideational environment that would reinforce the unfettered, centrally engineered instrumentalism of machine production. The parallel between mass production and an orderly, geometric style, they contended, would constitute an "honesty" of design, a rejection of the pretentious decadence of kitsch.

From early on, however, the machine-made *look* that they strived for was, in most cases, no more than a look, a superficial impression. Ironically, the mathematical austerity of their designs was not easily fabricated by mass-production machines, and their effective execution required the patient and time-consuming skills of handcraftsmen. At its inception, then, "honesty" of design deviated from the hard truth; it was more a call to order than the incontrovertible outcome of the factory process. Architectural historian Peter Blake has noted that many of the formative architectural "monuments of the modern movement" were laboriously handcrafted by traditional artisans: masons, cabinet makers and blacksmiths, using decidedly preindustrial materials. The sheer planes of bold geometric structures were achieved with "stucco smoothed over terra-cotta brick." The stark, angular doors and windows were, likewise, carefully handcrafted.[40] While the appearance of these structures promoted the technical and ethical superiority of the factory environment, the execution of these structures relied on crafts that industrial engineering sought to nullify and replace.

Functionalism, then, was designed to convey an impression, to communicate an aura of rational perfection and universal order. As architectural critic Alexander Tzonis has observed, "we have the paradox that most theories of architecture whose task was rationalization have in common their pre-occupation with visual order, the look of the product. There is a greater concern that the building should *look* rational rather than that rational methods should be employed in its design."[41]

The development of unifying *corporate images* in the twentieth century provides insight into the articulation of the "rational look," and into the ideological content it expresses. When Peter Behrens came to work at AEG in 1907, he complained that most product design, to that point, was nothing but a shoddy imitation of handcrafted "historic styles," now stamped out by machines. Called in to provide AEG with an all-embracing corporate identity, Behrens attempted to move beyond the anachronistic tribute to creative handcrafting. On 29 August 1907, he explained his mission to the *Berliner Tageblatt:*

> I have been commissioned by [AEG] to produce new designs for the products manufactured by the company. . . . In the manufacturing process until now, the emphasis has been . . . on the technical aspects. The determining factor in . . . external form has been the taste of the individual Werkmeister, and this was true of all firms concerned with the production of technical goods. From now on, however, the tendency of our age should be followed and a manner of design established appropriate to machine production. This will not be achieved through the imitation of handcraftsmanship, of other materials and of historic styles, but . . . through the most intimate union possible between art and industry. This could be done by concentrating on and implementing exactly the technique of mechanical production in order to arrive by artistic means at those forms that derive directly from and correspond to the machine and machine production.[42]

As industry was subsuming or eradicating customary crafts within an increasingly centralized, mechanized process, Behrens's approach to design would canonize the integrity of the machine at the expense of the hand. As one admirer noted in 1913, Behrens's approach to design promoted the ideals of "basic mathematical harmony . . . absolute precision of all the elements . . . [and] unity of all the assembled parts."[43] True to the panoptic principles of factory production, his design work at AEG enshrined the total coordination of a system. Whether designing products, or exhibition halls, or a typeface for a letterhead, or an advertising or corporate trademark, Behrens's workshop turned out a consistent look that denied the intrusion of individual decision making; it allowed for no tangible expression of "individual stylistic direction." The visual message of the look was shaped to mask even Behrens's creative contribution to its delineation.[44] Gabriele Heidecker, writing on Behrens's publicity materials and typography, discusses the development of one of his typefaces:

> The particular characteristics of the new AEG script (and thus the firm's image) could not be based on the individual style or the calligraphic capriciousness of one artist.
>
> The desire to avoid any individualistic traits in the new script led at first to a "fifth Behrens script" based on the surviving variations of the classic Roman script. The aim was to invoke the dignity of the script so that the architecture, the general form, and the sequence of these newly redesigned letters summoned up the image of work and performance. Like the products and the factories, the lettering was to achieve this directly, concretely, and in a modern manner that, at the same time, was to be exclusive to the AEG. In the resulting Behrens Roman script, the designer avoided . . . any suggestion of an individual "poetic flourish."[45]

Here the aestheticization of panoptic order is laid out clearly. The typeface was designed to glorify the corporate structure, while eradicating all evidence of individual autonomy within. The disciplinary motif of "work and performance" was also consistent with panoptic doctrines. The primacy of standardized identity as an aesthetic principle was analagous to the ideal of the regimented and "docile body."

Within the delineation of a modern style, this call for impersonality was recurrent. Walter Gropius, in discussing the Bauhaus approach to design, spoke of the need to elevate the principle of standardization as an aesthetic ideal. To achieve this, he argued, it was necessary to suppress "the designer's personal mark," to create an image that appears to have sprung forth, as if by magic, out of the mechanical process itself.[46]

Speaking of corporate typography, Moholy-Nagy also argued that an effective design must convey the efficiency of the machine. "For the really contemporary typographer," he explained, "the typeface is not merely a means of conveying meaning, but an optical disposition of space urging the reader to recognize the essentiality of clarity, brevity, and precision."[47]

Perhaps the most direct expression of these imagistic tendencies came from a modern architect, a character, in Evelyn Waugh's 1924 novel *Decline and Fall*. A straightforward exponent of rational modernism, he described the task of architecture in the following terms: "The problem of architecture as I see it is the problem of all art: the elimination of the human element from the consolidation of form. The only perfect building must be the factory, because that is built to house machinery, not men." In their kinship to the ideas of Le Corbusier, Behrens, Gropius, and others, and in their unencumbered clarity, these words remind us that fiction is often the most direct source for the discovery of the truth.

These formative insights of the modern design movement have become corporate rule of thumb. For those of us who inhabit a world decorated by corporate images and logos, these insights should strike a familiar, if disconcerting, chord. Beyond serving as recognizable trademarks, logos are also designed to express an air of technical dominion, of sublime completion and control. When one looks at Eliot Noyes's orchestration of the IBM image, beginning in the 1950s, or at the expensively nurtured "looks" of other major corporations, the accent on precision, preeminence, and depersonalization is evident. Even though a trademark or a product design may express the *personality* of a given corporation, the designs bear no visible trace of human intervention. The creative force, itself, is attributed to the corporate mechanism, while the creative work of people working within that mechanism is denied. Here, rational modernism, as a "technology of representation," reveals itself, without apology, as an aestheticization of power. Even that which is a product of the hand, or the imagination of a commercial artist or designer, is represented as the product of nothing less than a perfect, smoothly running system.

The unbroken smoothness that characterizes much corporate design bears out the idea of technical perfection, of an aesthetic beyond the capacities of human creation. "It is well known," wrote Roland Barthes in 1957, "that smoothness is always an attribute of perfection because its opposite reveals a . . . typically human operation of assembling: Christ's robe was seamless, just as the airships of science fiction are made of unbroken metal."[48]

When the banner of "functionalism" was first raised by the European modernists, it implied an approach to design which would faithfully reflect both the manufacturing process employed in the production of a product, and the ultimate use to which that product would be put. Functionalist design would effect an imagistic synchronicity between the engineering principles of mass production and the practical exigencies of everyday life in the machine age. In both areas, the factory and the machine would provide the most suitable visual idiom.

From the beginning, however, the look of the factory was aestheticized, divorced from any overt association with the coercive discipline or social conflict that were encompassed by factory life. As Le Corbusier, for example, took the look of the factory, he ignored the oppres-

In a context where individual craftsmanship was still highly valued, trademarks often expressed respect for the creative capacities of the human hand. This is seen in the late-eighteenth-century seal of the General Society of Mechanics and Tradesmen (*top*). "By Hammer & Hand all Arts do Stand," declares the logo, while ornamental detail suggests hand-tooled workmanship. This ethic is still seen—now as a nostalgic visual reference to a bygone era—on the trademark of Arm & Hammer Baking Soda (*left*).

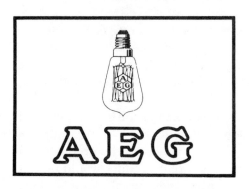

In Peter Behrens's design for an AEG corporate logotype (*left*), we see the beginnings of a consciously depersonalized corporate iconography, one which evinces the aura of technical perfection. In late-twentieth-century corporate iconography, the repudiation of the human hand is nearly complete. The flawless, inorganic look of the digitized IBM logo (*bottom*) combines the evanescence of abstract value with a thoroughly depersonalized visual corporate image: this is the aesthetic expression of a totally integrated corporate identity, and suggests no human intervention whatsoever.

siveness of factory work. For him the factory was simply a part of "the most noble quarters of our towns."[49] Similarly, as Peter Behrens designed a typeface that would dramatize the shift from handwork to mass production, the psychic cost of routine, unthinking factory labor was unacknowledged. By separating the "nobility" of industrial form from the social content of factory life, surface departed from its substance. As applied to architecture, industrial design, or to the various media of corporate image, panopticism was now transformed into a gallery of utopian visions of transcendent perfection.

During the 1930s, when the visual idiom of functionalism migrated from the drawing boards of European modernists, to the styling departments of American corporations, even the hygienic order of the disembodied factory fled. The look of progress, and of technical perfection, was taking on a life of its own.

In the construction of a coalescent corporate image, the seamless contours of progress were an implicit assertion that the corporation encompassed and exercised the full extent of technological possibility, coupled with the full extent of judgment. As Ronald Reagan benevolently pledged, while hosting television's General Electric Theater during the 1950s, "At General Electric, progress is our most important product."

If the overarching image of a corporation points our eye's mind toward the center of an apparently rational and well-intentioned system, the design of consumer products can ratify the prerogatives of that system in the details of everyday life. In the carefully calculated design of many consumer goods, the technological supremacy of the corporation is made seemingly accessible to the consumer. While at work many people spend their lives performing routine and minuscule elements within an impenetrable bureaucratic or productive maze, the design of many products—particularly appliances and other electronic items— suggests that with the purchase of the product, *you will have your hands on the controls.* In a world where a genuine sense of mastery is elusive, and feelings of impotency abound, the well-designed product can provide a symbolism of autonomous proficiency and power. Often this symbolism is nothing more than a gesture.

In the industrial design community of the United States, the iconography of mastery has developed and changed since the 1950s. With the end of the Second World War, and the ascendency of the United States as the economic and technological leader, the entry of high-tech design into the realm of the home was nothing less than tangible evidence that America provided the "best way of life" possible. Employing a visual idiom drawn loosely from what President Eisenhower termed the "military-industrial complex," designers enthusiastically worked to build an environment that was replete with strategically located "command centers." The earnest embrace of technological symbolism can be heard in the following description of the control panels on cooking and laundry appliances, published in *Industrial Design* magazine in April of 1965:

> If . . . [the housewife's] job looks as complex as a jet pilot's it is because the controls are arbitrarily being designed for effect, rather than use . . . a perfectly valid objective, both from a sales and from a functional point of view: there is no doubt that an appliance looks like a better buy if it looks versatile and powerful, and the customer may even feel her personal load lightened to the extent that the equipment . . . resembles a genie.

Indicating an appreciation of technological symbolism as a "function" in and of itself, the writer ends the piece by commenting that "certainly the top models this year, bristling with lights and dials and buttons, appear to *do* more than the economy models."[50]

A similar set of considerations went into the design of early hi-fi equipment. Gleaming, brushed metal exteriors, complemented with an impressive array of dials and controls, this first generation of high-fidelity equipment was designed with some sensitivity to people's ambivalence toward technology. The equipment designers sought to express an aura of technical empowerment without crossing the boundary into technological intimidation. As Eric Larrabee, writing in *Industrial Design,* explained, "they had to look technical, but not too technical." The equipment, he continued, was "consciously intended to satisfy the electronics enthusiast without disconcerting his wife."[51] Of course the training his wife was getting in the kitchen would, in time, expand her margins of tolerance.

Meanwhile, in the automotive industry, the look of military airplanes and rockets was being applied to the shell of the family car. At General Motors, design director Harley Earl launched an age of tailfins by drawing inspiration from the Lockheed P-38, twin-engined fighter plane, and later from the Douglas F-4D Skyray.[52] At Chrysler, automotive dashboards were trimmed to suggest the cockpit controls of a jet fighter, while body shapes were inspired by the "visual vocabulary" of rockets and jet aircraft.[53] In each automotive design, the notion of popular access to the most advanced levels of technology was visually and deliberately reinforced.

Ten years later, the impulse toward technological representation continued, but it was becoming somewhat less literal and more stylistically refined. A 1965 article on the design of new photographic equipment notes that one camera "has Bauhaus graphics and a moderately complicated look," while the designers of another camera are "attempting to create the look of a complex precision optical instrument."[54]

Today the iconography of technical empowerment continues, but the visual idiom has changed. The early, postwar technical look was still locked into a metallic and mechanical vision of technology, whereas contemporary design reflects the decline of the mechanical ideal, the ascendency of information industries, microelectronics, and plastic petrochemical compounds. Sleek digital clocks mete out the day, minute by minute, while digital watches keep the utopian allure of the "space age" close at hand. Computer-controlled kitchen appliances are designed to suggest a smooth, effortless, beeping, electronic atmosphere. The glowing graphic read-outs which emanate from the barely visible blackness of the stereo imply a frictionless marriage between the new-tech motif and the evanescence of abstract value; an up-to-the-minute aesthetic recipe. Likewise, the "new age" rhetoric of endless possibility, which cloaks the high-tech information industries, inspires a smooth, beige, nearly organic fluidity in the casings of home computers.

In each case, the tacit claim made by this technical aesthetic is democratic; it asserts that the prerogative of technical perfection is potentially available to everyone, in their homes, for the right price. It is a recognizable, if deceptive, symbol of social and economic status. As the emulation of ornamental grandeur had been essential to the construction of a middle-class appearance in the late nineteenth century, access to "state of the art" technology has become an essential fixture of middle-class identity in the twentieth. In each context, the realm of consumer products provides the owner with the appearance of being "plugged-in" to the dominant channels of power. In both situations, also, this appearance constitutes an implicit agreement with the system of power being represented.

THE GREENING OF PANOPTICISM

In the fall and winter of 1986–87, the Brooklyn Museum mounted an exhibit called "The Machine Age in America: 1918–1941." The title suggested the beginning, and the end, of an infatuation. A gleaming installation of architectural models, photographs, prototypes, consumer products, and artworks, the exhibition displayed the influence of the machine and the mechanical ideal in the interwoven realms of art, architecture, and industrial design during a formative moment in the development of American consumer society. Critics and commentators expressed nostalgia and amusement at the naive faith in the machine that emanated from the assembled items of the exhibit.

The exhibition catalog remarked that the show looked to a time when there was a belief in "a new age," new processes of production, new machine-made materials, new electric sources of power and light, and a new way of life in which "even human beings were viewed as machines."[55] An underlying faith held that the machine would perfect and deliver the products and diversions of that new way of life, while people (consumers) would sit back, each in their own mechanized home, and enjoy them. Culminating with the utopian spectacle of the 1939 World's Fair ("World of Tomorrow"), a pristine conception of a totally administered future was taking hold.

In part, the friendly cynicism expressed by commentators on the exhibition came from their belief that we have moved beyond that innocent time, into an age of postmodernism, and postmodern style. If the 1930s was still a time when—as architectural critic Bruno Taut then described it—people believed that "practical value" and perfect, mechanical "efficiency" would give forth their "own aesthetic law," now is a time when aesthetic lawlessness is in vogue, when ornament and color and gratuitous "poetic flourishes" have experienced an indiscriminate reinvigoration.[56] Veneers are employed by architects, product designers, and other packagers of the packaged society, without apology.

Atop AT&T's corporate headquarters in New York (designed by Philip Johnson), the superfluous and silly scrollwork of a Chippendale chair crowns an oft-cited monument to a new, postmodern sensibility. The application of chintzy pastels to the surfaces of other buildings, or radios, or jackets with wide, empty shoulder pads, provides similar evidence of stylistic change. Ridiculous and discordant juxtapositions abound, as when Warner Communications published an annual report to stockholders, employing a hygienicized punk-rock style. The disembodied, decontextualized use of facades has emerged as a social principle. A *dis*honesty of expression, a *dis*honesty of materials, has become the visual lingua franca. As one successful industrial designer I interviewed semi-earnestly told me, "Style is everything. There is no substance anymore." If it was true—as one 1933 critic of rational modernism had argued—that "the International Style has never learned how to play," the surfaces of the so-called postmodern design seem to testify that the play principle has been rediscovered as a guiding cultural force.

To a certain extent, the "work break" that permeates the self-promotions of postmodernism is a response to criticisms that were voiced even as the "machine age" was taking hold in America. While many leading architects and industrial designers were claiming the machine, instrumental reason, and aesthetic depersonalization as their stars of Bethlehem, others were shocked and disturbed by this development, and by its lack of what Lewis Mumford called "social evaluation."

Early on in the twentieth century, the tall building was emerging as the archetypal symbol of the "new age." Nonetheless, during the 1910s and 20s, when real estate speculation elevated the New York skyline with the floor-upon-floor repetitions of skyscraper office buildings, some architects and critics began to question the motivations and functions behind this newly emerging modern form. Writing in *American Architect,* which served as a provocative and critical forum during the period, Harvey Corbett condemned the instrumental, pecuniary motivations that were shaping the new urban, architectural environment. "Speculative interests," he argued in 1926, "were keen to realize the income bearing possibilities of tall buildings and in greed for dollars, built so high and so closely that health and beauty of the cities were menaced. Narrow streets became canyons where sunlight only appeared for brief minutes at noonday."[57]

During the 1930s, with the Depression, unqualified enthusiasm for the modern industrial system gave way to increasing criticism and calls for a more human-centered conception of progress.

Frederick Ackerman, an architectural advocate of human-scale communities, where architecture would be intimately responsive to the needs and aspirations of people living within them, questioned the verbiage of "functionalism" directly. Writing in 1932, Ackerman noted that "during the last decade . . . need and effective demand played little or no part in the promotion of structures representing in total an investment of billions of dollars." Pointing to the recent crash of the economy, and the collapse of a superinflated real estate market that had led the way, Ackerman added that the now largely unrented, unoccupied office buildings' "utter uselessness had to be dramatized by such events as followed October 1929." Ackerman conceded that by building upward on a small parcel of land the skyscraper was the ideal form for inflating land values. He questioned, however, whether any other functions were being served:

> The tremendous surge of activity surrounding the erection of these structures was utterly unrelated to consideration of use; and strange as it may seem, it was during this period that the theory of utility and functional expression revived and burst into flower.
>
> The bulk of this excess *functional* architecture was in truth functional only in a most peculiar and limited sense. The structures served the end

of floating some billions of real estate bonds and of jeopardizing the utility of and the investment in a very large amount of property adjacent to these new creations.

Despite all the endless talk about the planning of communities they continue to grow in response to the exigencies of speculation.[58]

If Corbett and Ackerman focused on *form following profit,* Frank Lloyd Wright saw the skyscraper environment as an example of form following power. Although Wright, over a long career, offered many contradictory insights, in 1932 he spoke of the skyscraper as the embodiment of social control, a panoptic work environment. He described skyscrapers as "human filing cabinets" in which human life is geared to the grindstone, and human imagination denied its freedom. Desiring to develop a more ethical, organic, and spontaneous environment, Wright questioned the urban grid to its core:

> Why shouldn't mankind be allowed this freedom [of imagination]? Why should vested interests hang on to him, to milk him as cattle are herded and lined up in stanchions to be milked? The skyscraper as the typical expression of the city is the human stable, stalls filled with the herd, all to be milked by the system that keeps the animals docile by such fodder as it puts in the manger and such warmth as the crowd instills in the crowd.

Noting that many people felt energized by the urban spectacle, Wright responded, "Many in the herd of human beings have sunk so low as to seem to like it. But the bovines, too, stand waiting at the gate."[59]

Beyond seeing the skyscraper as an aestheticization of panoptic power, Wright also understood it as an expression of form seeking profit. "The skyscraper envelope," he pronounced in a lecture in 1930, "is not ethical, beautiful, or permanent. It is a commercial exploit or a mere expedient. It has no higher ideal of unity than commercial success."[60] The concentrated, vertical agglomeration of skyscrapers that constituted the modern metropolis was, for Wright, a socioaesthetic form inseparable from the history of concentrated power: "Monarchy was centralization. The city is centralization. Our capitalistic system, as it stands to fall, is centralization. And centralization is no longer practical." For Wright, a democratic society demanded a different scale, a different trajectory of social life. "Decentralization and reintegration are the need and the purpose of the machine age," he argued. "Buildings were once forts, and cities were fortifications. Democracy makes the fort a mockery." Prophetically, given the aerial firebombings and nuclear bombings that were to come during the Second World War,

Wright added that "modern warfare . . . makes concentrations in cities only nuclei for wholesale murder."[61] As a speculation in 1932, Wright's observation may allow us to better understand psychological fears of the city which fueled the postwar flight to the suburbs. Given the gruesome images of urban devastation which became familiar during World War II, the migration to suburban "security" becomes more comprehensible. Beyond the flight from the problems of city life, the widespread images of war had also escalated people's sense of ultimate urban danger.

As the preeminent symbol of the machine age, the skyscraper was a logical target of critics. Yet in addition to this focused critique of closely packed tall buildings, there were more general examinations of the rational modern faith. Ralph Walker, writing in the architecture and design magazine *Pencil Points* (December 1936), offered an "analysis of order" that directly confronted Le Corbusier's notion of the "regulating line" as a "guarantee against wilfulness." Le Corbusier's conception, Walker argued, was nothing more than "the controlled disciplinary order of social dictation." Like much formal architecture, Le Corbusier's machines for living were the result of architectural plans imposed from the top down, "in line with the mass thinking of our post-war heritage; that thinking which presupposes daily life supplied and controlled by others." Questioning the intrinsic power relations of formal architecture, Walker, like Ackerman and Wright, argued that building design and construction must go beyond the panoptic rigidity of instrumental reason and engage with the people for whom the building is intended. Decrying the "disciplinary order" of rational modernism, Walker spoke in favor of a revised conception of "order," one intimately informed by "a cultural appreciation, a knowledge of people and an understanding of human needs and desires." Calling for the reinvigoration of human-scale aesthetics, Walker insisted that "architectural creation achieves order only through the ability to intellectualize the sensations of the tenant."[62] From the beginning of the century, rational modernism had signaled a simultaneous death knell for ornamental kitsch on the one side, and popular, vernacular forms on the other. Now, in the lengthening shadow of economic catastrophe, there was an impassioned plea for a reassessment of values, for the revitalization of vernacular concerns within architecture and design.

Such sentiments moved beyond the fringes of the architectural profession. The overwhelming scale of modernist monumentalism was coming under more general attack as a conspicuous symbol of predatory economic power, and of an increasingly dehumanized physical environment. In 1933, Walter Lippmann deemed the newly constructed Radio City a quintessential expression of these depersonalizing tendencies. For Lippmann, the quantitative size of the theater posed a qualitative problem. Its sheer size, he argued, was conceived without any consideration of how much an audience is able to take in. The Music Hall, in its Art Deco grandeur, was a theater built without concern for the limits and capacities of the human senses. Radio City, he intoned, is a "striking example of the complete dissociation of means and ends . . . a monument to a culture in which material power and technical skill have been divorced from human values and the control of reason." In order for audiences to appreciate entertainments in Radio City, he prophesied, it would be necessary to redefine entertainment, to launch spectacles which, themselves, assumed the scale of *mass production:*

> What they have done is to build a theater which is so long that from the back rows the performers look like pygmies and is so wide that from the nearer seats the eye cannot encompass the whole stage. For such a theater it would be necessary to create some radically new kind of spectacle, some sort of show in which the individual performer was disregarded, because few in the audience can really establish any relation with him, and to substitute gigantic dolls or the mass effect of regiments of people.

Anticipating the lavish stage shows, and the panoptically coordinated, high-kicking Rockettes, Lippmann saw Radio City as the ultimate aestheticization of modern, industrial social relations. "It is the very essence of materialism," he concluded, "to make human values fit the equipment instead of adapting the equipment to human taste."[63]

By the 1940s, the search for a human-scale community had become a recurrent refrain as critics, and inhabitants, encountered the megalopolis. Once touted as the prefigurative forms of a transcendent new age, sheer geometric edifices were now beginning to be seen as rock and iron cages. The lure of the city was beginning to be broken. Writing about Stuyvesant Town, a middle-income, urban housing project, built and owned by Metropolitan Life in New York, Lewis Mumford saw the structures as visual expressions of totalitarian social control. The "unbroken facade of brick . . . absolutely uniform in every detail, mechanically conceived and mechanically executed, with the word 'control' implicit in every aspect of the design," was, in Mumford's estimation, "the architecture of the POLICE STATE."[64] The *machine age* was starting to rust, and with it, much of the urban iconography it had generated.

Within the emerging critique of rational modernism, there was a refrain that spoke to deeply felt popular needs. The development of corporate capitalism had created technological wonders, but it had also forged a culture that was increasingly standardized, marked by mechanical regimentation, bureaucratic rationality, and the dense anonymity of metropolitan life. In the face of these tendencies, a longing for a more "organic," simpler way of life was taking hold.

The architectural historian Sibyl Moholy-Nagy wrote of the distinction between "formal architecture" and "vernacular architecture," which sheds light on these longings. The former, she explained, reflects the "official . . . history of a culture," while the latter "testifies to the aspirations" of anonymous people, "their unending struggle for physical and spiritual survival."[65] If corporate modernism expressed an "official" history of progress, by the 1930s and 1940s a hunger for vernacular community was mounting.

Western movies satisfied this hunger by carrying audiences back to a mythological past, when open land, fierce independence, and a deep distrust of vested interests shaped the possibilities and character of frontier life. More immediately in the 1940s, however, it was the growth of the suburbs, and of the suburban idea, which seemed to offer escape and rebirth.

The attraction of the suburbs was not new. From the late nineteenth century, the option of an "out-of-town" residence had begun to emerge as a desired prerogative of middle-class life. Usually developing around the nuclei of old, existing villages, these suburbs contained homes where well-off men could shield their wives and children from the social ills and congestion of the city, and to which they, themselves, could retreat for comfort at day's end.[66] Consistent with Ira Steward's perceptive characterization of middle-class life, these communities housed people for whom "the achievement of prestige or status" was important, and who entered into patterns of "competitive consumption" (often on credit) in order to position themselves socially.[67] Through the 1930s, however, this way of life was available only to those relatively few who could afford to assemble and maintain it.

From the 1940s, though, a revitalized economy began to fertilize visions of a new way of life for "the masses." The war created civilian shortages, both of labor and essential building materials; the postwar era witnessed the flowering of the suburbs as an option for many people who had previously inhabited cities. Cities remained centers for poverty, and black people were systematically excluded from the suburban dream, but large numbers of whites, newly provided with the mass-produced mantle of middle-classness, made the move. Between 1945 and 1960, it is estimated that more than 30 million people migrated to a new way of life. Still in process, this population shift affected demographic patterns and social attitudes among a wide sweep of the American electorate.

Even before the end of the war, the coming of suburban living was in the air. Ideas about decentralization and vernacular community, as raised by Ackerman, Wright, and others, had combined with new approaches to mass-produced housing, to give shape to a suburban ideal. The war had started the economy up again, and while war production occupied factories through 1945, mass magazines and advertising had promoted a vision of postwar life that united prosperity, consumer goods, and single-family home ownership as a white American birthright.

In September of 1945, a writer in *Pencil Points* discussed how mass magazines had, throughout the war, "whet[ted] the public appetite for something better than it has been used to." "Houses for the people," as presented in the magazines, were filled with new products (televisions, washing machines, and so on) and were framed by "contemporary design ideas," the writer noted. In the "Letters to the Editor" columns of the magazines, people were expressing a "backlog of needs and desires" to which these new homes, and suburban communities, would respond. "We have been keeping a scrapbook of ideas for our postwar home," wrote one woman to the *Ladies' Home Journal.* "We have visions of nothing else but one of these homes after the war," confided another. A third responded excitedly to pictures of a home that had appeared in the magazine, and announced that "I am going to have one just like it."[68] Given the deprivations of the war and the Depression, along with the spiritual deprivations of the dominant modernist vision, the suburb, as an idea, encapsulated a mix of frontier and technological utopianism.

On the surface, the suburbs appeared to offer a tonic for the preponderant conditions of the *machine age,* a dramatic break from the anonymity and density of urban existence. The semiological contours of the suburbs conveyed a symbolic antidote for the ills of industrial civilization. If the city and its iconography evoked work and commercial priorities, the suburbs were a place where leisure provided the official leitmotif. If the metropolis was an overwhelming realm of rock and steel megaliths, the suburbs were defined by small-scale, single-family housing, and by grass and land. If the city had relegated vernacular, architectural forms to the dustbin of history, the suburbs seized on the inspiration of vernacular housing ("Cape Cod" and "ranch" styles) in delineating their identifiable look. No longer agglomerated within an urban mass, the suburbanite laid claim to individuality.

More than a hundred years before, Karl Marx had predicted that industrial capitalism would reduce more and more people to the impoverished status of propertyless, proletarian renters. The suburbs were a deliberate attack on that assumption; they conferred property ownership on their inhabitants and infused them with symbolic entitlements of a "middle class." In 1948, almost as if in response to Marx's prediction, William Levitt, builder of Levittowns, argued that "no man who owns his own house and lot can be a Communist. He has too much to do."[69] Underlying Levitt's contention was a recognition that those who entered the suburban way of life left all signs of poverty behind them, in the city. For a newly emergent white middle-class, blacks and others who remained among the urban poor were out of sight and, for the most part, out of mind. So, too, were extreme concentrations of wealth. The very structure of these new suburbs posed the appearance of an egalitarian, middle-class American consensus. The maintenance of this appearance was predicated on the erasure of social memory. As Harry Henderson—one of the first journalists to write on the suburban phenomenon—observed in 1953, the suburbs seemed to offer a new physics of existence, one where all ties to familiar understandings of the past had been severed:

> Socially, these communities have neither history, tradition, nor established structure—no inherited customs, institutions, "socially important" families, or "big houses." Everybody lives in a "good neighborhood"; there is, to use that classic American euphemism, no "wrong side of the tracks." Outwardly, there are neither rich nor poor, and initially there were no older people, teen-agers, inlaws, family doctors, "big shots," churches, organizations, schools, or local governments.

Symbolic of the break from social memory, Henderson noted, is the conspicuous absence, in suburban homes, of family heirlooms.[70]

Yet despite an imagistic and geographical break from the urban locus of industrial society, the suburbs of postwar America were intimately entwined with the fortunes of that society. Beyond the fact that most of what Kenneth Jackson has called the "crabgrass frontier" was economically dependent on the city, the suburbs themselves were, in many ways, the embodiment of what corporate modernism had been calling for. While surfaces expressed a return to a simpler, preindustrial way of life, the underpinning of the new image was industrial mass production with a vengeance. Although rational modernists had long claimed that their aesthetic precepts would create a "machine for living" in the modern age, the impact of their cool, stark lines was limited, for the most part, to costly corporate and public architecture. With a reinvigorated economy after the war, and with the systematic orchestration of suburban desire, however, the "machine for living" warmed up and entered everyday life.

Writing in the 1940s, industrial designer Walter Dorwin Teague summarized those things which would permit the United States to realize itself as a "land of plenty." At the top of his list was mass-produced housing. "What our vast, shifting, wage-earning population needs . . . is a bright, shining, handsome, completely equipped, up-to-date machine for living, costing between $1,000 and $2,500." Key to this development, he argued, would be the adaptation of mass-production methods to the problem of home construction. "Through prefabrication," he explained, "a complete, basic, domestic machine will be made available at a popular cost, just as the low-cost cars provided basic transportation."[71]

It was William Levitt, in Levittown, Long Island, who led the way in the construction of this new "machine." The tract houses he built were designed to convey a nonindustrial aura, but the heart of Levitt's approach to development was mass production. Up until the mid-1940s, the mass production of housing had been limited to the military, where rows upon rows of barracks were lined up in regiments, identically and instrumentally ordered. Such panoptic approaches to construction had also been used on high-yield, experimental chicken farms, where a monotonous sea of coops would be laid out for continual monitoring, and for optimal production efficiency. Levitt, who had produced housing for the military during the Second World War, began in 1945 to apply "assembly line building techniques" to the construction of "civilian buildings."[72] He began with a folksy, Cape Cod design, but the cornerstone of his operation was large-scale industrialism. The homes he built and the items that filled them were products of the assembly line. Clifford Edward Clark, Jr., the historian of *The American Family Home,* describes Levitt's construction methods in some detail.

Levitt's enormous success was built on careful use of standardization and economies of scale. . . . William Levitt achieved a great advantage by buying large quantities of appliances directly from the manufacturer. When lumber, lighting switches, and nails were expensive and in short supply, he set up his own subsidiary companies to produce them. The actual construction of the homes took place on an assembly-line basis and was broken down into twenty-six steps. At a central warehouse, lumber was precut to size, plumbing fixtures were preassembled, staircases were prefabricated, and kitchen cabinets were built. At the site, after the concrete foundation slabs were poured, teams of workers went from house to house and worked upon preassigned task. Some put up the walls, others put in the kitchens. Still others tiled the bathrooms in the special decorator colors that Levitt praised in his ads. . . . Using these methods, Levitt was able to complete a new house every fifteen minutes at a cost that lower-middle-class Americans could afford.[73]

Though the cost of the house was considerably higher than Walter Teague's projection (Levitt homes sold for $7,900 in 1946), Levittown and other similar "projects" were very close approximations of what Teague had listed as a basic requirement for a "land of plenty." The increased availability of low-term consumer credit after the war, from the Veterans' Administration and other sources, also sweetened the pie of the American dream, making the flight to the suburbs all the more possible.

If the suburbs spoke to certain antimodern yearnings, they were also permeated by contradiction. The suburban ideology challenged the anonymous regimentation of panopticism, yet the suburbs, themselves, were the product of a panoptic process. In Levittown the architect was transformed from the designer of a single structure to an industrial engineer; his plans and his design set production standards for the assembly line. Routine, unskilled labor comprised 80 percent of the work done at the construction site.[74] At the warehouse factory, staircases, window frames, and plumbing were assembled by unskilled workers who, following a systematic breakdown of operations, performed fragmentary tasks of "fitting and nailing." At the site, a similar breakdown of the labor process was enforced.

Construction was organized according to processes innovated by Henry Ford on the automotive assembly line, and the promotion of Levittown followed trails blazed by advertising and consumer engineering. As John Liell, an early student of Levittown's development, remarked, Levitt's sales department "substituted salesmanship for craftsmanship."[75] Kitchens were designed to correlate with magazine advertisements and illustrations; sales materials were replete with artist's drawings which suggested spacious, relatively secluded houses, surrounded by lush foliage. Explaining the patent imagistic deception of his promotional materials, Levitt opined that "the masses are asses."[76]

Deception was not limited to advertising. Following precepts of consumer engineering developed in the 1920s and 1930s by Earnest Calkins, Roy Sheldon, Egmont Arens, and others, the play of images permeated the suburban idea, and the suburban product.

From a critical distance, one could observe that the homes themselves were laid out in a monotonous gridwork, a panoptic organization of horizontal space whose prior applications had included penal institu-

In Chicago, in 1931, the Century of Progress exposition provided visitors with a futuristic environment, designed to show them an optimistic vision of things to come. Among the exhibits were several technologically appointed "homes of the future," built of modern industrial materials, and suggesting a new way of life that lay in the not-too-distant future. Elsewhere at the fair—apparently remote from issues of post-Depression housing—was a model poultry farm (*below*) used for egg-laying contests. In retrospect, the model poultry farm may have provided fairgoers with a truer crystal ball—as proven by this modern housing development (*above*).

tions, military barracks, and chicken coops. Environmental uniformity was an underlying principle of construction; developers invariably built on "flat land because it cuts construction costs."[77] Here, they were following the efficiency of the geometric plane which stood at the core of rational modernism.

Yet within the grid, there was a game of appearances which, in ensemble, suggested another, less methodical way of life. As a mass-production designer, the architect also had the job of offering a kind of individuality that seemed at odds with the industrial routines of panopticism and standardization. Walter Teague, though he employed some of the lingo of Le Corbusier, added that "a romantic attitude toward the domestic machine is understandable and defensible." In this regard, Teague suggested that "some means of satisfying the buyer's romantic as well as practical needs" must be found.[78] Writing as early as 1932, the architect Arthur T. North had argued that "houses cannot be built like automobiles." The standardized product of the assembly line may be appropriate for automobiles, he argued, but a home must have a greater sense of individuality. Defending his profession's honor, North conceded that "it should be possible to incorporate the desirable elements of individualism in a low-cost, prefabricated, contractor-produced house— a house that retains an architectural 'flavor' in its design."[79]

With the development of Levittown and other "planned communities," however, a lesson from automotive production was translated for mass-production home building. During the 1920s, General Motors had surged past Ford to the pinnacle of the American auto industry by instituting model and color diversity as a marketing answer to Henry Ford's durable, practical, but uniform Model T. By the mid-1940s, a nascent mass-produced housing industry discovered their own approach to standardized diversity. Writing in *Architectural Record,* in November 1944, Randolph Evans—an innovator and early designer of suburban tract communities—spoke of a factory approach to production, employing crews who "could work with their eyes closed," which was able to produce a wide variety of *looks* on "one floor plan." By applying "surface variations," or by reversing or rotating the garage, these crews could assemble "seventy-two possible combinations," or, to borrow from North, *seventy-two architectural flavors!* If one were merely looking for construction efficiency, Evans noted, "it would be logical to develop the . . . unembellished style loosely called modern." If productivity includes market conditions, however, "it would sell better with a peaked roof, some shutters, and . . . some scroll-saw work, too."[80]

In addition to the techniques of standardized diversity, other devices were employed to communicate the powers of suggestion. The widely used "ranch-style" motif, which mixed ideas taken from Frank Lloyd Wright's "prairie houses" with an odd assortment of other stylistic elements, provided an eclectic connotation of open space. These prefabricated units were generally smaller than most houses of the 1920s, although imagistic elements suggested otherwise.[81] Low-pitched rooflines, picture windows, and open-plan styling (where rooms opened up into other rooms, or onto outdoor patio space) gave "small houses a 'bigger' look and a greater sense of spaciousness."[82] In Levittown, where streets were at first laid out in a graph-paper grid of straight lines, later sections added curves to the streets, creating an illusion of greater separation between houses, while allowing more houses to be built along a street.[83]

As these superficial variations suggested diversity, the postwar growth of the suburbs began to standardize the American landscape as never before:

> The architectural similarity extended beyond the particular tract to the nation as a whole. Historically, each region of the country had developed an indigenous residential style—the colonial-style homes of New England, the row houses of Atlantic coastal cities, the famous Charleston town houses with their ends to the street, the raised plantation homes of the damp bayou country of Louisiana, and the encircled patios and massive walls of the Southwest. This regionalism of design extended to relatively small areas; early in the twentieth century a house on the South Carolina coast looked quite different from a house in the Piedmont a few hundred miles away.[84]

By the 1960s, continues Kenneth T. Jackson, "the casual suburban visitor would have a difficult time deciphering whether she was in the environs of Boston or Dallas." The "ranch style, in particular, was evocative of the expansive mood of the post–World War II suburbs and of the disappearing regionality of style. It was almost as popular in Westchester County as in Los Angeles County."[85]

The standardized eclecticism of these postwar suburban developments cannot be separated from many of the new consumer products that were found in and around them. Here, too, there was a discordant array of surfaces. Brightly colored or pastel, often covered by a veneer of newly introduced surface materials (Formica, Naugahyde, Con-Tact paper, and so on) Thomas Hine calls the whole phenomenon "populuxe," the indiscriminate play of surfaces that connoted the arrival of modern luxuries for the people. Hine's incisive panorama of consumer goods includes peach refrigerators; two-tone automobiles with rocket fins in the rear and chrome "bullet shaped" breasts protruding above the front bumper; potato chips whose modernistic ridges suggested corrugated board; Davy Crockett coonskin caps; and an endless clash of shapes, colors, textures, and meanings which, together, announced that the American century had arrived, and that masses of new, suburban homeowners had achieved that longed-for goal of middle-class status.[86]

If the automobile was a motivating force of suburban life, television was its centerpiece. As early as 1932, an *American Architect* article predicted that the influence of "entertainment instruments . . . on homes of the future" would eventually lead to the "development of some room of the house as the 'theatre' of the home."[87] By 1950, many suburban developers had taken the prediction to heart and were including the lure of built-in televisions in the houses they sold. (In the case of veterans' homes, these built-ins were covered as part of a government-subsidized mortgage.) The television was being installed as a powerful fixture in postwar life, insinuating an unprecedented image-machine into the home. According to an article that appeared in *Architectural Forum* in 1950, many large-scale builders hoped that these built-in TVs would "hasten the demise of the expensive fireplace as the living room focus, and ultimately replace it."[88]

In the early 1930s, Frank Lloyd Wright had called for a process of "decentralization and reintegration," which would signal a break from the consolidated city and the consolidated power that built it. With the development of postwar suburbs, populuxe consumerism, and the constantly flickering icy hearth of television, American business had fashioned its peculiar response to Wright's plea. In the suburbs, a decentralized mode of life was taking root, reflecting an emerging social pattern of what Raymond Williams has called "mobile individualism." In television, a powerful tool of reintegration was emerging, one that unified an increasingly individuated population around similar images, similar information, similar celebrities, and similar products. In this sense, television was the cornerstone of suburban panopticism; it organized an individuated population around the hub of a relatively centralized source of authority. On television, the goods and life-style of a populuxe world were continuously visible. From sit-coms to commercials, the material accoutrements of the suburban dream were a conspicuous part of the picture. In the suburbs, the power of TV as a force of integration was evident early. Harry Henderson, writing in 1953, described the new suburban developments as "the first towns in America where the impact of TV is so concentrated that it literally affects everyone's life. Organizations dare not hold meetings at hours when popular shows are on. In addition, it tends to bind people together, giving the whole community a common experience."[89]

This, then, was the postmodern moment, the point when the earnest pleas of rational modernism gave way to a self-conscious and promiscuous play of images. In the nineteenth century, kitsch had been an unreflective and eclectic pursuit of what people understood to be traditional style. By the 1920s and 1930s, consumer industries had already begun to develop a systematic approach to product design, but the smooth, metallic call of the modern still shaped the multitude of consumer products. With the postwar suburbs—the official containers of a newly packaged way of life—the indiscriminate collage of disembodied images applied a thin, if playful, facade of individuality to an essentially conformist environment. It was just a matter of time before a gratuitous gesture of architectural humor would be added to top off a floor-upon-floor corporate office tower, and have the promotional chutzpah to call itself "postmodern."

Though the surface of suburban life had made a similar gesture of escape from the mechanical routine, even its innovator knew that its inner essence was structured by that routine. Responding in 1958 to critics who accused Levittown of conformity, William Levitt revealed his essential kinship to Le Corbusier and other proponents of rational modernism:

> It seems to me incredibly myopic to focus on the thread of uniformity in housing and fail to see the broad fabric of which it is a part—the mass production culture of America today. To fuss about uniformity in housing touches on only so small a part of the truth as to be without meaning. It is not just our houses that are uniform but the furniture and appliances we put in them, the clothes we wear, the cars we drive.
>
> This isn't something to grieve over. It's something to glory in—just so long as we keep in mind the difference between material values and those of the mind and spirit. The reason we have it so good in this country is that we can produce lots of things at low prices through mass production. And with mass production, of course, uniformity is unavoidable.[90]

What Levitt failed to say was that in the perpetual play of images that shaped the mass-produced suburbs, and in the ever-changing styles that kept the market in consumer goods moving, "material values" and values of "mind and spirit" were becoming increasingly interchangeable and confused.

CHAPTER TEN

Form
Follows Waste

Nothing survives—
But the way we live our lives . . .

—JACKSON BROWNE,
"Daddy's Tune"

CONSPICUOUS CONSUMPTION

In May of 1987 the good ship *Mobro,* a garbage scow, set sail from Long Island carrying a cargo of 6,200,000 pounds of baled refuse. Drawing its load primarily from the suburban town of Islip, the *Mobro* headed out to sea in search of an underwater dumping ground. By the time the barge had reached the warm waters of the Gulf of Mexico, it was still laden with debris. Despite repeated assurances that the garbage was "nonhazardous," authorities all along the coast refused to provide haven for this homely freight. Unable to secure dumping arrangements on the journey southward, the *Mobro* reversed course in the hope that somewhere along the way a site might be found. More than a month later summer had come, but the problem had not yet been solved; the scow still floated aimlessly with its 3,100-ton cargo, now in New York Harbor. On the 29 June, the *New York Times* designated the *Mobro* a national "symbol," emblematic of a serious "solid waste crisis" facing the United States.

The bizarre odyssey of the *Mobro* seemed to capture the attention of the mass media but, considering the dimensions of the crisis, this garbage without a home was but a drop in the bucket. Each day of the year, New York City alone disposes of 14,329 tons of garbage, more than four and a half times the amount sitting on the *Mobro*'s deck. Miami generates 7,445 tons; Los Angeles, 6,193 tons; Chicago, 5,985 tons; and Dallas, 1,948 tons of garbage per day. Around the world, similar patterns prevail. The daily refuse of Tokyo is estimated at 12,500 tons; Mexico City, 8,000 tons; London, 6,831 tons; Cairo, 4,270 tons; and Rio de Janeiro, 4,000 tons; collective evidence that waste has arrived as an international standard of "progress."[1]

Much of what gets thrown away is packaging, the provocatively designed wrappings that we have come to expect on nearly everything we purchase. In the United States in 1984, more than 37 percent of the debris tossed into municipal waste systems was made up of paper and paperboard products. Glass, metal, and plastics—largely from disposable containers—comprised another 26.5 percent.

But it is not just packaging. Increasingly, products which in the past would have been considered "durables" quickly find their way into the trashbin. These include wristwatches, telephones and other electronic devices, razors, pens, medical and hospital supplies, cigarette lighters, and, recently, cameras. General Electric and GTE sell lamps "that sell for under $25 and are designed to be discarded when the bulbs burn out." Predictions abound that automobile engines will soon be made of plastic and will be "less expensive to replace than to repair." The "machine for living" will follow suit. "In the 21st century," one futurist forecasts, "we'll begin to see prefabricated homes that will be manufactured from inexpensive materials, will take only days to put up, and will be thrown out and replaced rather than repaired."[2]

From a marketing point of view, disposability is the golden goose. It conflates the act of *using* with that of *using up*, and promotes markets that are continually hungry for more. Business economists, sociologists, and psychologists argue that, beyond being highly profitable, throwaway products satisfy the peculiarities of the modern temperament. Joseph Smith, a consumer psychologist, contends that the popular appeal of disposable products "reflects our changing social values; there's less emphasis on permanence today." Trend watcher Faith Popcorn, president of the Brain Reserve, concurs: "People just don't get attached to things the way they used to."[3]

It might even be argued that disposability satiates transhistoric human drives. Along these lines of thought, John Rader Platt, professor of physics at the University of Chicago, has raised the issue of the "fifth need of man":

The needs of man, if life is to survive, are usually said to be four—air, water, food, and, in the severe climates, protection. But it is becoming

History

In a world of rich and poor, history weighs heavily in the symbolism of wealth and power. Social class becomes the ability to claim history as property.

For people whose day-to-day meets squalor, history of either the past or the future is an unattainable luxury. Each day is imprisoned by the terms of necessity. History offers little promise of relief.

For the increasingly desperate middle class—bent on survival—history is *culture*; a panorama of elusive images, played before their eyes, to consume, if possible. Only the future is truly worth owning, and money is spent to perpetuate and propel these people forward. Life insurance!

Only extreme wealth can afford to *own* the past. The past is already spent, gone. To own and maintain it is a luxury which shows that one's present and future are already taken care of. With their vast surplus, the rich buy up the past. They place it in their homes; in the name of "public service" they place it in their museums—for the rest of us to worship, but not to touch. Once artifacts of daily life, old objects return as rare treasures. Ancient automobiles, survivors in a world of perpetual junkyards, are but reminders of the disposable culture. Those that can keep the old "new" have beaten the system that the rest of humanity inhabits. A **Model T** in the age of microchips is a price one pays—an *investment*—for owning a sense of continuity, of security across the generations.

No one else owns history like the rich: in houses, in clothes, in objects—*antiques*. To own history, they believe, is to possess a deed on the future.

No wonder Karl Marx claimed **history** for the wretched of the earth. By assigning guardianship over history to the working class, the world of symbols was overturned. It is only by claiming a deed to history that the future will be ours.

Billboards of the Future

clear today that the human organism has another absolute necessity.
. . . This fifth need is the need for novelty—the need, throughout our
waking life, for continuous variety in the external stimulation of our eyes,
ears, sense organs, and all our nervous network.[4]

In view of Platt's amendment to the four needs of man, the consumption of ever-new disposable might be seen as feeding primordial human hungers.

Yet if disposability satisfies one hunger, it jeopardizes the others. The pollution of the oceans raises questions of how much more deep-sea dumping can go on without destroying the human food supply or, more generally, the global ecosystem. The disposal of trash in landfills has reached a point of near saturation. The *New York Times* reports that

according to the experts, there is no room to dig landfills in many areas.
Where sites are available, apprehension about the contamination of underground water supplies has been a deterrent. Landfills pose other hazards, including the generation of methane and other gases. . . .

A recent survey by the Federal Environmental Protection Agency found that half of all municipalities will run out of landfill space within 10 years and that a third of all municipalities will run out within five.

Ecologically safe alternatives to dumping are hard to find. Large municipal incinerators can each burn more than a *Mobro*-full of refuse per day, and can "reduce the volume of trash by up to 90 percent," but emissions of gaseous pollution and toxic ash may "make this cure for the garbage problem far worse than the disease."[5]

The ever-mounting glut of waste materials is a characteristic by-product of modern "consumer society." It might even be argued that capitalism's continual need to find or generate markets means that disposability and waste have become the spine of the system. To *consume* means, literally, "to destroy or expend," and in the "garbage crisis" we confront the underlying truth of a society in which ongoing market priorities and enormous productive capacities have engaged human needs and desires, without regard to the long- or even short-term viability of life on the planet.

If the immanent course of consumerism is one of continuous expenditure and exhaustion, it must be acknowledged that for most people living within consumer society, waste is seen as an inherent part of the processes by which they obtain replenishment and pleasure. To some extent, this perception is reinforced, without ceremony, by the far-reaching maze of the market society itself. In societies where home production and localized subsistence agriculture provided people with most of their essential material needs, the sources that people drew from, as well as the constant need to maintain available resources as much as possible, were immediate, legible pieces of their reality.

In large measure, a consumer society begins to erode this cycle. While providing many people with new standards of material life, the retail, wholesale, or "black" market in goods makes "where things come from" increasingly abstract, apparently insignificant. The most pressing contingencies weighing on the consumer are those enforced by the obligatory system of abstract value, available cash, or credit. Simultaneously, the normalization of waste and modern networks of disposal tend to make "where things go" more or less inscrutable, seemingly inconsequential. The often-cited difficulty that *moderns* have in dealing with the life-process issues of birth, aging, and death, may, to some extent, reflect the falling rate of ecological literacy. We buy our chicken, cut up in a plastic tray, in a modern supermarket with canned music piped in. After we are all done, we place the bones, along with the plastic tray, along with all other genera of waste, into a large plastic garbage bag which we place outside to be carted off. On those occasions when we *do* pass a dump site, there is little sense of personal belongings. It does not occur to us that it is *our* refuse.

The customs of rural and preindustrial life militated against the systematized obsolescence which is commonplace within modern commercial culture. The historical roots of this improvident sensibility lie, for most people, in the social development of industrial capitalism, and in the apparently inexhaustible capacities of mass production.

Historically, the majority of people lived by economic assumptions that were starkly at odds with those that guide the present. Writing of "anonymous," vernacular housing of colonial America—from the vantage point of the mid-1950s, when suburban living and populuxe culture were on the unimpeded rise—Sibyl Moholy-Nagy illuminated some of the differences:

> We think today of economy as the minimum provision at the maximum profit, but the settler never thought of economic shortcuts. To be "economical" did not mean to save, but to prevent waste . . . [to] use . . . the best resources available. . . . Economy in indigenous architecture means maximum advantage of all given factors.

"Cost and speed, two driving forces of technological building," she added, "have affected rural building like a plague."[6] Another historian of vernacular culture, Bernard Rudofsky, concurs. "The built-in obsolescence of our commercial architecture," he wrote, "contrasts strongly with the virtual everlastingness of some rural constructions. . . . These days, buildings have a shorter life span than the men who build them."[7]

By the end of the nineteenth century, the customary rules of economy appeared, to many, to have been broken. In addition, new techniques, materials, and colorful chemical dyes foretold a world of universal abundance, where all might come to enjoy prerogatives customarily available only to elites.

Much of late nineteenth- and twentieth-century social thought is premised on the coming of what historian Warren Susman termed "a newly emerging culture of abundance."[8] To some extent, socialist thought has been fertilized by this expectation. For Karl Marx, writing at mid-nineteenth century, "the rapid improvement of all instruments of production" under capitalism was creating the material conditions which, ultimately, made communism possible. For the capitalist market, this enormous productive capacity would lead to a crisis of "overproduction," a crisis which, Marx observed, "in all earlier epochs would have seemed an absurdity." If market demand were replaced by the rule of "each according to his need," however, the industrial potential developed by capitalism would become the source of material well-being for the proletarians of the world.[9]

In the Freudian tradition of psychoanalytic thought, another vision of redemption is raised. For Freud, the historical development of human culture and civilization permitted people "to make the earth serviceable to them, to protect them against the tyranny of natural forces, and so on." But not without a price. The repression of instinctual sexual drives was the price exacted in the creation of civilization:

> It is impossible to ignore the extent to which civilization is built up on renunciation of instinctual gratifications, the degree to which the existence of civilization presupposes the non-gratification (suppression, repression or something else?) of powerful instinctual urgencies.[10]

Against this backdrop, the ability to alleviate millennia of material want, and to replace human toil with mass-production machinery, raises the possibility of desublimating erotic drives, of returning to the "pleasure principle," of allowing *eros* to grow within the shelter of a new and "permanent *order.*"[11]

In the United States, where both of these traditions have exerted an important if limited influence, another vision of the cornucopian promise of mass production was expressed by the social theorist of abundance Simon Patten. Writing in 1892, when most socioeconomic thought still "defended the assumption of scarcity" as an irrevocable part of the human condition, Patten was an outspoken pioneer in the belief that "enough goods and services would be produced in the foreseeable future to provide every human being with the requisites of survival."[12]

Patten enthusiastically greeted the coming of a new standard of living for an ever-expanding middle class in the United States. A "new basis of civilization" was coming into existence, he argued, one that would improve the material conditions of more and more people's lives, while opening up endless opportunities for psychological gratification. Old practices of saving and preservation, Patten observed, were on the wane, as was the customary way of life that had nurtured those traditional values. Mass production had raised all kinds of previously unimaginable possibilities, and the new standard of living would be drawn from among its myriad creations, propelled by the continual consumption of goods:

> The standard of life is determined, not so much by what a man has to enjoy, as by the rapidity with which he tires of the pleasure. To have a high standard means to enjoy a pleasure intensely and to tire of it quickly.[13]

In Patten's statement we see the beginnings of an outlook that responded to issues raised by socialist and psychoanalytic thought, but grounded itself squarely within the mechanisms of a newly developing, middle-class consumer economy. If, as Sibyl Moholy-Nagy argued, traditional cultures located the satisfaction of needs in a perspective that disapproved of waste, Patten's vision of the future embraced the principle of waste, and saw human gratification as the product of continual obsolescence.

DYNAMIC OBSOLESCENCE

Writing in the early 1930s, Walter Benjamin had remarked that mankind's "self-alienation has reached such a degree that it can experience its own destruction as an aesthetic pleasure of the first order."[14] It is in the representation and aestheticization of waste that the modern phenomenon of style plays its most ubiquitous and persistent role. In the market, the underlying invocation of nearly all of contemporary style is to consume, use up, and consume again.

If, on some "newsworthy" occasions, we are confronted with disquieting images of waste (toxic dumps near the playground, dead marine life washing ashore, overflowing landfills, or other indications of impending ecological calamity), most ordinarily the representation of waste in consumer society offers a picture of provocatively evolving styles, social and technological progress, and the blessed good fortune of material abundance.

POISON IS MY POTION

le nouveau parfum et Bath & Body Essentials
par Christian Dior

Mankind's "self-alienation has reached such a degree that it can experience its own destruction as an aesthetic pleasure of the first order."
—WALTER BENJAMIN

In Hollywood films, waste has been elevated to the level of entertainment. Michael Wood's incisive description of the catastrophe or "great crash" scenes in Hollywood epics (*Gone With the Wind, The Ten Commandments, Ben-Hur,* and the like) offers an illuminating look at consumption as spectacle:

The idea of waste in these movies receives its fullest expression here. Here are costly sets, carefully built constructions going up in smoke, or toppling down in ruins, the very feats of engineering we have just been admiring are now thrown away. This is visible expense, like the crowds of extras, only more startling. This is money being burned. We may find out, if we inquire that the blazing sets are not the sets we have just seen but leftovers from other movies given false fronts, as was the case for the lurid burning of Atlanta in *Gone With the Wind*. But the effect in the film remains. *Something* is being consumed before our eyes, and the historical Rome was at least lived in for a while before it went under. Here is an elaborate imitation of Rome which is inhabited only for a couple of big scenes before the flames take over; a Rome built, in effect, in order to be burned. The camera can't lie in this respect: the unmistakable work of human hands collapses into genuine ashes or genuine dust.[15]

In less titanic films we often see the same thing on a smaller scale. The obligatory *chase scene,* which has become a cliché in American adventure movies, leaves total material ruin in its wake. Automobiles tumble over cliffs, smashing in flames; house and store fronts are demolished in an explosive spray of splinters and shards; innocent bystanders are "wasted." Industrial Light and Magic, along with lesser-known special effects companies, have carried the ephemeralization of matter to new and erotic levels of enjoyment.

Material destruction is only one kind of palpable waste that is celebrated in the consumer culture. Advertising provides a perpetual spectacle of another variant on the theme. Beyond encouraging us to dispose of that which we have and replace it with that which they are selling, "the commercial message" itself represents the normalization of waste and embodies the ideal of conspicuous consumption. Advertising expends huge amounts of money on messages which are, more often than not, frivolous. A thirty-second advertisement during "The Cosby Show," for example, costs $440,000 or more in 1987; in half a moment enough money is consumed to keep ten Nielsen families going for a year or more. When the whole nation is watching, as during the Super Bowl broadcast, a thirty-second spot begins to approach the million-dollar mark. In the weeks preceding the game these figures are publicized in newspapers, educating the audience about the scale of waste that they will be witnessing on this holiest of days.

The most visible and unremitting aestheticization of waste, however, is seen in the continually changing styles and packaging that, in order to stimulate sales, affects nearly every commodity. Here the principle of waste is not embedded in any particular image, but rather in the incessant spectacle that envelops the marketing of merchandise. To a large extent, the mass phenomenon of market-stimulated waste had its beginnings in the early decades of the twentieth century, when nascent American consumer industries and the advertising agencies that served as their public spokesmen methodically attempted to promote sales by assailing the "customs of ages" which had encouraged thrift and the careful preservation of resources. By the early 1920s, the advertising industry had begun to publicly define itself as both "the destroyer and creator in the process of the ever-evolving new."[16]

Yet if the advertising industry was beginning to see itself as the promoter of profitable consumptive behavior, the productive apparatus was not necessarily tuned to this priority. Aside from the fashion industry which, even in the late nineteenth century, was gearing mass-produced fashion to seasonal cycles of stylistic change, many industries still approached production with little systematic attention to the marketing potential of style.

Perhaps more than any other person, it was the advertising man, Earnest Elmo Calkins, who raised the strategy of rapid, planned stylistic change as an element of twentieth-century American business thinking. Calkins took aim at "the Puritan tradition" within American industry, a tradition that had achieved wonders in the area of technological efficiency, yet had little appreciation of the aesthetic dimension. His model for the outmoded "Puritan" businessman was Henry Ford. While many saw Ford as the father of the modern age, Calkins focused on what he saw as Ford's retrograde tendencies. In going after Ford, Calkins selected as his text a remark that Ford had made "that he would not give five cents for all the art the world had produced."[17]

> There is no doubt that Mr. Ford was sincere in what he said about art. He believed that the homeliness of his car was one of its virtues. He correctly read the minds of his fellow citizens, who suspected that mere prettiness camouflaged the fact that sterner virtues were lacking. The Ford car was homely, but it did its work. And standing firmly on this belief Henry Ford broke all records of production, distribution, and sales in a country where such things are a religion.[18]

By the mid-1920s, however, Ford's puritanical commitment to "homeliness" could no longer command an increasingly competitive market. By adding "design and color to mechanical efficiency," Calkins noted, Ford's primary competitor in the production of inexpensive cars, Chevrolet, seized the largest share of the market.

Employing the story of Ford as an object lesson, Calkins began to articulate a business strategy that not only added the question of style to the business agenda, but recommended ongoing, methodical style change as the key to business prosperity. Writing in *Modern Publicity* in 1930, Calkins compressed his strategy into one extraordinarily direct paragraph:

> The purpose is to make the customer discontented with his old type of fountain pen, kitchen utensil, bathroom or motor car, because it is old fashioned, out-of-date. The technical term for this idea is obsoletism. We no longer wait for things to wear out. We displace them with others that are not more effective but more attractive.[19]

For Calkins, the practice of obsoletism was not limited to product design. It combined packaging, store display, advertising, and other elements into a coordinated sales campaign.

In 1892 Simon Patten had predicted that a standard of living premised on volatile patterns of obsessive consumption would yield "intense pleasure" to the consumer. Obsoletism was built on a very different assumption. It sought to erect a visible environment of change in which the profit margins of business would neatly mesh with a nurtured condition of consumer dissatisfaction, perpetual feelings of disorientation and self-doubt.

By the 1930s, as the Depression intensified the ferocity of corporate competition for sales, the ideas laid out by Calkins became rules of thumb. Writing in *Consumer Engineering* in 1932, Roy Sheldon and Egmont Arens contended that modern conditions had forced a reassessment of meanings:

> The dictionary gives obsolescence as the process by which anything—a word, a style, a machine—becomes antiquated, outworn, old-fashioned, falls into disuse—ceases to be used. But this definition is itself rapidly becoming obsolete. It expresses a pre-war point of view, [it] is passive.

For Sheldon and Arens, it was necessary now to conceive of "obsolescence as a positive force," a resource to be used to drive the market forward.[20]

This kind of thinking was reflected in the practices of business itself. Reporting to the President's Research Committee on Social Trends in 1933, Robert Lynd noted that a "speeding up of the tempo of style change as well as a broadening in the scope of fashion influence to new commodities and through new sections of the population occurred during the 1920s as an accompaniment of increasing prosperity and wide diffusion of wealth." Perhaps not surprisingly, the spread of rapid style change was most conspicuous in the women's apparel industry:

> Formerly there were definite seasonal changes in style of women's apparel. Now many New York stores report that there are no seasons, but a change in merchandise from month to month. Fifteen years ago a manufacturer was safe in preparing volume sales models that were fash-

ionable in Fifth Avenue shops the year before. Today it is frequently less than a week after a model has been shown in the window of one of the exclusive couturiers of 57th Street or Fifth Avenue that it appears at $6.95 or $3.95 in the 14th Street serve-yourself stores.[21]

Sheldon and Arens were particularly aware and enthusiastic about the role of the mass media in this development:

> Obsolescence . . . is seething through the life of the nation. Every day the latest fashions in clothes, in furniture, in automobiles, in coiffures is flashed on the screen before 16,000,000 intent watchers. Heralded in the newspapers, illustrated in the magazines, described over the radio, the latest wrinkle and the newest gadget are pushing and crowding into people's lives, not casually or with the leisurely pace of prewar days, but with the haste and bustle—and also the gaiety—characteristic of the modern American *tempo.*[22]

If, during the 1930s, the practice of "progressive obsolescence" (as it was then called, perhaps to conform to New Deal ideology) was part of a sometimes desperate attempt to build markets in a shrinking economy, the period following World War II saw obsolescence installed as a basic underpinning to the "populuxe" ideal of suburban prosperity. Articulating the boom mentality of the period, industrial designer J. Gordon Lippincott hailed obsolescence as a fundamental American birthright. Writing in 1947, Lippincott noted that "we have become so used to change that as a nation we take it for granted. The American consumer *expects* new and better products every year. . . . His acceptance of change toward better living is indeed the American's greatest asset. It is the prime mover of our national wealth."[23]

Yet even amid this nascent period of suburban boosterism, it was clear to Lippincott that citizen expectations may not be enough. Back in the 1930s, Sheldon and Arens had noted that many people were resistant to the economy of waste. "Scratch a consumer," they wrote, "and you find an opponent of consumptionism and a fear of the workings of progressive obsolescence."[24] By the late 1940s conditions had changed, but Lippincott still spoke of the need to combat thrift-oriented thought:

> The major problem confronting us is how to *move this merchandise to the American consumer.* The major problem therefore is one of stimulating the urge to buy! . . . Our willingness to part with something *before* it is completely worn out is . . . truly an American habit, and it is soundly based on our economy of abundance. It must be further nurtured even though it is contrary to one of the oldest inbred laws of humanity—the law of thrift—of providing for the unknown and often-feared day of scarcity.[25]

Here, in the clarity of Lippincott's words, we confront the inner logic of the spectacle of waste: the live-for-the-moment ideology that primes the market and avoids the question of the future, except insofar as that *future* is defined by *new, improved* items for purchase. Lippincott's argument displays an uninhibited instrumentalism that is rarely seen, even in the writings of other promoters of obsolescence, but which helps to explain the fissure between commercial visions of "the good life" and the planetary garbage dump that accrues in its wake:

> The method capable of *stimulating* this flow of merchandise is the key to our future prosperity. . . . The outstanding factor in such stimulation is a mass buying-psychosis. This we have always experienced during years of prosperity. The prime job that national advertising, research, and the industrial designer are doing in common is the breaking down of *new sales* resistance. . . . This is chiefly mental conditioning . . . [the] job of convincing the consumer that he needs a new product before his old one is worn out.[26]

During the 1950s, the appeal to "mass buying-psychosis" accelerated as never before. The suburbs were a symbolic escape from the rhythms of industrial society; they also were the locus of systematic obsolescence as a *way of life*. At the center of the system lay the automobile which, during the 1950s, became a public laboratory in waste. Perhaps more than anyone else, Harley Earl—who coined the phrase "dynamic obsolescence" to describe the design approach he innovated at General Motors' Styling Department—expressed big business's approach to style and market stimulation in the mid-1950s:

> Design these days *means taking a bigger step every year.* Our big job is to hasten obsolescence. In 1934 the average car ownership span was 5 years; now it is 2 years. When it is 1 year, we will have a perfect score.[27]

In the economic boom years between the end of the Second World War and 1960, the cycle of aestheticized waste accelerated and touched the lives and aspirations of more and more people. Fueled by higher incomes for many, and by the availability of consumer credit, the cycle of superficial change that emanated from corporate design departments was frequently cited as a conspicuous sign of American "abundance" and "progress."*

---

*Clearly, not all product change is stylistic. The postwar era has witnessed the emergence of important new technologies from the transistor to the microchip. These new developments have been part of a reordering of everyday life on basic levels. Still, the filter of style through which even significant technological advances are often seen, makes the distinction between actual technical improvement and style obsolescence difficult to discern.

"Color is the yearmark of 1955," announced the trade journal *Industrial Design*. It is "the most conspicuous symbol in designing and consuming." Within this trend toward more and more color, the article continued, "a new kind of elegance emerges for a middle-class classless society." At the heart of this populuxe elegance, the journal concluded, lay "a healthy self-indulgence, a new interest in simple routines and humble objects, a belief in the ceremonial enjoyment to be found in everyday occasions."[28]

MERCHANDISE AND MEMORY

From the 1930s onward, as many among the vanguard of American industrial designers laid out their personal recipes for a successful styling strategy, one necessary ingredient was mentioned repeatedly. Industrial design was largely a task of creating commercially appealing surfaces, but its effective accomplishment depended upon its ability to touch something deep in the consumer. Product designs, packages, or corporate symbols, they advised, must be able to be impressed on the *memory;* they must endure in the minds of prospective consumers.

For Henry Dreyfuss, even newly designed goods must, in some way, evoke prior goods and memories. This way, new sales would be built upon an implicit visual message of continuity with the past:

> Almost without exception, our designs include an ingredient we call survival form. We deliberately incorporate into the product some remembered detail that will recall to the users a similar article put to similar use. . . . People will more readily accept something new, we feel, if they recognize in it something out of the past. . . . By embodying a familiar pattern in an otherwise wholly new and possibly radical form, we can make the unusual acceptable to many people who would otherwise reject it.[29]

The rapid social, cultural, and stylistic changes intrinsic to industrial consumerism were, in many respects, mowing down the grasses of the past. Nonetheless, Dreyfuss contended that successful merchandising depended upon the ability of a design to evoke a symbolic restoration of that which, in fact, the design was intended to displace.

From a somewhat different vantage point J. Gordon Lippincott realized that effective packaging design was predicated on the ingredient of "memory value." Observing that "Americans are picture and cartoon conscious," Lippincott advised that packaging that draws a mental association between the product being sold and a potent visual symbol "will aid memory value" and stimulate sales.[30] Typical of Lippincott's candor, the phrase *memory value* encapsulated the modern approach to human remembrance which sees it as a potential commercial resource. (Kodak advertising, which promises you "the stories of your life" if you purchase their film, is but one strong example of this marketing strategy.)

Writing retrospectively of his work as a designer of corporate symbols, Raymond Loewy sounded a similar note. The designer of many of the world's most familiar logotypes—including those for Exxon, Shell, and BP petrochemical products; Nabisco; Lucky Strike cigarettes; and the modern update of Coca-Cola—Loewy explained that "I'm looking for a very high index of visual memory retention. In other words, we want anyone who has seen the logotype, even fleetingly, to never forget it, or at least to forget it 'slowly,' you might say."[31]

The idea that a product, or the images that surround it, must be established as a fixture in public memory is also a cardinal rule of advertising and promotion. Even irritating catch-phrases, such as "Please don't squeeze the Charmin!" or "How do you spell relief?" are valued by advertisers by simple virtue of their tested and proven *recall*.

It is curious that this fixation on *memory,* on *being remembered,* is expressed by an apparatus of representation which, while it hopes to preserve an aura of corporate perpetuity, is deeply involved in a process of market-enforced ephemeralization and superficial change. It is this paradox, the tension between the incessant provocation of popular memory and the uninterrupted spectacle of cultural flux, which has helped to shape the peculiar quality of contemporary consciousness. The mind becomes cluttered with disconnected but "memorable" images, random cultural waste materials whose only common denominator is that they once appeared amid the volatile marketplace of style. Along the way, the distinction between memory and "trivial pursuits" becomes obscure.

Even as the machinery of the "ever-evolving new" is perpetually in search of the "memorable," the particular sources—or aesthetics—from which commercially "memorable" images are drawn are unimportant. In a society where the skinning of the visible world has become commonplace, any skin, any visual connotation, may be drawn into service. The only requirements for appropriation into the style market are these:

1 The image must be able to be *disembodied, separated from its source.*
2 The image must be capable of being *"economically" mass produced.*
3 The image must be able to *become merchandise,* to be promoted and sold.

Given these three essentials, the market in style is extraordinarily plastic—capable of being molded, of receiving form.

The essential quality of a consumer society—marked as it is by the continuous cultivation of markets, obsessive/compulsive shopping, and premeditated waste—has made ever-changing style a cardinal feature of economic life, and *of popular perception.* Suspended in this cultural miasma, the "memories" of style are many, but as they unfold, historical recollection—the ability to comprehend social forces at work, to draw meaning from a social environment—is reduced to a flickering procession of familiar images. (With television, "picture" newspapers, and "life-style" magazines as the primary fountains of public information, this perspective is only reinforced.)

In housing design, in furniture, in assorted bric-a-brac, and—systematically—in the changing styles of automobiles, appliances, and clothing, we confront a visual representation of passing time. Other elements contribute to the impression as well. Films, faces, musical refrains, and dance-steps, and various fads and crazes that have been "picked up" by the media, each occupies its pictorial place in a fragmentary and essentially stylistic depiction of "an era." This transvaluation of memory is of great significance. As style becomes a rendition of social history, it silently and ineluctably transforms that history from a process of human conflicts and motivations, an engagement between social interests and forces, into a market mechanism, *a fashion show.*

This inversion can be exemplified in the ways that the style industries have appropriated, and changed, the trappings of various social movements of the last twenty-five years. From the 1960s onward, a loosely defined "alternative" or "oppositional" culture has materialized, concerned with questions of war, the environment, racial and sexual equality, global inequities, and of an overly *commercialized* and *superficial* consumer culture. In the midst of its ebbs and flows, this oppositional culture has expressed itself in a number of ways. Widely defined political activism, challenging the dominant structures of social, economic, and political power, has been its recurrent mode of expression, along with a rejection of the prevalent values and iconography of the primarily white, "middle-class" consumer culture. These ideas have led to attempts to shape a new, alternative culture, whose symbols would reject the "official society" and its rules, while pointing—hopefully—toward a more authentic and democratic way of life.

These countercultural trends have, at times, caught the style industries by surprise. During the 1960s, and at other moments since then, the rise of alternative subcultures has generated renegade styles—verbal expressions, ways of dress, music, graphics—which particularly captivated young people, traditionally seen as the most lucrative sector of the style-consuming public. This sense of having fallen behind, and the attempt to catch up, shows up in the trade literature of the style industries.

Early in 1967, as a radical "youth culture" was capturing international attention, Daniel Moriarty (editor and publisher of *Madison Avenue*, "The Magazine for New York Advertising") published a sixteen-question quiz for admen over twenty-five, designed to familiarize them with "what's happening with the Now Generation." In the glib patter of his introduction, it is clear that Moriarty saw the "youth culture" as both an antiestablishment challenge and a potential resource to be mined:

> This quickee quiz may seem as irrelevant as hell, but there are millions of teeny-boppers, hippies and Harvard sophs in Fat City with bread in their jeans and a lot of ways to spend it. You'd better know what they're talking about—or you may find yourself out of the gang. As America's great folk-poet-philosopher [actually, a New York disc jockey] Murray the K tells us, *attitudes are everything,* baby.

From the questions asked in the quiz, however, it is clear that "what they're talking about" or their "attitudes" were of little concern. The primary focus was on stylistic elements of the "Now Generation," codes that could be deciphered and transformed into merchandising know-how and phrase-book fluency. Questions included these:

1 To "blow your mind"
  a. refers to sniffing glue.
  b. refers to a sudden lapse of memory at exam time.
  c. means to be overwhelmed by an idea or event. . . .

5 Eddie Albert (you remember Eddie Albert) recently sang "Don't Think Twice" on the Dean Martin Show. The song was written by:
  a. Bob Dylan.
  b. Peter, Paul and Mary.
  c. Monti Rock IV. . . .

7 Buffy Sainte-Marie and Phil Ochs are
  a. leading singer-composers.
  b. student leaders at Berkeley.
  c. inventors of skin jewelry. . . .[32]

This countercultural trivia quiz, written during some of the most protracted protests against US involvement in the Vietnam War, displays a conspicuous absence of political and/or social content. The counterculture is reduced to a disembodied constellation of styles.

The same thing can be seen in the December 1969 issue of *Hear, There & Everywhere,* a newsletter for department store promotion executives, and others in the business of predicting, promoting, and selling style. "Can You Rap with the Soul Generation?" asked newsletter editor Samuel J. Cohen. "How many English languages do you speak? Better add soul and rock 'n roll. A hip (not hep) business man should have a nodding acquaintance with such talk." Again, a quiz followed, this one focusing on "soul generation" vocabulary:

Check a or b for correct meaning. . . .

1 HEAVY
    a. meaningful
    b. villain. . . .

11 RAP
    a. knock opponent
    b. a conversation

2 EGO-TRIP
    a. soulful
    b. self-centered. . . .

12 BUMMER
    a. sponger
    b. negative experience, bad job experience[33]

10 FREAKED
    a. left early; quit
    b. fainted

Here, as in the *Madison Avenue* quiz, language and style are lifted out of context, transformed into a meaningless, if potentially profitable, style.

The impact of this process can be seen if we look at the evolution of language from popular expression to an essentially commercial idiom. An example of this trajectory can be seen in the uses of the phrase "right on" from the 1960s onward. In what writer Claude Brown has described as "the language of soul," the expression was part of a call and response tradition which has survived among black Americans for more than three hundred years.[34] Until the mid-1960s, the phrase's use had remained relatively exclusive to black communities in the United States, just one way that black people shared common understandings, especially about their historical experiences. In 1968, as the phrase gained currency in the black liberation struggle, Black Panther party leader Bobby Seale defined it in this way:

Right on: Right on time. Black people used to say "right on time" a long time ago. It is a shortened form of identifying something that's said or done as really true and really right.[35]

As blacks and whites came together in the political movements of the 1960s, the phrase moved across color lines and became a common expression of the counterculture. As politicians and commercial interests attempted to appeal to young people, it was natural that they tried to appropriate the idiom of youth, to express symbolic affinity to the sensibility, if not the political outlook, of the young people they were addressing. One of the first of the mainstream authorities to use the term was President Lyndon Johnson, and—following the linguistic guidelines set in the just-quoted "quizzes"—other politicians and advertising copywriters began to follow suit. Full circle came when Bic ballpoint pens used the phrase "Write on!" in one of its ad campaigns. The idiom of subculture had entered the market place of style. In the process, meaning was lost. It had been reduced to the status of a *commodity*. Whatever significance or value the expression may have had in the context of its earlier development, that value was now outweighed by its exchange value, its ability to make something marketably "hip." When its marketability had been consumed, the phrase—like so much else—achieved the status of cultural waste matter. Admen and style merchants moved on to something *new*.

Similarly, in January of 1970, as the ecology movement was beginning to develop, *Hear, There & Everywhere* began to scan its linguistic market potential. *"The Hottest Word, Philosophically,* economically during the next 10 years," predicted editor Samuel Cohen, "will be ENVIRONMENT; it will be the key word to retail profit, merchandising, promotion."[36] Ironically, a term that was gaining currency as part of a growing awareness of the pollution and waste intrinsic to the consumer economy was now seen as a "hook" that could help to promote more and more consumption, more and more waste. From "Natural" foods to "Energy Saving" air conditioners, *environmentalism* was turned into a style; its meaning turned upside-down.

The ability to appropriate and "commodify" meaning is a continual feature of the style market. In the 1970s and 1980s, the transition of "punk" from an angry social statement to a *couture* style provides a good example. As "punk" culture arose in working-class Britain, the renegade style provided angry, often unemployed youth with a powerful and—to outsiders—shocking vehicle of expression. Through their antistyle, explains Dick Hebdige in his wonderful book on the subject, the *skinheads* and *punks* were, in their own way, enacting a kind of "conspicuous consumption." While they "conspicuously refused" the consumption patterns of middle-class propriety, they simultaneously adorned themselves in their own style, using commodities to "mark the subculture off from more orthodox cultural formations." Hebdige calls this popular appropriation of commodities *bricolage,* describing a process in which the marketplace provides raw materials which a subculture then uses to construct its own, improvisational meanings.[37]

Hebdige's insight offers important texture to the discussion of style because it allows us to see the ways in which popular movements or subcultures can seize meanings from the mainstream culture and turn them against themselves. This process of *bricolage* can be heard in the words of Stefan J——, a twenty-one-year-old skinhead, interviewed in 1983:

> [The skinhead style is] . . . a way of making a statement. The removing of hair and the wearing of Dr. Martin's . . . combat boots was a reaction to the long-haired hippie style which had gone from being the rebellious style to a conformist one. I myself have been criticized by a folkie hippie type person as being militaristic simply because of my ¼ inch buzz-cut hair. . . . The early skinheads were saying . . . that they wanted to be rebellious but in their own way. Considering the heat I catch just walking down the street, skinhead seems still to be damn rebellious.

To J——, the renegade style of the *skins* was a conspicuous rejection of the conventions of style which, to him, deluded people. The *skin* defined his image as part of a commitment to struggle and authenticity.

> Skinhead has so far been restricted to the very lowest classes of whichever society it has been a part of. The fashion statement made is one where expensive clothing and fancy hairdos do not exist. . . .
>
> By giving what seem to be expensive and upper class styled clothes to the mass of people these persons feel as if they are of a nobility. If one doesn't have the correct style or make you ain't gonna cut it among those who believe in conforming to the power structure of . . . society. To a skin, one way of rejecting the power structure is to get rid of as many fashionable things as possible.[38]

In Stefan J——'s testimony, there is an air of autonomous culture. While buying Dr. Martin's combat boots may constitute consumption, the commodity is being employed as part of an oppositional cultural politics. By the fall of 1986, however, Eddie R——'s testimony attests to the enormous rapacity and plasticity of the style industries. If punk was initially a popular appropriation of marketplace items, Eddie's description of "Punky's Underground Fashions from London," where he works, shows that *bricolage,* itself, may become a marketable resource:

> I work for a mail order clothing company that imports clothes from Europe. . . . The clothes [that "Punky's" sells] are basically "punk" wear.

Practically everything is black, has spikes or buckles on it. . . . Originally the clothes were very underground, worn only by a handful of "anarchists" who wanted to set themselves off from the rest of . . . society . . . to rebel against a culture they hated, a value and moral system they disagreed with. . . . Their clothes had meaning. The spikes represented violence, fighting back with power. The chains and buckles represented how they felt like prisoners of their society . . . how they felt bound to something. . . . Most people . . . were very afraid of punks. . . . This has all changed now. . . . Somebody saw profit in this "style" of clothing and decided to market. . . .

Even though the clothes are copies of the original . . . punks . . . the meaning of the clothes has disappeared. Nowadays most people think it is cute to dress a "little punky."

As punk became marketable style, it became its opposite. Initially a rejection of conformist fashions, and of the false status that they carry, its appropriation by "Punky's Underground" and other outlets of the style market transforms it into an item of competitive consumption with an inflated price. Nowhere is this more evident than in Eddie's description of "an official Punky's sweatshirt," sold by catalog:

In the catalog it looks very stylish. The model is very good looking and has that "I'm going places, I'm really cool and with it" look. In short, that "I must have" look. We're always running out of stock with them. People are willing to spend $49.00 for a sweatshirt. All it is is a regular sweatshirt that you could buy at K-Mart for $10.00, with a PUNKY's patch on the side. "PUNKY's" which really signifies nothing now has meaning. A simple $10.00 sweatshirt is now worth $49.00 because it's something new, it's *in style,* something that people will hopefully talk about.[39]

As punk becomes a market style, it also enters the cycle of waste upon which the market is built. Its appropriation signals its eventual disposal. This recurrent disposal relegates social history to the dustbin of images past; nevertheless, these images can, at any time, be revived for commercial recycling. They provide the raw material for commercialized displays of nostalgia, and they also provide us with a way of seeing, if not comprehending, the past.

Recuperated as a marketable style, the past may be invested with a multiplicity of instrumental meanings. Three 1980s recyclings of "the sixties" provide a case in point. Both are advertisements.

In the first, a magazine ad selling Frye boots, "the sixties" are a romantically longed-for, exciting time. "RETURN WITH US TO THOSE THRILLING DAYS OF YESTERYEAR," invites page one of the ad, above a scatter of peace pins, lifted from the drawer of imagistic history. When

The 60's was the wild look.

The 70's was the let it be look.

The 80's is the neat look.

Here's how you can get it.
First of all, get your hair cut well
and shampoo often. Then, before you comb and style,
use **Vitalis Liquid** or light **Vitalis Clear Gel** to put back
the manageability shampooing and blow drying can strip away.
The result will be hair that looks neat and natural;
well-groomed but soft to the touch.
If you have fine or thinning hair,
try **Vitalis Dry Texture**
for a full-bodied, natural look.
And to hold today's neat look all day,
use **Vitalis Super Hold** or
Regular Hold,
the pump sprays that give your hair
long-lasting control
that's always soft and natural,
not stiff or sticky.

Vitalis Men's Haircare.

(Don't let your hair
let the rest of you down)

©1984 Bristol-Myers Co.

the page is turned, a two-page spread offers a symphony of images and memorabilia. A photo-montage of Jimi Hendrix/Hare Krishna/March on Washington/JFK/Man on Moon/1969 Mets/Flower Power/One Man One Vote/Psychedelic Ties/Beatles' Rolls Royce/Woodstock/No More War provides a visual whiff of higher ideals, pristine optimism, *the sixties*.

Below, a text narrates the visual panorama of times gone by:

> It was a decade unlike any other in the history of this country.
>
> Ten years that have affectionately become known as the 60's.
>
> A decade of enormous social change, political upheavals, and where the activities of the day ranged from the ridiculous (how many people could squeeze into a Volkswagen) to the sublime (meditating along with your favorite Maharishi).
>
> It was a decade that saw man first walk on the moon. And the New York Mets win their first World Series, a feat many saw as even more improbable.
>
> A decade in which four guys from England came west to the U.S. and changed music forever. And 400,000 people from all across America traveled north, to upstate New York, and a piece of history known simply as Woodstock.

Shorn of content or coherent meaning, the decade is presented as procession of evocative captions, the suggestion of a time we long for, a time lost. The events have taken on a stylistic quality, and style takes on the quality of an event:

> Finally, it was a decade in which hemlines got shorter, ties got wider, and the official uniform was faded jeans, T-shirts and a pair of Frye boots.
>
> It was a uniform that symbolized a belief on the part of those who wore it (did anybody not?) in things that were simple, honest and enduring.

The advertisement speaks of the 1960s as a time of "simple, honest and enduring" values, a caring, down-to-earth evocation that has a seductive appeal within a society where *investment banking* and a *condo* are most commonly represented as the goals and ideals of youth. Yet as a collection of stylized images, retrieved from the cultural garbage dump, those *higher values*, themselves, become no more than a commodity, something to be purchased. They have been recycled only for their potential as *exchange value*. History becomes incomprehensible as people's own collective past comes back to them in the hollow, if appealing, form of a sales pitch. As the advertisement concludes, the emptiness of its overture becomes evident:

FORM FOLLOWS WASTE

So to the often asked question these days, "Where can you find those values that were so important to us all back in the 60's?", we have our own answer.

At any of the stores you see listed below. In men's sizes 7–13, and women's 5–10.

As an eviscerated piece of visual currency, the stylized 1960s—or any historical period, for that matter—may be used in a variety of ways, each instrumental to a product, idea, or life-style being sold. As the Frye boots ad employs the image of "the sixties" to offer a nostalgic return to "the good old days," an advertisement for Vitalis Men's Haircare products uses the image of "the sixties" to represent a *primitive* stage in human development, one that its product helped to *civilize.* The ad sets up a vertical sequence of pictures—one representing the 1960s, the next representing the 1970s, and the bottom, most elegantly photographed of the three, representing the 1980s. The top photo shows a young man with an open collar and long, tousled hair, characterizing the "wild look"; part of a natural historical progression toward a slicked-down, coat-and-tie "neat look" for the 1980s in the last picture. The social forces, issues, and conditions of the 1960s, or of the 1980s, are reduced to a *look,* a visual cliché which is then employed in an argument for order, discipline, and, of course, hair cream. Within this stylized dialectic, Vitalis ascends to the position of historical agency, emancipating us from the chaos of those *troubled times,* and that *uncombed hair.*

The same ability to transform social movements into easily manipulated visual clichés is seen in a 1987 television commercial for *Changing Times* magazine. *Changing Times,* which began in 1952, now seeks an upscale, yuppie market. To solidify this approach, the commercial offers up the counterculture of the 1960s and 1970s as its sacrificial lamb. The spot opens on a hippie, circa 1967, who proclaims "Capitalism stinks, man." He is now president of a high-tech firm and worth $3 million, according to a message typed on the screen. Next, a woman cursing the establishment at a 1973 protest rally. Now she runs the Little Lady Charm school.

According to the historical narrative of the commercial, both of these people have outgrown the naiveté of their youth and have come into their own as embodiments of the status quo. The issue of "capitalism" and why it "stinks" is packaged as the lead-in to a punch line, as does the issue being protested by that young woman in 1973.

Even though the ads for Frye, Vitalis, and *Changing Times* represent different positions on a left-to-right politico-stylistic spectrum, the recycled images that they employ float without any reference to society. Yet in the absence of a deeper, critical interpretation of social forces, such superficial recyclings become a surrogate for comprehending history; they take on a phantom veracity. In the case of the 1960s, style is often offered as an adequate way of understanding social opposition to the established order. Even sympathetic reveries can degenerate into a babble of surfaces. An example of this can be found in the February 1987 issue of *Details* magazine, in a special feature on the return of 1960s style:

> The Sixties style set the world swinging to a youthquake of delicious dissent. And in this very moment in time, in both fashion and furniture, its influence has come fabulously full circle. . . .
>
> The Sixties. Never in modern history had we taken such a giant step in attempting to discover what we were all about.
>
> Now. Now it happened—black was beautiful, the liberated spirit was recognized, women had their own cigarette. . . .
>
> Hegel wrote that what we learn from history is that we learn nothing from history. What it does teach us, however, is the ability to focus, to chronicle, to become our own historians. . . .
>
> What the Fifties suppressed the Sixties demanded. We wanted to know everything, run the full gamut of emotions—we were accessible yet inaccessible, vulnerable yet tough, approachable yet unapproachable. Every experience was a delight, a discovery. The initial change was titillating and infectious, a welcome stranger.
>
> It was the age of the new dilettante, the age of self-indulgence yet the age of a shared esthetic—the institution of the skin-and-bone body, the white go-go boot, the unisex hair dresser and the intoxicating breath of liberation uncompromising.
>
> This quality of feeling solidarity, this quality of being in step with being out of step, living in the fishbowl—always observing, being observed. . . . The writing on the wall, the graffiti. . . . So alien. . . . These new heroes on every level—the Warhols, the Malcolm X's, the Mary Quants, the Twiggys—heroes of those who shared our dreams.[40]

This is the quintessence of waste as history, history as style; a pulsating parade of provocative images, a collage of familiar fragments, an *attitude* of rebellion and liberation, the *Life* magazine illustrated *History of the Civil War . . .* on LSD. This mix of pomposity and fluff, with its claim of our discovery of how to become "our own historians," this kind of pastiche, ultimately, tells us nothing. At best it is a palette of hues and styles, waiting to be applied to merchandise, waiting to be sold. The 1960s will sell Frye boots; the "spirit of the Czar," cleansed of blood and history, provides a romantic setting for a couple sipping Wolfschmidt vodka.

As this happens, history disintegrates as a way of comprehending the world; it becomes an incomprehensible catalog display. It shifts from the realm of human subjects engaged in social relations, motivated by interest, circumstance, and experience, to the realm of objects, discrete commodities to be bought and sold. Popular historical retrospectives capture decades in terms of how things looked. Memory is encapsulized in *Depression glass*. The past can be evoked through the assembly of style. Hollywood is very good at this; sepia tones and gaslights produce that Gay Nineties feel; Giorgio Armani suits are perfect for Chicago gangsters. Even people become understood in these terms. Roosevelt, Bogart, and Hitler; each captures the style of the 1930s and 1940s in a different way. . . . Together they embody the spirit of a decade!

Style can encode our apprehension of the past; it can occupy our present and give shape to our expectations for the future. Much of our daily experience reinforces the notion of people as marketable objects; such versions of past and future assume a certain validity, if not truth.

In his novel *1984*, George Orwell depicted a future world in which historical memory lay in ruins, in which people could not look or imagine beyond the "official" version of *what is*, and of *what is possible*. The parade of disposability that marks today's consumer society is in no way as gray, or bleak as that delineated by Orwell. In its imagistic variety and its polychromatic glitter, it conveys an aura of sensuality, gaiety, even utopian promise. Yet while the two worlds may be worlds apart stylistically, in substance there are some disquieting affinities. Insofar as our perception of past, present, and future is unable to see beyond the facades of the style market, then Orwell's admonition may still deserve consideration: "Who controls the past controls the future. Who controls the present controls the past."

The Political
Elements of Style

The given facts that appear . . . as the positive index
of truth are in fact the negation of truth. . . . Truth
can only be established by their destruction.

—HERBERT MARCUSE,
Reason and Revolution

In American society today—where "image management" has become both a lucrative business and a matter-of-fact "necessity" in commerce, industry, politics, and interpersonal relations—style has ripened into an intrinsic and influential form of *information.* In countless aspects of life, the powers of appearance have come to overshadow, or to shape, the way we comprehend matters of substance.

In the world of business, the utility of style has made its mark, even in unanticipated places. One example is in the publication of annual financial statements, a legal requirement for public corporations imposed by the Securities and Exchange Commission in 1934. More and more companies "consider style to be as important as the bottom line" in the publication of annual reports. Gini Sikes, reporting in *Metropolis (The Architecture & Design Magazine of New York),* explains that "annual reports are now the domain of designers who often slip in fantasy between the facts and figures":

> The audience for annual reports extends beyond stockholders and employees. Executives use them as calling cards, salesmen as credentials, personnel departments as recruiting tools, and financial analysts as a

means of evaluating a company's performance. Thus, there's no limit to the kinds of visual metaphors used to express corporate character. . . .

In annual reports it's what's up front that counts. The opening pages can be visual corporate propaganda in its purest form. The reality you see is the reality the firm wants you to see, often by showing rather than telling. Chief executive officers (CEO) are primped for portraits as lovingly as pet poodles, and oil rigs are lit as theatrically as the set of Miami Vice next to breezy, easily scanned prose. The real story lies in the back pages' financial figures, a territory frequently neglected by designers—perhaps in the hopes that shareholders will do the same.[1]

The styling of annual financial reports ranges from "incidental" details to the overall image a corporation wishes to convey. In terms of detail, it may be something as subtle as the paper stock upon which the report will be printed. As one CEO explained, offering an argument on behalf of heavy-coated stock, "When you give someone an annual report it's like shaking hands. You want to project a firm handshake."[2]

At times, a report's design may be an attempt to establish a venerable corporate "personality." "In 1959," Sikes discloses, "Litton was a five-year-old company struggling to look like the billion-dollar industrial conglomerate its founder Tex Thornton was scheming to build." Robert Miles Runyan, an award-winning graphic cosmetician from California, was commissioned by Litton to design their annual reports:

> To create the feeling of an already established, traditional company, Runyan used photographs of antiques, historical documents such as the Bill of Rights and the Declaration of Independence, and text set in a classical serif face. Copy on one spread, for example, was illustrated with scientific instruments and discussed Litton's role in America's battle for worldwide technological leadership. The goal was to show how Litton fit into the framework of the major social and economic trends of the time—the big picture. As Litton grew, so did the grandiosity of Runyan's concepts. The 1962 report displayed a stunning photograph of the Acropolis in Athens; inside was an essay about democracy.[3]

Another place where style has become an indispensable, perhaps dominant, ingredient, is in public speaking. The practice of rhetoric and public address, which once prided itself on its ability to employ reason in the communication of information and ideas, has—in large measure—devolved into a hollow technique of pretense.

Dorothy Sarnoff, an "image consultant" who runs a company called Speech Dynamics, argues that recognition of the *style factor* is, today, essential to effective speech making. Reinforcing the ever-diminishing attention span demanded of people living in the shadow of the "ever-evolving new," Sarnoff explains that "surveys have revealed that only

8 percent of the audience pays attention to the content of a speech, 42 percent to the speaker's appearance, and 50 percent to how the person speaks." Keeping these figures in mind, the purposeful construction of a compelling style (physical appearance and mode of delivery) becomes a far more important part of training than research or the preparation of a coherent argument. As reported in the *New York Times Magazine*, "Ms. Sarnoff teaches her students to sit and stand with the upper torso and rib cage held high, because 'it gives you enormous presence, even when sitting silently in a meeting.' " The effective cultivation of gesture is also a plus. "Animation is the greatest cosmetic in the world," notes Sarnoff. A colleague in image training, Kevin Daley (who runs an outfit called Communispond) concurs. "People want to *appear* convincing, enthusiastic and committed to what they're saying. . . . All of those things are communicated physically rather than verbally." Given the fact that conviction, enthusiasm, and commitment are here defined as a play of appearances, it is little wonder that these trends were reported in the "Beauty" column of the *Times*. [4]

The variety of circumstances in which style has become the preponderant form of publicly accessible *information* is endless. Corporations are involved in a wave of much-publicized name and logo changes, attempting to communicate a more up-to-date, "informatic" image, or to "distance themselves from a debt-ridden affiliate."[5]

To attract recruits for the Clandestine Service, the CIA distributes a small brochure that is "discreet—matte gray in color, with a small seal of the Central Intelligence Agency tucked into one corner." The minute you lay your eyes on it, you know that it is intended for "your eyes only." To extend the aura of caution and confidentiality, there are no photographs inside the booklet; no names, no faces, no identifiable locations. The inner text, however, appeals to the spy novel reader in all of us:

> The Clandestine Service . . . the cutting edge of American intelligence. Its operational terrain is the human mind, where people—alone or together—make decisions, develop intentions, decide to go to war, make peace, change history.

Underlining the exclusive and secretive design motif of the Clandestine Service brochure, other recruiting literature from the CIA provides a stylistic contrast: "Most of the C.I.A. brochures are large and glossy, with color photographs—what one might expect from I.B.M., perhaps, or a large bank."[6]

On television, producers of "Miami Vice" announce that—in a move to bolster up flagging ratings—they have decided to make a shift from predominantly pastel hues, to deeper, richer colors for the fall 1987 season.[7]

In those television markets where "Wheel of Fortune" competes for viewers with the evening news, the majority of viewers choose to be informed by Vanna White who, in a sparkling evening gown, reveals precisely which letters lurk behind which squares.

On Broadway, the "mega-spectacle" has, in large measure, replaced plays with even a hint of character development or plot.

In automobile production, following years in which critics repeatedly questioned shoddy and hazardous manufacture, the industry has responded by offering the *look* of quality in a much-heralded "Euro-styling" blitz.

Heading for job interviews, young college grads are instructed by their advisors to "dress for success." All of these, and more, are examples of what Paul Goldberger, architectural critic for the *New York Times,* has described as "visual overkill in our culture." For Goldberger, the overarching primacy of disembodied style reveals a growing "tendency to place visual priorities above all else, . . . to seek an easy, spectacular visual 'fix.' "[8]

As a form of information (or dis-information) style places us on slippery and dangerous ground. Where style has become a visible world of memorable "facts," easily appended as a facade to almost anything, it has emerged as a powerful element in what Herbert Marcuse once described as "the closing of the universe of discourse." As style becomes increasingly ubiquitous, other ways of knowing, alternative ways of seeing, become scarce. The ability to stylize anything—toothpaste, clothing, roach spray, dog food, violence, other cultures around the world, ideas, and so on—encourages a comprehension of the world that focuses on its easily manipulated surfaces, while other meanings vanish to all but the critical eye. Most notably, as the evanescent becomes increasingly "real," reality becomes increasingly evanescent.

Like the authoritarian language "Newspeak," in Orwell's *1984,* style is capable of holding two contradictory ideas simultaneously without any apparent conflict or opposition.

WAR IS PEACE as camouflage battle fatigues join the iconography of high fashion.

FREEDOM IS SLAVERY when manacles or "slave bracelets" are worn as the shiny accoutrements of liberated sensuality.

IGNORANCE IS STRENGTH as a fetching young woman in a Calvin Klein jeans commercial proudly announces "when you lose your mind, it's great to have a body to fall back on."

As a form of information, style creates a consciousness that is seductively at war with much of our experience. That is part of the point; style addresses deep-seated desires, it promises to release people from the subjective conditions of their experience. Psychoanalyst Joel Kovel says that "style is the ego's homage to the id."[9] Christian Dior—in a 1986 advertisement—says that style "comes from a dream, and the dream is an escape from reality." Perhaps because it emits this primal, unconscious kind of attraction, style—as a form of *information*—discourages thought.

This discouragement of thought seems at odds with the widely promulgated idea that we are living through the dawn of a "new information age," in which people will have unlimited access to information and computers will process this information with the speed of light. Despite these promotional claims, the myth of the information age is riddled with contradictions.

Herbert Schiller has argued that one of the prime characteristics of the so-called new information society has been the steady "enfeeblement of the public's access to information." The last two decades have certainly witnessed the emergence of many innovative technologies for collecting, storing, and transmitting information. At the same time, however, sources of political, economic, scientific, and technical information—many formerly available in public libraries and depositories—are increasingly the province of commercial enterprise, collected, packaged, and sold for profit, to those who can afford to pay for it:

The commercialization of information, its private acquisition and sale, has become a major industry. While more material than ever before, in formats created for special use, is available at a price, free public information supported by general taxation is attacked by the private sector as an unacceptable form of subsidy. . . . An individual's ability to know the actual circumstances of national and international existence has progressively diminished.[10]

Yet as access to coherent information has ebbed, the flow of stylistic *information* has become torrential. Going with the flow, even those agencies that claim to provide the public with knowledge and information about the world we inhabit have become increasingly stylized. As style becomes information, information becomes style.

Nowhere is this trend more evident than in television news. "Newsroom" sets are styled to create the look of a command center, to offer an imagistic sense of being "plugged-in" to what is happening, to convey authority. Television journalists are selected and cultivated for their looks, their screen presence. From an authoritative, medium-shot vantage point, sitting behind a formidable desk, the anchorperson is constructed to transmit an appearance of incorruptibility, and of omniscience. On occasion, the camera moves in for a close-up, to impress a connotation of gravity upon a story, to show the audience that this newsperson *cares*. From opening logo to sign-off, all information, all stories are filtered through a veil of appearances. The Christine Craft affair, in the early 1980s, in which an anchorwoman was removed from a news program because she did not fit the correct image mold, is a case in point. In a business where anchorwomen are expected to appear both cool and attractive, beauty does—indeed—become truth.

Over and above this play of appearances, the *truth* is also continually subjected to the forces of the marketplace. The ratings system, which determines the advertising fees that can be charged for commercials, assures that the news program must weigh its informational responsibilities against its ability to attract a large "market share" of the audience. In the process, information devolves into *info-tainment*.

The contradiction between truth and *commercial truth* can be observed in a 1985 advertising campaign for New York City's "Channel 7 [ABC] Eyewitness News." Atop one of the billboards for the campaign, there is a familiar portrait of Thomas Jefferson, a widely recognized paragon of integrity. Next to his picture, his forceful words declare: "We are not afraid to follow the truth wherever it may lead." Beneath Jefferson's wise face, sits the portrait of another great patriot, Kaity Tong, anchorwoman for "Eyewitness News." Her words, in the same boldface type in which Jefferson's appeared, proclaim: "We're here to tell you the truth." Below, in smaller typeface, we get a closer look at what she means:

The truth is, there's nothing on television more important, more entertaining, more thrilling than the true human drama of the news.

If Jefferson speaks for the Age of Reason, Tong speaks for the Age of
Hype. The operative words here—*entertaining, thrilling, drama*—are
a giveaway as to what is meant by *truth*. In the ratings game, the
news—out of economic necessity—must be transformed into a drama,
a thriller, entertainment. Within such a context, the *truth* is defined as
that which sells.

The news itself is sculpted to conform to a totally administered stylistic environment. George Fasel, a public relations man in New York, has
described the formulaic presentation of news content in terse but familiar terms:

> News stories are presented by brand-name journalists in short and easily
> digestible gobbets. Commercial interruptions are frequent, not only for
> financial reasons but also so that the program can be absorbed in manage-
> able portions. And issues are often presented in terms that are easily
> comprehended, as in a game show: Who won?[11]

Remote, on-location news footage and interviews are presented to
maintain a fast pace, and to avoid any lingering questions or doubts
about what has been presented. In the use of edited news footage, a
story is constructed to provide a dramatic impact with strong visual
effect, even if this comes at the expense of deeper understanding.
"Bites" taken from longer interviews are selected for their economy of
language, and are required to end on a vocal downbeat. This communi-
cates a sense of completion, suggesting that the person has finished
what he or she has been saying, and that what you are seeing is all that
there is to be seen. Jump-cuts between bites of an interview are avoided
for the same reason. Editing style is designed to suggest that there are
no "outtakes" on the cutting room floor.

Within such a stylistic environment, the news is beyond comprehension. Stories are presented as a series of jagged bits. Segues between
tragedy and farce are the glue that holds the whole thing together. The
interconnectedness of facts, their actual relations within the world, are
never developed. The highly stylized signature of the news program
offers the only overarching principle of cohesion and meaning. Again,
surface makes more sense than substance. The assembled facts, as
joined together by the familiar, formulaic, and authoritative personality
of "The News," becomes the most accessible version of the larger reality that most Americans have at their disposal. Consciousness *about the
world* is continually drawn away from a geopolitical understanding of
events as they take place in the world. As nations and people are daily
sorted out into boxes marked "good guys," "villains," "victims," and

"lucky ones," style becomes the essence, reality becomes appearance.

With the development of picture newspapers and magazines, each filled with regular entertainment features, print journalism has, to a large extent, moved in the same direction. *USA Today*—the national newspaper—with its color photographs, its easy-reading bullet style of newswriting, and its spectacular computer graphic weather maps, is television news adapted to the medium of newsprint. With circulation rates and advertising revenues at the heart of each issue, once again we see information shaped by the laws of the market; the truth becomes that which the most people will buy.

If the news helps to promulgate an ongoing cognitive confusion, closely related are the dominant channels of political influence. As far back as the presidency of Andrew Jackson, when the vote was extended beyond the propertied classes, political style makers have negotiated between the objective power and interests of ruling elites on the one hand, and rising popular democratic aspirations on the other. Social inequalities of wealth and opportunity were transformed, by the hoodoo of political promotion, into a consensual notion of "common interest."

Summing up various sources, historian Edward Pessen has described the birth of modern campaign politics during the Age of Jackson:

> Demagogy of the most transparent sort became the practice. Always aware that the ordinary man had the vote, the politician "tried to identify himself with the common people, to wear old clothes, to claim a log-cabin origin, and conceal his superior education." After plying their audience with free whiskey, politicians would "speak grandiloquently of 'the sovereign people.'"
>
> Demagogic speechmaking was everywhere supplemented by a kind of showmanship which added a "dramatic function" to politics. A series of theatrical devices were used to stimulate mass enthusiasm, featuring parades, rallies, barbecues, and lavish dispensation of hard liquor.[12]

These nineteenth-century political developments and campaign approaches shaped the contours of American party politics well into the twentieth century. In more recent years, political style has become the product of coordinated and carefully managed sales campaigns.

With the end of the Second World War, the systematic stylization of politicians, policies, and political ideas became commonplace. To some extent this development was rooted in the 1920s, when the emergence of vast consumer industries, and a modern advertising and marketing system, gave rise to the general field of consumer engineering. Pioneers of merchandising believed that if only the psychological mechanisms, the instinctual buttons of *the masses* could be known and pinpointed, surefire marketing appeals could be designed and/or constructed. People were coming to be understood as an "audience" to be monitored, analyzed, shaped.

By the 1930s and 1940s, this predilection took on a decisively political orientation. The rise of "mass movements" of the right and the left, and the entry of the United States into World War II, gave impulse and funding to propaganda research, whose utility was twofold. First, through the gathering of social scientific data, the successes of *enemy* propaganda could be evaluated, understood, and potentially contained. More relevant to contemporary image building, research could also be used in the construction of alternative propagandas, or—to use the more current jargon—as a tool of "image management."

The arrival of this kind of thinking can be seen in Edward Bernays's 1947 essay "The Engineering of Consent." Sigmund Freud's nephew and one of the founders of the modern field of public relations, Bernays presented a new vision of democracy. With film and radio already established, and with television rapidly becoming one of the central fixtures in the American way of life, Bernays redefined the Bill of Rights to include "the right of persuasion":

> The tremendous expansion of communications in the United States has given this Nation the world's most penetrating and effective apparatus for the transmission of ideas. Every resident is constantly exposed to the impact of our vast network of communications which reach every corner of the country, no matter how remote or isolated. Words hammer continually at the eyes and ears of America. The United States has become a small room in which a single whisper is magnified thousands of times.

For political leaders, or for those aspiring to political power, he argued, "these media provide open doors to the public mind":

> Such leaders, with the aid of technicians in the field who have specialized in utilizing the channels of communication, have been able to accomplish purposefully and scientifically what we have termed "the engineering of consent."

Here we have the kernel of Bernays's newly conceived democracy, his unflinching ability to conflate ideological management techniques with the idiom of social and political liberty:

> The engineering of consent is the very essence of the democratic process, the freedom to persuade and suggest. The freedoms of speech, press, petition and assembly, the freedoms which make the engineering of consent possible, are among the most cherished guarantees of the Constitution of the United States.[13]

In one brief and prescient treatise, Bernays had outlined the modern contours of American politics. Today, the "engineering of consent" has become business as usual.

From the 1950s onward, within the context of an ever more pervasive consumer culture, electoral politics have become one more market of promotable and consumable items. Advertising agencies regularly participate in the packaging of governmental policies for public scrutiny and consumption. A whole field of media consultancy has emerged, to advise candidates and office holders in matters of leadership style. Much of this represents the employment of techniques first developed within the field of product merchandising, now applied in the political arena. Like sit-coms, political speeches, debating tactics, and campaign commercials are regularly tested for second-by-second audience reaction, to guide the pacing and flow of political messages and appeals, to produce a more marketable product.[14] In a theater which, at every turn, obscures underlying realities, the manufacture of political fictions has become the norm. In the resulting realm of superficial meanings, democracy itself becomes style; popular political involvement becomes structured by a pattern of spectatorship and consumption.

This fractured consciousness—torn between the substantive perception of social and political issues, and the inviting concoctions of appearance peddlers—is relied upon by those in power. More and more, public politics has devolved to the status of image marketing. Nowhere can this be more clearly seen than in the political career of Ronald Reagan. In 1947, Edward Bernays had asserted that the building of political constituencies, in a modern, mass-mediated society, required the systematic "engineering of consent." Ronald Reagan and his presidency represent the unequivocal triumph of that approach to politics. Reagan was trained for political life as a Hollywood actor and, later, on television and in the field as a pitchman for the General Electric Corporation. Given the contemporary parameters of the political spectacle, he is the logical president, the template for future aspirants and incumbents.

Reagan's apprenticeship in Hollywood provided him with a proven repertoire of images and appeals. At times we can close our eyes and hear the impassioned and honest tones of Spencer Tracy. When an aura of simple trustworthiness is called for, he can draw upon his folksy Jimmy Stewart routine, replete with a shake of the head and an implied "Aw, gee." As the unyielding executioner of social programs he becomes the "last angry man," true to his own inner sense of justice, painfully misunderstood. As the assassin of women's rights, he opts for the antiseptic mainstream; he and Nancy become Ward and June

Cleaver. As a militarist he assumes the pose of the indignant good guy, out to right the world's wrongs. In defining America's enemies, world struggles for power are couched in the familiar idiom of *Star Wars,* or some medieval costume drama. We are implored to join a heroic crusade against the dread "Evil Empire," or to throw in our lot with the "freedom fighters" south of the border. The plots are all familiar, tried and true. The Hollywood narrative supplies a stylistic model for political consciousness.

This tendency toward cinematic cliché has been an earmark of Reaganism more generally. It is this Hollywood touch, for example, which has underwritten the reemergence of militarism, and of the soldier-hero, in American society over the past decade. Following a period in which antiwar sentiments had become widespread among the population, the war lost in Vietnam can now be won, by Rambo, on the screen. Even Oliver North, who is a real soldier, captivated people on a primarily imagistic level. Polls taken after his legendary testimony before the Irangate-Contragate committee of Congress in 1987 indicated that people responded to his apparent boyish sincerity, despite revelations that he had repeatedly lied to Congress and to the people of the United States. His earnestly transmitted loyalty to God and Country effectively overshadowed the fact that he was ruthless player in an intelligence/military plot to undermine and bypass the structures of constitutional democracy. Like Ronald Reagan, Oliver North's stylistic affinity to Jimmy Stewart permitted people who were polled to say that although they rejected everything he did, they also thought that he was "inspirational."

This commitment to the politics of image permeates the Reagan administration's response to criticism. Even though the deregulation of business opened the way for windfall profits, and reduced attention to industrial or environmental health and safety, the argument that Reaganism favors the rich is characterized by White House aides as a problem of "perception." As thirty years of long-struggled-for civil rights legislation is systematically dismantled, the conviction that Reaganism is insensitive or hostile to minorities is addressed, likewise, as a problem of "perception." This attitude represents the ascendancy of politics as pure public relations. By reducing all social issues to matters of perception, it is on the perceptual level that social issues are addressed. Instead of social change, there is image change. Brief shows of flexibility at the surface mask intransigence at the core.

The impulse to dissociate images from social experience, or to present images as a surrogate for experience, is reiterated throughout our culture. The perpetual repetition of this dynamic—affecting our sense

World of toil

Facade

Plate 46

Appearances

In a world of strangers . . . appearances become all. We buy . . . or are encouraged to buy . . . to make an impression . . . our stock in trade. We consume the face of personality. At times, American architecture reinforces this principle of society: the oath of abundance.

On Third Avenue, in New York City, *Bloomingdale's* stands. It is an icon to the world of appearance. Appearance: a medium of exchange. From a distance, an inner truth is revealed.

(See Plate 46, above) The facade is one of smooth modernity, the *covenant* of lubricated leisure. Yet we see what the intimate passers-by cannot. The facade is applied as a mask over the structure of 19th-century industrialism. The world of toil and its bleak experience is covered by the look and promise of eternal pleasures.

Today, more and more Americans are standing across the street. As the facade lapses into a distance, the 19th century returns. Sweatshops; home work; pauperism. Greed and hunger meet once again. So it is written on the face of *Bloomingdale's*.

Billboards of the Future

of self and of society—has created a world in which style has emerged as the predominant expression of meaning. The danger is this: as the world encourages us to accept the autonomy of images, "the given facts that appear" imply that substance is unimportant, not worth pursuing. Our own experiences are of little consequence, unless they are substantiated and validated by the world of style. In the midst of such charades, the chasm between surface and reality widens; we experience a growing sense of disorientation.

From the middle of the nineteenth century onward, the rise of a mass market in images has had an unprecedented impact on the ways people have perceived, experienced, and behaved within the world. To a large extent, the flourishing diversity of images has opened people's eyes to a wide variety of new possibilities, new ways of imagining. As these new possibilities have been raised, however, they have also been played upon the surfaces of life; underlying meaning has been masked, while concrete possibility and evanescent style have become, too often, confused with one another.

The way out of this confusion is difficult to imagine. It is too much a part of the social history of our time. For meaningful alternatives to come into being, however, the dominance of surface over substance must be overcome. There must be a reconciliation of image and meaning, a reinvigoration of a politics of substance. Only then will people be able to ensure that the imagery of pleasure is joined to the experience of pleasure; that seductive images of the "good life" are rooted in the principles and practices of a human community; and that images of freedom, satisfaction, and social resistance are meaningfully engaged with the resources and real options available to us in the world we inhabit.

Notes

INTRODUCTION   **Shoes for Thought**

1 See Stuart Ewen, "The Political Elements of Style," in Jeffery Bucholtz and Daniel Bertrand Monk, eds., *Beyond Style: PRECIS,* no. 5 (Fall 1984), pp. 125–33.

2 This research led to the publication of "Fashion and Democracy," a major section in Stuart Ewen and Elizabeth Ewen, *Channels of Desire: Mass Images and the Shaping of American Consciousness* (1982).

3 Only much later would I realize that Strunk and White were very much part of the picture, that at the very time that these two were arguing against adjectives, and calling for a lean and streamlined use of language, architects, industrial designers, fashion designers, girlie magazines, and other arbiters of public image were also counseling aesthetic spareness, a sense of *less being more.* Only later would I realize that style is an essential way that individual and social ideas get expressed, and that it jumps across the gaps that often appear to divide one arena from another within society.

4 As quoted in chapters that follow, these papers provide unusual, poignant, and rarely detailed maps of connection between individual identity and the broader phenomenon of style in contemporary culture. Without these students' generous contribution, an important element of this book would be lacking. To protect the privacy of these people, and because their stories often represent outlooks and experiences shared with others, I have disguised all Style Project names throughout this book. Those willing to be fully named are listed in the Acknowledgments.

5 Style Project, written testimony A8. The following quotations are from Style Project, written testimonies A22, A10, A5, A3, B15, and B2, respectively.

6 Ralph Ellison, "The Little Man at Chehaw Station," *American Scholar* (Winter 1977), pp. 37–39.

CHAPTER ONE   **". . . Images Without Bottom . . ."**

1 Style Project, written testimony A6.

2 Ibid., written testimony A9.

3 Ibid., written testimony A10.

4 Ibid., written testimony A2.

CHAPTER TWO **Goods and Surfaces**

1 Oliver Wendell Holmes, "The Stereoscope and the Stereograph," *The Atlantic Monthly* 3 (June 1859), reprinted in Beaumont Newhall, ed., *Photography: Essays and Images* (1980), pp. 53–54.

2 Naomi Rosenblum, *A World History of Photography* (1984), pp. 94, 155.

3 Holmes, "The Stereoscope and the Stereograph," p. 60, emphasis added.

4 Ingrid Brenninkmeyer, "The Sociology of Fashion" (1962), p. 32. See also Stuart Ewen and Elizabeth Ewen, *Channels of Desire* (1982), pp. 122–25.

5 Arnold Hauser, *The Social History of Art*, 4 vols. (1951), 1:201.

6 Marcel Thomas, "Manuscripts," introductory essay to Lucien Febvre and Henri-Jean Martin, *The Coming of the Book* (1958), p. 6.

7 Ibid., p. 47.

8 Brenninkmeyer, *The Sociology of Fashion*, pp. 58–59.

9 Sidney Mintz, *Sweetness and Power* (1985), p. 93.

10 Ibid., pp. 92–94.

11 Siegfried Giedion, *Mechanization Takes Command* (1948), pp. 47–49.

12 Arthur J. Pulos, *American Design Ethic* (1983), p. 123.

13 Egon Friedell, *A Cultural History of the Modern Age: The Crisis of the European Soul from the Black Death to the World War*, 3 vols. (1954), 3:300–301.

14 Peter Blake, *Form Follows Fiasco* (1974), p. 31.

15 Georgine Oeri, "Aspen," report on the fourth Aspen Design Conference, *Industrial Design* 1 (August 1954), pp. 109–13.

16 James W. Shepp and Daniel B. Shepp, *Shepp's World's Fair Photographed* (1893), p. 27.

17 John F. Kasson, *Amusing the Million* (1978), pp. 23–24.

18 John Berger, *Ways of Seeing* (1972), p. 106.

19 Janet Byrne, *American Ephemera* (1982), pp. 2–4.

20 Oliver Wendell Holmes, "Doings of the Sunbeam," *The Atlantic Monthly* 12 (July 1863), reprinted in Beaumont Newhall, ed., *Photography: Essays and Images* (1980), p. 64.

21 Ibid., pp. 63–64.

CHAPTER THREE **The Marriage Between Art and Commerce**

1 Tilmann Buddensieg and Henning Rogge, *Industriekultur: Peter Behrens and the AEG*, trans. I. B. White (1984), p. x.

2 Ibid., p. 2.

3 Ibid., pp. x, 2.

4 Paul S. Boyer, *Urban Masses and Moral Order in America, 1820–1920* (1978), p. 264.

5 Walter Lippmann, *Drift and Mastery* (1914), pp. 52–53.

6 George Mowry, ed., *The Twenties: Fords, Flappers and Fantasies* (1963), p. 15. See also Stuart Ewen, *Captains of Consciousness* (1976), for a fuller discussion of the rise of modern advertising.

7 C. Wright Mills, *The Power Elite* (1956), p. 84.

8 Earnest Elmo Calkins, "Beauty The New Business Tool," *The Atlantic Monthly* 140 (August 1927), pp. 147–48, emphasis added.

9 Ibid., p. 149.

10 Ibid., p. 151.

11 Ibid., p. 152.

12 Robert S. Lynd, "The People as Consumers," in Report of the President's Research Committee on Social Trends, *Recent Social Trends in the United States* (1933), p. 878.

13 Egon Friedell, *A Cultural History of the Modern Age: The Crisis of the European Soul from the Black Death to the World War,* 3 vols. (1954), 3:475–76.

14 Harry Dexter Kitson, "Understanding the Consumer's Mind," *The Annals* 110 (November 1923), pp. 131–38.

15 Roy Sheldon and Egmont Arens, *Consumer Engineering* (1932), p. 97.

16 Ibid., pp. 100–101, emphasis added.

17 Harold Van Doren, *Industrial Design* (1940), pp. 121–22.

18 Jean Abel, "An Explanation of Modern Art," *California Arts and Architecture* 37 (June 1930), pp. 34–35.

19 Van Doren, *Industrial Design,* p. xviii.

20 J. Gordon Lippincott, *Design for Business* (1947), p. 19.

21 Raymond Loewy, *Industrial Design* (1979), p. 8.

22 Roland Barthes, *The Fashion System* (1983), p. 300.

23 J. Gordon Lippincott and Walter Margulies, "We Couldn't Have Done It in Wichita," *Industrial Design* 7 (October 1960), p. 103.

24 Sheldon and Arens, *Consumer Engineering,* pp. 61, 63.

25 Ibid., pp. 13–14.

CHAPTER FOUR   **Chosen People**

1 Alexis de Tocqueville, *Democracy in America,* 2 vols. (1945), 2:51–52.

2 Edward Pessen, *Jacksonian America* (1969), p. 53.

3 Alan Dawley, *Class and Community* (1976), pp. 151, 171.

4 Ibid., p. 149.

5 Ibid., p. 150.

6 Ibid., pp. 150, 284.

7 See title essay in Herbert Gutman, *Work, Culture and Society in Industrializing America* (1977).

8 Karl Marx and Frederick Engels, *The Communist Manifesto* (1948), pp. 15–16.

9 Karen Halttunen, *Confidence Men and Painted Women* (1982), p. 29.

10 Ibid., p. 29.

11 Eric Foner, *Free Soil, Free Labor, Free Men* (1970), pp. 16–17.

12 Halttunen, *Confidence Men and Painted Women,* p. 29.

13 Ibid., p. 64.

14 Ibid., p. 66.

15 Harriet Beecher Stowe, "The Lady Who Does Her Own Work," *The Atlantic Monthly* (1864), reprinted in Gail Parker, ed., *The Oven Birds* (1972), p. 187.

16 Foner, *Free Soil,* p. 23.

17 Ira Steward, "Poverty," Massachusetts Statistics of Labor, House Document 173, pp. 412–14.

18 Ibid., pp. 412–14. Ira Steward understood that this "middle class" performed an important political function in American society, erecting a buffer zone between extremes of wealth and poverty. "If men have nothing but a bare living," Steward observed, "they are in a condition to believe, at any critical moment, that they have something to gain from public disorder." Thus, the middle class's identification with the interests of the status quo forged an important alliance between them and the rich, one which might lead to agitation and rebellion among the pauperized classes. The conservative proclivities of an indebted middle class, noted by Steward in the 1870s, have been an important feature of the U.S. in the 1980s, where credit has been extended to millions and where an increasingly in-debt middle class proudly emerged as foot soldiers for Reaganism.

19 George M. Beard, "Causes of American Nervousness" (1881), reprinted in Henry Nash Smith, ed., *Popular Culture and Industrialism* (1967), pp. 67–69.

20 Quoted in Marvin Meyers, *The Jacksonian Persuasion* (1957), pp. 126–27.

21 Foner, *Free Soil,* p. 24.

22 Beard, "Causes," p. 69. See also Erving Goffman, *The Presentation of Self in Everyday Life* (1959), p. 208.

23 Editors of *Fortune, Markets of the Sixties* (1958), pp. 116–17.

24 Ibid., p. 90.

25 Ibid., p. 123.

26 Thomas Hine, *Populuxe* (1986).

27 Quoted in Editors of *Fortune, Markets of the Sixties,* p. 123.

28 Joan Kron, *Home-Psych: The Social Psychology of Home and Decoration* (1983), p. 263.

29 Robert S. Lynd, "The People as Consumers," Report to the President's Research Committee on Social Trends, *Recent Social Trends in the United States* (1933), pp. 866–67, emphasis added.

30 Stuart Ewen and Elizabeth Ewen, *Channels of Desire* (1982), p. 214.

31 Ibid., p. 215.

32 Stanley Feldstein and Lawrence Costello, eds., *The Ordeal of Assimilation* (1974), p. 369.

33 Warren Susman, " 'Personality' and the Making of Twentieth Century Culture," in *Culture as History* (1984), pp. 271–85.

34 Elizabeth Ewen, *Immigrant Women in the Land of Dollars* (1985), p. 228.

35 Ibid., p. 67.

36 James W. Shepp and Daniel B. Shepp, *Shepp's World's Fair Photographed* (1893).

37 See Ewen and Ewen, *Channels of Desire,* pp. 109–251, for a more extensive discussion of the "democratization" of fashion.

38 Elizabeth Ewen, *Immigrant Women,* p. 69.

39 Quoted in Sibyl Moholy-Nagy, *Moholy-Nagy: Experiment in Totality* (1950), p. xv.

40 Elizabeth Ewen, *Immigrant Women,* p. 69.

CHAPTER FIVE   "The Dream of Wholeness"

1 Stuart Chase, *Prosperity: Fact or Myth* (1929), p. 65.

2 Estelle De Young Barr, "A Psychological Analysis of Fashion Motivation," *Archives of Psychology* 171 (June 1934), pp. 9–10.

3 Roland Barthes, *The Fashion System* (1983), pp. 254–55.

4 Harry Braverman, *Labor and Monopoly Capital* (1974), p. 90.

5 Ibid., p. 112.

6 Ibid., p. 113.

7 Ibid., pp. 112–21.

8 Herbert Gutman, *Work, Culture and Society in Industrializing America* (1977), pp. 55, 63.

9 Braverman, *Labor,* p. 103.

10 Ibid., p. 87.

11 Richard Schickel, *D. W. Griffith: An American Life* (1984), p. 28.

12 Charles W. Mears, *Salesmanship for the New Era* (1929), p. 52.

13 Ibid., p. 46.

14 Dale Carnegie, *How to Win Friends and Influence People* (1977), p. 28.

15 Ibid., pp. 72–74.

16 Erich Fromm, *Escape from Freedom* (1941), p. 243.

17 C. Wright Mills, *White Collar: The American Middle Classes* (1953), pp. 178–79, emphasis added.

18 Emmet Murphy, "Louis Grubb," *Communication Arts* (May–June 1980), pp. 58–62.

19 Casmera Norwich, "Parts Plus," *Photo/Design* 4 (July–August 1987), pp. 51–54.

20 Ibid.

21 Marshall McLuhan, *The Mechanical Bride* (1951), p. 96.

22 *Village Voice,* 24 April 1984, p. 34.

23 "Tonight Show," NBC-TV, 11 September 1986.

24 Joan Kron, *Home-Psych: The Social Psychology of Home and Decoration* (1983), p. 60.

25 Alfred Auerbach, "What Is Modern?" *Arts and Architecture* 65 (March 1948), pp. 28–29.

26 John Everard, "Advertising to Women by Photography," *Commercial Art and Industry* (July 1934), pp. 2–3.

27 Style Project, interview I-1.

28 Sergei Eisenstein, *Film Form* (1949), pp. 206–8.

29 Lewis Erenberg, *Steppin' Out* (1981), p. 179.

30 Hortense Powdermaker, "An Anthropologist Looks at the Movies," *The Annals* 254 (November 1947), p. 85.

31 Walter Benjamin, "The Work of Art in the Age of Mechanical Reproduction," in Hannah Arendt, ed., *Illuminations* (1968), pp. 222–23.

32 C. Wright Mills, *The Power Elite* (1956), p. 84.

33 Lorine Pruette Fryer, *Women and Leisure* (1924), pp. 173–74.

34 Warren Susman, *Culture as History* (1984), pp. 146–47.

35 Margaret Farrand Thorp, *America at the Movies* (1939), p. 113.

36 Ibid., pp. 90–91.

37 Ibid., p. 108.

38 Mills, *The Power Elite,* pp. 92–93.

39 Hortense Powdermaker, *Hollywood: The Dream Factory* (1951), p. 207.

40 The division of labor, as embedded in images of women, is discussed in Serafina K. Bathrick's forthcoming study of "monumental women," to be published by the University of Wisconsin Press.

41 Jean-Paul Sartre, *Being and Nothingness* (1956), p. 59.

42 Barthes, *The Fashion System*, p. 225.

43 Thomas G. Atkinson, *Psychological Laws Applied to Advertising* (1925), p. 12.

44 J. Gordon Lippincott, *Design for Business* (1947), p. 62.

CHAPTER SIX   Varnished Barbarism

1 David Reisman et al., *The Lonely Crowd* (1950), pp. 190–91.

2 Stuart Ewen and Elizabeth Ewen, *Channels of Desire* (1982), pp. 110, 117–28.

3 The historical relationship between plantation slavery and the rise of British capitalism is discussed lucidly in Eric Williams, *Capitalism and Slavery* (1944).

4 Robert La Cour-Gayet, *Everyday Life in the United States Before the Civil War, 1830–1860* (1969), p. 24.

5 Ishbel Ross, *Taste in America* (1967), p. 9.

6 William Taylor, *Cavalier and Yankee* (1963), p. 153.

7 Lewis Erenberg, *Steppin' Out* (1981), pp. 36–37.

8 Ibid., p. 48.

9 Ibid., p. 39.

10 Michael Wallace, "Visiting the Past," in Steven Brier et al., eds., *Presenting the Past* (1986), p. 141.

11 Arthur J. Pulos, *American Design Ethic* (1983), p. 195.

12 Eric Mendelsohn, "Architecture in a Changing World," *Arts and Architecture* 65 (March 1948), p. 37.

13 Pulos, *American Design Ethic*, p. 195.

14 Quoted in Grace M. Meyer, *Once Upon a City* (1958), pp. 28–29.

15 Ibid., p. 29.

16 Ibid., p. 30.

17 Ibid., pp. 39–40.

18 Sidney Mintz, *Sweetness and Power* (1985), pp. 157–58.

19 William Morris, *Selected Writings*, ed. G. D. H. Cole (1934), p. 492, emphasis added.

20 Le Corbusier, *Towards a New Architecture*, trans. E. Etchells (1927), p. 3.

21 Egon Friedell, *A Cultural History of the Modern Age: The Crisis of the European Soul from the Black Death to the World War*, 3 vols. (1954), 3:298–99.

22 J. Huizinga, *In the Shadow of Tomorrow* (1936), p. 204.

23 Edith Wharton and Ogden Godman, Jr., *The Decoration of Houses* (1897), pp. xxii, 196–98.

24 Ibid., p. 198.

25 Ibid., p. 2.

26 Ibid., p. 14.

27 Morris, *Selected Writings*, pp. 478, 489–90.

28 Ibid., p. 484.

29 Ibid., pp. 484, 492.

30 Louis H. Sullivan, *Kindergarten Chats and Other Writings* (1947), p. 191.

31 Louis H. Sullivan, *Democracy* (1961), pp. 135–36, 387.

32 Ibid., pp. 387–88.

33 Ayn Rand, *The Fountainhead* (1943), pp. 44–45. Peter Keating, Roark's Beaux Arts antagonist throughout the book, is based roughly on Stanford White.

34 Sullivan, *Kindergarten Chats,* p. 187.

35 John F. Kasson, *Amusing the Million* (1978), p. 17.

36 Louis H. Sullivan, *The Autobiography of an Idea* (1956), p. vii.

37 Adolf Loos, "Ornament and Crime" (1908), reprinted in Ulrich Conrads, ed., *Programs and Manifestoes of Twentieth Century Architecture* (1964), p. 19.

38 Ibid., pp. 22–23.

39 Ibid.

40 Sheldon Cheney and Martha Candler Cheney, *Art and the Machine* (1936), p. 48.

41 Pulos, *American Design Ethic,* p. 153.

42 Vincent Scully, Jr., *Modern Architecture* (1974), p. 18.

43 Joan Kron, *Home-Psych: The Social Psychology of Home and Decoration* (1983), p. 136.

44 Carl E. Schorske, "Revolt in Vienna," *New York Review of Books,* 29 May 1986, p. 24.

45 Kathy Torrence, *An Art Nouveau Album* (1981), p. 6.

46 Peter Selz and Mildred Constantine, eds., *Art Nouveau* (1975), p. 22.

47 In J. M. Richards and Nikolaus Pevsner, eds., *The Anti-Rationalists* (1973), p. 143.

48 Selz and Constantine, *Art Nouveau,* pp. 123, 22.

49 Le Corbusier, *Towards a New Architecture,* pp. 3, 288–89.

50 Tilmann Buddensieg and Henning Rogge, *Industriekultur: Peter Behrens and the AEG,* trans. I. B. White (1984), p. 212.

51 Le Courbusier, *Towards a New Architecture,* p. 3.

CHAPTER SEVEN Mechanical Sentiments

1 Quoted in Brent C. Brolin, *The Failure of Modern Architecture* (1976), p. 46.

2 Ibid., p. 49.

3 Basset Jones, "The Modern Building Is a Machine," *The American Architect—Architectural Review* 125 (30 January 1924), p. 97.

4 Sheldon Cheney and Martha Candler Cheney, *Art and the Machine* (1936), frontispiece.

5 Arthur J. Pulos, *American Design Ethic* (1983), pp. 159–60.

6 Alfred Auerbach, "What Is Modern?" *Arts and Architecture* 65 (March 1948), pp. 28, 62, 9.

7 Frank A. Randall, *History of the Development of Building Construction in Chicago* (1949), p. 12. See also Philip Johnson, *Writings* (1979), p. 218.

8 See, especially, Siegfried Giedion, *Mechanization Takes Command* (1948); also, Joseph Rykwert, *The First Moderns* (1980).

9 Sibyl Moholy-Nagy, *Moholy-Nagy: Experiment in Totality* (1950), pp. 141–42.

10 *Munsey's Magazine* (July 1905), p. 390.

11 Tilmann Buddensieg and Henning Rogge, *Industriekultur: Peter Behrens and the AEG,* trans. I. B. White (1984), p. 187.

12 Le Corbusier, *Towards a New Architecture* (1927), p. 45.

13 Ibid., p. 1.

14 Ibid., p. 41.

15 Ibid., pp. 276–77.

16 Ibid., pp. 11, 13.

17 Ibid., pp. 4–7.

18 Ibid., p. 289.

19 Walter Gropius, "Education Toward Creative Design," *American Architect* 150 (May 1937), p. 27.

20 Walter Gropius, *The New Architecture and the Bauhaus* (1965), p. 47.

21 Gropius, "Education Toward Creative Design," p. 27.

22 Walter Gropius, "Sociological Premises for the Minimum Dwelling of Urban Industrial Populations" (1929), reprinted in *Scope of Total Architecture* (1961).

23 Moholy-Nagy, *Moholy-Nagy,* p. xii.

24 Ibid., p. 19.

25 Ibid., p. 21.

26 Hayden Herrera, *Frida* (1983), pp. 134–35.

27 Earnest Elmo Calkins, "Beauty The New Business Tool," *The Atlantic Monthly* 140 (August 1927), p. 153.

28 Ibid., p. 154.

29 Philip Johnson, *Writings* (1979), p. 29.

30 Talbot Faulkner Hamlin, "The International Style Lacks the Essence of Great Architecture," *American Architect* 143 (January 1933), pp. 12–16.

31 Herrera, *Frida,* p. 115.

32 Roy Sheldon and Egmont Arens, *Consumer Engineering* (1932), p. 2.

33 Harold Van Doren, *Industrial Design* (1940), p. 13.

34 Pulos, *American Design Ethic,* p. 393.

35 Calkins, "Beauty The New Business Tool," p. 147.

36 J. Gordon Lippincott, *Design for Business* (1947), p. 209.

37 Van Doren, *Industrial Design,* pp. 90–91.

38 Henry Dreyfuss, *Designing for People* (1955), p. 77.

39 Van Doren, *Industrial Design,* p. 137.

CHAPTER EIGHT   Form Follows Value

1 Walter Benjamin, "The Work of Art in the Age of Mechanical Reproduction," in Hannah Arendt, ed., *Illuminations* (1968), p. 244.

2 See Andre Bazin, *What Is Cinema?* 2 vols. (1971), 2:47–60.

3 Cesare Zavattini, "Some Ideas on the Cinema" (1953), reprinted in Richard Dyer MacCann, *Film: A Montage of Theories* (1966), p. 218.

4 David Cook, *A History of Narrative Film* (1981), p. 380.

5 Robert Musil, *The Man Without Qualities* (1953), p. 11.

6 Helen Merrell Lynd, *On Shame and the Search for Identity* (1958), p. 16.

7 Georg Lukacs, *History and Class Consciousness* (1971), p. 100.

8 *New York Times,* 30 August 1986, p. 1.

9 *New York Times,* 12 October 1986, sec. 12, p. 1.

10 *New York Times,* 9 January 1987, p. D1.

11 Leonard Silk, "Symbolism vs. Reality," *New York Times,* 9 January 1987, p. D2.

12 *New York Times,* 11 January 1987, sec. 3, p. 1.

13 Quoted by Silk, "Symbolism," p. D2.

14 Le Corbusier, *Towards a New Architecture* (1927), p. 87.

15 J. Huizinga, *In the Shadow of Tomorrow* (1936), and Egon Friedell, *A Cultural History of the Modern Age: The Crisis of the European Soul from the Black Death to the World War* (1954), offer prime examples of this outlook.

16 Gareth Stedman Jones, review of Jean-Christophe Agnew, *Worlds Apart, The Nation,* 28 June 1986, pp. 896–98.

17 Mikhail Bakhtin, *Rabelais and His World* (1968), pp. 9, 19.

18 Arnold Hauser, *The Social History of Art,* 4 vols. (1951), 1:200, 232–44.

19 Christian Norberg-Schulz, *Meaning in Western Architecture* (1980), p. 98.

20 Arthur J. Pulos, *American Design Ethic* (1983), p. 110.

21 Quoted in Humphrey Jennings, *Pandaemonium* (1985), p 261.

22 Friedell, *A Cultural History of the Modern Age,* p. 99.

23 Tilmann Buddensieg and Henning Rogge, *Industriekultur: Peter Behrens and the AEG,* trans. I. B. White (1984), p. 223.

24 Ibid., p. 217, emphasis added.

25 Le Courbusier, *Towards a New Architecture* (1927), p. 143.

26 Vincent Scully, Jr., *Modern Architecture* (1974), p. 20.

27 Walter Gropius, *New Architecture and the Bauhaus* (1965), p. 29.

28 Sibyl Moholy-Nagy, *Moholy-Nagy: Experiment in Totality* (1950), pp. 27–28, 127, emphasis added.

29 Ibid., pp. 141–43.

30 Style Project, interview I-2.

31 Harvey Wiley Corbett, "The Birth and Development of the Tall Building," *American Architect* 129 (5 January 1926), p. 37.

32 Egerton Swartwout, "Definition in Modern Architecture," *The American Architect—The Architectural Review* 125 (2 January 1924), p. 7.

33 Lewis Mumford, *The Culture of Cities* (1938), p. 243.

34 Frank Lloyd Wright, *The Future of Architecture* (1953), pp. 161, 164.

35 Frederick Ackerman, "Forces That Influence the Profession's Future," *American Architect* 141 (May 1932), pp. 30–31.

36 Anne Hollander, *Seeing Through Clothes* (1978), p. 154.

37 *New York Times,* 16 April 1987.

38 Bakhtin, *Rabelais,* p. 26.

39 Lewis Erenberg, *Steppin' Out* (1981), pp. 214–15.

40 Jessica Ruth Johnston, "The Double Bind" (1983), pp. 7–11.

41 Hillel Schwartz, *Never Satisfied* (1986), p. 160.

42 Elizabeth Ewen, *Immigrant Women in the Land of Dollars* (1985), p. 201.

43 Johnston, "Double Bind," p. 30.

44 Ibid., p. 44.

45 Raymond Loewy, *Industrial Design* (1979), p. 150.

46 Ibid., p. 135.

47 *New York Times,* 11 February 1988, p. B9.

48 Therese Bertherat and Carol Benstein, *The Body Has Its Reasons* (1979), pp. 44–45, 50.

49 Kim Chernin, *The Obsession* (1981), pp. 9, 18.

50 Style Project, interview I-7.

51 Chernin, *Obsession,* p. 20.

52 Ibid, p. 52.

53 Kent C. Bloomer and Charles W. Moore, *Body, Memory and Architecture* (1977), p. 44.

CHAPTER NINE   Form Follows Power

1 This and the preceding quotations are from Guy Endore, "Men of Iron" (1940), reprinted in Thomas N. Scortia and George Zebrowski, eds., *Human Machines* (1975), pp. 3–11.

2 This and the preceding quotations are from (Tokyo) National Institute for Research Advancement Electronics Research Group, *NIRA Report* 2, no. 2 (20 December 1985), pp. 130–31.

3 George A. Lundberg et al., *Leisure: A Suburban Study* (1934), p. 3.

4 *New York Times,* 3 June 1987, p. A27.

5 Ellington Darden, *The Nautilus Bodybuilding Book* (1986), pp. viii–ix.

6 Style Project, interview I-13.

7 Michel Foucault, *Discipline and Punish* (1977), p. 138.

8 Ibid., p. 135.

9 Ibid., pp. 135–36, 138.

10 Ibid., p. 136.

11 Henry Dreyfuss, *Designing for People* (1955), p. 26.

12 James B. Gilbert, *Work Without Salvation* (1977), p. 157.

13 Dreyfuss, *Designing for People,* p. 46.

14 Ibid, pp. 37–38.

15 Ibid., p. 27.

16 Ralph M. Barnes, *Motion and Time Study* (1963), pp. 214–17.

17 Christian Norberg-Schulz, *Meaning in Western Architecture* (1980), p. 200.

18 As quoted in *Arts and Architecture* 65 (May 1948), p. 31.

19 Elton Mayo, "The Irrational Factor in Human Behavior: The 'Night-Mind' in Industry," *The Annals* 110 (November 1923), p. 123.

20 Ibid., p. 117.

21 Ibid., pp. 122–26.

22 Humphrey Jennings, *Pandaemonium* (1985), pp. 98–99.

23 Michel Foucault, *Discipline and Punish,* p. 206 ("power of mind over mind" comes from Jeremy Bentham, *Panopticon*).

24 Ibid., pp. 102–3.

25 Robert Rydell, *All the World's a Fair* (1984), p. 2.

26 Ibid., pp. 44–45.

27 Paul S. Boyer, *Urban Masses and Moral Order in America, 1820–1920* (1978), pp. 182–83.

28 Jennings, *Pandaemonium,* p. 262.

29 Boyer, *Urban Masses,* p. 183.

30 Martha Buskirk, "Stanford White's Washington Memorial Arch: Civic Beauty and the Development of Urban Order" (paper delivered at Society of Architectural Historians, Philadelphia, 9 November 1985), pp. 1–2, 10.

31 Ibid., pp. 12–13.

32 Boyer, *Urban Masses,* p. 183.

33 Ibid., pp. 272–73, 275.

34 Walter Gropius, "Education Toward Creative Design," *American Architect and Architecture* 150 (May 1937), pp. 26–30; Brent C. Brolin, *The Failure of Modern Architecture* (1976), p. 58.

35 Raymond Williams, *Keywords: A Vocabulary of Culture and Society* (1983), p. 201.

36 Tilmann Buddensieg and Henning Rogge, *Industriekultur: Peter Behrens and the AEG,* trans. I. B. White (1984), p. 242.

37 Quoted in Talbot Faulkner Hamlin, "The International Style Lacks the Essence of Great Architecture," *American Architect* 143 (January 1933), pp. 12–16.

38 Le Corbusier, *Towards a New Architecture* (1927), p. 277.

39 Ibid., p. 67.

40 Peter Blake, *Form Follows Fiasco* (1974), pp. 40–41.

41 Alexander Tzonis, *Towards a Non-Oppressive Environment* (1972), p. 87.

42 Buddensieg and Rogge, *Industrielkultur,* p. 207.

43 Ibid., p. 187.

44 Ibid., p. 34.

45 Ibid., p. 178.

46 Brolin, *The Failure of Modern Architecture,* p. 54.

47 Sibyl Moholy-Nagy, *Moholy-Nagy: Experiment in Totality* (1950), pp. 37–38.

48 Roland Barthes, *Mythologies* (1972), p. 88.

49 Le Corbusier, *Towards a New Architecture,* p. 54.

50 *Industrial Design* 12 (April 1965), pp. 87–89.

51 Eric Larrabee, "Machines That Make Music," *Industrial Design* 1 (June 1954), p. 27.

52 Thomas Hine, *Populuxe* (1986), pp. 83, 85.

53 Ibid., p. 87.

54 *Industrial Design* 12 (November 1965), pp. 25–31.

55 Brooklyn Museum, *The Machine Age in America* (1986), p. 25.

56 Hamlin, "The International Style," p. 12.

57 Harvey Wiley Corbett, "The Birth and Development of the Tall Building," *American Architect* 129 (5 January 1926), p. 37.

58 Frederick Ackerman, "Forces That Influence the Profession's Future," *American Architect* 141 (May 1932), pp. 30–31.

59 Frank Lloyd Wright, "America's Tomorrow," *American Architect* 141 (May 1932), p. 76.

60 Frank Lloyd Wright, *The Future of Architecture* (1953), p. 164.

61 Wright, "America's Tomorrow," p. 16.

62 Ralph Walker, "An Analysis of Order," *Pencil Points* 17 (December 1936), p. 689.

63 Walter Lippmann, "Radio City," *American Architect* 153 (March 1933), p. 18 (originally published in the New York *Herald Tribune* in 1932).

64 Lewis Mumford, *From the Ground Up* (1956), p. 109.

65 Sibyl Moholy-Nagy, *Native Genius in Anonymous Architecture* (1957), p. 19.

66 Harry Henderson, "The Mass Produced Suburbs," *Harpers,* November 1953, p. 25.

67 George A. Lundberg et al., *Leisure: A Suburban Study* (1934), p. 17.

68 K. R., "Houses for the People," *Pencil Points* 26 (September 1945), pp. 59, 62–63.

69 Kenneth T. Jackson, *Crabgrass Frontier* (1985), p. 231.

70 Henderson, "Mass Produced Suburbs," pp. 26–27.

71 Walter Dorwin Teague, *Land of Plenty* (1947), pp. 183, 194.

72 Editors of the *Wall Street Journal, How They Sell* (1965), pp. 87–88.

73 Clifford Edward Clark, Jr., *The American Family Home* (1986), p. 222.

74 Ibid., p. 222.

75 John Liell, "Levittown: A Study in Community Development" (1952), p. 110.

76 Ibid., p. 111.

77 Henderson, "Mass Produced Suburbs," p. 26.

78 Teague, *Land of Plenty,* p. 183.

79 Arthur T. North, "Houses Cannot Be Built Like Automobiles," *American Architect* 142 (December 1932), p. 20.

80 Randolph Evans, "House Design for the Mass Market," *Architectural Record* 96 (November 1944), pp. 74, 79.

81 Gwendolyn Wright, *Building the American Dream* (1981), p. 251.

82 Clark, *American Family Home,* pp. 221–23.

83 Editors of the *Wall Street Journal, How They Sell,* pp. 94–95.

84 Jackson, *Crabgrass Frontier,* p. 240.

85 Ibid.

86 Thomas Hine, *Populuxe* (1986).

87 Lee McCanne, "Every House Will Have Its Own Theatre," *American Architect* 141 (May 1932), p. 46.

88 "They Want Television," *Architectural Forum* 92 (April 1950), p. 187.

89 Henderson, "Mass Produced Suburbs," p. 28.

90 Rosalind Baxandall and Elizabeth Ewen, "Picture Windows" (unpublished manuscript, 1987), p. 3. My entire discussion of the suburbs is indebted to the authors of this paper.

CHAPTER TEN   Form Follows Waste

1 *New York Times,* 29 June 1987, p. B8.

2 *New York Times,* 31 May 1987, sec. 3, p. 19.

3 Ibid.

4 John Rader Platt, "The Fifth Need of Man," *Horizon* 1 (July 1959), p. 106.

5 *New York Times,* 29 June 1987, p. B8.

6 Sibyl Moholy-Nagy, *Native Genius in Anonymous Architecture* (1957), pp. 170–71.

7 Bernard Rudofsky, *The Prodigious Builders* (1977), pp. 269, 271.

8 Warren Susman, *Culture as History* (1984), p. xx.

9 Karl Marx and Frederick Engels, *The Communist Manifesto* (1948), pp. 9–21.

10 Sigmund Freud, *Civilization and Its Discontents* (1930), pp. 33, 43.

11 See Herbert Marcuse, *Eros and Civilization* (1955).

12 Simon Patten, *The New Basis of Civilization* (1968), p. ix.

13 Simon Patten, *The Consumption of Wealth* (1892), p. 34.

14 Walter Benjamin, "The Work of Art in the Age of Mechanical Reproduction," in Hannah Arendt, ed., *Illuminations* (1968), p. 244.

15 Michael Wood, *America in the Movies* (1975), pp. 178–80.

16 See Stuart Ewen, *Captains of Consciousness* (1976).

17 Earnest Elmo Calkins, "Beauty The New Business Tool," *The Atlantic Monthly* 140 (August 1927), p. 145.

18 Ibid., p. 146.

19 Quoted in Arthur J. Pulos, *American Design Ethic* (1983), pp. 357–58.

20 Roy Sheldon and Egmont Arens, *Consumer Engineering* (1932), pp. 52–53.

21 Robert S. Lynd, "The People as Consumers," in Report to the President's Research Committee on Social Trends, *Recent Social Trends in the United States* (1933), p. 878.

22 Sheldon and Arens, *Consumer Engineering*, pp. 52–53.

23 J. Gordon Lippincott, *Design for Business* (1947), p. 10.

24 Sheldon and Arens, *Consumer Engineering*, p. 57.

25 Lippincott, *Design for Business*, pp. 14–15.

26 Ibid., p. 16.

27 Jane Fiske Mitarachi, "Harley Earl and His Product," *Industrial Design* 2 (October 1955), p. 52.

28 "Trends," *Industrial Design* 2 (December 1955), pp. 35, 39.

29 Henry Dreyfuss, *Designing for People* (1955), pp. 59–60.

30 Lippincott, *Design for Business*, p. 157.

31 Raymond Loewy, *Industrial Design* (1979), p. 32.

32 *Hear, There & Everywhere*, no. 27, December 1969.

33 Ibid.

34 Thomas Kochman, *Rappin' and Stylin' Out* (1972), p. 135.

35 Bobby Seale, *Seize the Time* (1968), p. 411.

36 *Hear, There & Everywhere*, no. 28, January 1970.

37 Dick Hebdige, *Subculture: The Meaning of Style* (1979), pp. 102–4.

38 Style Project, written testimony A4.

39 Ibid., written testimony A1.

40 *Details* 5 (February 1987), pp. 85–89.

CONCLUSION   **The Political Elements of Style**

1 Gini Sikes, "Art and Allegory," *Metropolis* (May 1986), pp. 31–32.

2 Ibid., p. 40.

3 Ibid., p. 32.

4 *New York Times Magazine,* 22 March 1987, p. 56, emphasis added.

5 *New York Times,* 8 March 1987.

6 *New York Times Magazine,* 8 June 1986, p. 23.

7 *New York Post,* 23 July 1987, p. 88.

8 *New York Times,* 12 April 1987, p. 29.

9 Style Project, interview I-31.

10 *The Nation,* 4–11 July 1987, p. 6.

11 *New York Times,* 24 July 1987, p. A35.

12 Edward Pessen, *Jacksonian America* (1969), pp. 166–67.

13 Edward Bernays, "The Engineering of Consent," *The Annals* 250 (March 1947), pp. 113–14. In 1955 Bernays edited a collection of essays, also entitled *The Engineering of Consent,* in which nine public relations experts discussed the topic from a variety of instrumental vantage points. Notable among the contributers was Bernays's wife, Doris E. Fleischman, who (with Howard Walden Cutler) discussed the use of familiar visual themes and symbols to shape public opinions and attitudes. Their inventory of symbols will be familiar to anyone who has seen "Americana"-style advertising for Kodak, Pepsi-Cola, and other corporate brands, as well as 1984 Ronald Reagan campaign commercials.

14 *New York Times,* 25 July 1987, p. 8.

Bibliography

Abel, Jean. "An Explanation of Modern Art." *California Arts and Architecture* 37 (June 1930): 34–35.

Ackerman, Frederick. "Forces That Influence the Profession's Future." *American Architect* 141 (May 1932): 30–31.

Albrecht, Donald. *Designing Dreams: Modern Architecture in the Movies.* New York, 1986.

Allen, James Sloan. *Romance of Commerce and Culture.* Chicago, 1983.

Aronovic, Carol. "The One Hope for Low Rental Housing." *American Architect* 144 (January 1934): 20–24.

Atkinson, Thomas. *Psychological Laws Applied to Advertising: A Lecture.* Scranton, Penn., 1925.

Auerbach, Alfred. "What Is Modern?" *Arts and Architecture* 65 (March 1948): 28–29.

Bakhtin, Mikhail. *Rabelais and His World.* Cambridge, 1968.

Barnes, Ralph M. *Motion and Time Study: Design and Measurement of Work.* New York, 1963.

Barr, Estelle De Young. "A Psychological Analysis of Fashion Motivation." *Archives of Psychology* 171 (June 1934).

Barthes, Roland. *The Fashion System.* New York, 1983.

———. *Mythologies.* New York, 1972.

Bayley, Stephen. *In Good Shape: Style in Industrial Products, 1900–1960.* London, 1979.

Bazin, Andre. *What Is Cinema?* 2 vols. Berkeley, Calif., 1971.

Beard, George M. "Causes of American Nervousness" (1881). Reprinted in Henry Nash Smith, ed. *Popular Culture and Industrialism.* Garden City, N.Y., 1967.

Bel Geddes, Norman. *Horizons.* New York, 1932.

Bell, Philip, Kathe Boehringer, and Stephen Crofts. *Programmed Politics.* Sydney, Australia, 1982.

Benham, Reyner. *A Concrete Atlantis.* Cambridge, 1986.

Benjamin, Walter. "The Work of Art in the Age of Mechanical Reproduction." In Hannah Arendt, ed., *Illuminations.* New York, 1968.

Berger, John. *The Look of Things.* New York, 1974.

———. *Ways of Seeing.* London, 1972.

Berman, Marshall. *All That Is Solid Melts into Air.* New York, 1982.

Bernays, Edward L. "The Engineering of Consent." *Annals of the American Political and Social Science Association* 250 (March 1947): 113–20.

Bertherat, Therese, and Carol Benstein. *The Body Has Its Reasons.* New York, 1979.

Blake, Peter. *Form Follows Fiasco: Why Modern Architecture Hasn't Worked.* Boston, 1974.

Bloomer, Kent C., and Charles W. Moore. *Body, Memory and Architecture.* New Haven, Conn., 1977.

Bonellie, Helen-Janet. *The Status Merchant: The Trade of Interior Decoration.* New York, 1972.

Bookchin, Murray. *The Limits of the City.* New York, 1974.

Boorstin, Daniel J. *The Image: A Guide to Pseudo-Events in America.* New York, 1961.

Bossom, Alfred C. "Fifty Years Progress Toward an American Style in Architecture." *American Architect* 129 (5 January 1926): 43–49.

Bowen, Hugh M. "New Directions in Human Engineering." (Special Issue: "The Changing Face of America.") *Industrial Design* 12 (September 1965): 128–29.

Boyer, Paul. *Urban Masses and Moral Order in America, 1820–1920.* Cambridge, 1978.

Braudel, Fernand. *The Structures of Everyday Life.* New York, 1985.

Braverman, Harry. *Labor and Monopoly Capital.* New York, 1974.

Brenninkmeyer, Ingrid. "The Sociology of Fashion." PhD dissertation. Freiburg, 1962.

Brolin, Brent C. *The Failure of Modern Architecture.* New York, 1976.

Brooklyn Museum. *The Machine Age in America, 1918–1941.* New York, 1986.

Brown, Richard D. *Modernization: The Transformation of American Life, 1600–1865.* New York, 1976.

Buddensieg, Tilmann, and Henning Rogge. *Industriekultur: Peter Behrens and the AEG.* Translated by Iain Boyd White. Cambridge, 1984.

Burghardt, Walter J. *The Image of God in Man According to Cyril of Alexandria.* Washington, D.C., 1957.

Bush, Donald J. *The Streamlined Decade.* New York, 1975.

Buskirk, Martha. "Stanford White's Washington Memorial Arch: Civic Beauty and the Development of Urban Order." Paper delivered at Society of Architectural Historians, Philadelphia, 9 November 1985.

Byrne, Janet S. *American Ephemera.* New York, 1982.

Calkins, Earnest Elmo. "Beauty The New Business Tool." *The Atlantic Monthly* 140 (August 1927): 145–56.

Carnegie, Dale. *How to Win Friends and Influence People.* New York, 1977.

Chase, Stuart. *Prosperity: Fact or Myth?* New York, 1929.

Cheney, Sheldon, and Martha Candler Chevey. *Art and the Machine: An Account of Industrial Design in Twentieth Century America.* New York, 1936.

Chernin, Kim. *The Obsession: Reflections on the Tyranny of Slenderness.* New York, 1981.

Clark, Clifford Edward, Jr. *The American Family Home, 1800–1960.* Chapel Hill, N.C., 1986.

Coburn, Elmer Poswell. "Economics—The New Basis of Architectural Practice." *American Architect* 143 (September 1933): 50–54.

Cole, Rex, and C. D. Frazer. *Rex Cole on Salesmanship.* New York, 1935.

Colean, Miles. "The Architect's Stake in Private Enterprise." *Architectural Record* 103 (June 1948): 97–99.

Cook, David A. *A History of Narrative Film.* New York, 1981.

Corbett, Harvey Wiley. "The Birth and Development of the Tall Building." *American Architect* 129 (5 January 1926): 37–40.

Cross, Whitney R. *The Burned Over District: The Social and Intellectual History of Enthusiastic Religion in Western New York, 1800–1850.* New York, 1965.

Darden, Ellington. *The Nautilus Bodybuilding Book.* Chicago, 1986.

Dawley, Alan. *Class and Community.* Cambridge, 1976.

Deetz, James. *In Small Things Forgotten: The Archeology of Early American Life.* Garden City, N.Y., 1977.

Dreyfuss, Henry. *Designing for People.* New York, 1955.

Dudley, Drew. "Molding Public Opinion Through Advertising." *Annals of the American Political and Social Science Association* 250 (March 1947): 105–12.

Editors of *Fortune. Markets of the Sixties.* New York, 1958.

Editors of *Wall Street Journal. How They Sell.* New York, 1965.

Eisenstein, Elizabeth. *The Printing Press as an Agent of Change.* 2 vols. Cambridge, 1979.

Eisenstein, Sergei. *Film Form.* New York, 1949.

Ellison, Ralph. "The Little Man at Chehaw Station." *American Scholar* (Winter 1977): 37–39.

Endore, Guy. "Men of Iron" (1940). Reprinted in Thomas N. Scortia and George Zebrowski, eds. *Human Machines.* New York, 1975.

Erenberg, Lewis A. *Steppin' Out: New York Night-Life and the Transformation of American Culture, 1890–1930.* Westport, Conn., 1981.

Evans, Randolph. "House Design for the Mass Market." *Architectural Record* 96 (November 1944): 74–79.

Everard, John. "Advertising to Women by Photography." *Commercial Art and Industry* 17 (July 1934): 1–6.

Ewen, Elizabeth. *Immigrant Women in the Land of Dollars.* New York, 1985.

Ewen, Stuart. *Captains of Consciousness.* New York, 1976.

Ewen, Stuart, and Elizabeth Ewen. *Channels of Desire: Mass Images and the Shaping of American Consciousness.* New York, 1982.

Farber, Bernard. *Guardians of Virtue: Salem Families in 1800.* New York, 1972.

Farrell, Morgan G. "The One Room Apartment Arrives." *American Architect* 125 (18 June 1924): 553–58.

Febvre, Lucien, and Henri-Jean Martin. *The Coming of the Book.* London, 1976.

Feldstein, Stanley, and Lawrence Costello, eds. *The Ordeal of Assimilation.* Garden City, N.Y., 1974.

Fitch, James Marston. *American Building: The Forces That Shape It.* Boston, 1948.

————. *Walter Gropius.* New York, 1960.

Foner, Eric. *Free Soil, Free Labor, Free Men.* New York, 1970.

Forty, Adrian. *Objects of Desire: Design and Society from Wedgwood to IBM.* New York, 1986.

Foster, Stephen. *Their Solitary Way: The Puritan Social Ethic in the First Century of Settlement in New England.* New Haven, Conn., 1971.

Foucault, Michel. *Discipline and Punish: The Birth of the Prison.* New York, 1977.

Frankl, Paul. *Principles of Architectural History: The Four Phases of Architectural Style, 1420–1900.* Cambridge, 1969.

Fraser, Kennedy. *The Fashionable Mind: Reflections on Fashion, 1970–1981.* New York, 1981.

Freud, Sigmund. *Civilization and Its Discontents.* Garden City, N.Y., 1930.

Friedell, Egon. *A Cultural History of the Modern Age: The Crisis of the European Soul from the Black Death to the World War.* 3 vols. New York, 1954.

Fromm, Erich. *Escape from Freedom.* New York, 1941.

Fryer, Lorine Pruette. *Women and Leisure: A Study of Social Waste.* New York, 1924.

Fussell, Paul. *Class.* New York, 1983.

Genovese, Elizabeth Fox, and Eugene D. Genovese. *Fruit of Merchant Capital.* New York, 1983.

Genovese, Eugene. *The Political Economy of Slavery.* New York, 1965.

Gerth, H. H., and C. Wright Mills, eds. and trans. *From Max Weber.* New York, 1958.

Giedion, Siegfried. *Mechanization Takes Command.* New York, 1948.

Gilbert, James B. *Work Without Salvation.* Baltimore, 1977.

Glogg, John. *The Missing Technician in Industrial Production.* London, 1944.

Goffman, Erving. *The Presentation of Self in Everyday Life.* New York, 1959.

Goldberger, Paul. *On the Rise: Architecture and Design in a Postmodern Age.* New York, 1983.

Gowans, Alan. *Images of American Living.* Philadelphia, 1964.

Gropius, Walter. "Education Toward Creative Design." *American Architect and Architecture* 150 (May 1937): 26–30.

————. *The New Architecture and the Bauhaus.* Cambridge, 1965.

————. *Scope of Total Architecture.* New York, 1962.

————. "Toward a Living Architecture." *American Architect and Architecture* 152 (January 1938): 21–22.

Groves, Ernest R. *Personality and Social Adjustment.* New York, 1924.

Gutman, Herbert G. *The Black Family in Slavery and Freedom.* New York, 1976.

————. *Work, Culture and Society in Industrializing America.* New York, 1977.

Halttunen, Karen. *Confidence Men and Painted Women: A Study of Middle Class Culture in America, 1830–1870.* New Haven, Conn., 1982.

Hamlin, Talbot Faulkner. "The International Style Lacks the Essence of Great Architecture." *American Architect* 143 (January 1933): 12–16.

Harbeson, John F. "The Automobile and the 'Home' of the Future." *Annals of the American Political and Social Science Association* 116 (November 1924): 58–60.

Hauser, Arnold. *The Social History of Art.* 4 vols. New York, 1951.

Hebdige, Dick. *Subculture: The Meaning of Style.* London, 1979.

Henderson, Harry. "The Mass Produced Suburbs." *Harpers* (November 1953): 25–32.

———. "Puzzled American Collection: The Mass Produced Suburbs, Part II. " *Harpers* (December 1953): 80–86.

Henry, Jules. *On Sham, Vulnerability and Other Forms of Self-Destruction.* New York, 1973.

Herrera, Hayden. *Frida: A Bibliography of Frida Kahlo.* New York, 1983.

Hill, Christopher. *The World Turned Upside Down.* Middlesex, 1972.

Hine, Thomas. *Populuxe.* New York, 1986.

Hobsbawn, E. J. *The Age of Capital, 1848–1875.* New York, 1975.

Hochschild, Arlie. *The Managed Heart.* Berkeley, 1987.

Holden, Thomas S. "Prologue to Progress." *Architectural Record* 103 (January 1948): 87–91.

Hollander, Anne. *Seeing Through Clothes.* New York, 1978.

Holmes, Oliver Wendell. "Doings of the Sunbeam." *The Atlantic Monthly* (July 1863). Reprinted in Beaumont Newhall, ed., *Photography: Essays and Images.* New York, 1980.

———. "The Stereoscope and the Stereograph." *The Atlantic Monthly* (June 1859). Reprinted in Beaumont Newhall, ed., *Photography: Essays and Images.* New York, 1980.

Horkheimer, Max. *Dawn and Decline.* New York, 1978.

Huizinga, J. *In the Shadow of Tomorrow.* New York, 1936.

Hulten, K. G. Pontus. *The Machine as Seen at the End of the Mechanical Age.* New York, 1968.

Huxtable, Ada Louise. *The Tall Building Reconsidered.* New York, 1985.

"Interior Architecture: Nineteen Twenty-eight Contributions to a Modern America Style." *American Architect* 135 (5 January 1929): 31–48.

Irwin, Will. *Propaganda and the News: Or, What Makes You Think So?* New York, 1936.

Jackson, Kenneth T. *Crabgrass Frontier: The Suburbanization of the United States.* New York, 1985.

James, M. H. "The Automobile and Recreation." *Annals of the American Political and Social Science Association* 116 (November 1924): 32–34.

Jenks, Charles. *The Language of Post-Modern Architecture.* New York, 1984.

———. *Modern Moments in Architecture.* New York, 1985.

Jennings, Humphrey. *Pandaemonium, 1660–1886: The Coming of the Machine as Seen by Contemporary Observers.* New York, 1985.

Johnson, Philip. *Writings.* New York, 1979.

Johnston, Jessica Ruth. "The Double Bind." MA Thesis, California State University, Fullerton, 1983.

Jones, Basset. "The Modern Building Is a Machine." *The American Architect—The Architectural Review* 125 (30 January 1924): 93–98.

Jones, Gareth Stedman. Review of Jean-Christophe Agnew, *Worlds Apart: The Market and the Theatre in Anglo-American Thought. The Nation* (28 June 1986): 896.

Jordan, Winthrop D. *White Over Black.* Chapel Hill, N.C., 1968.

K. R. "Houses for the People." *Pencil Points: Progressive Architecture* 26 (September 1945): 59–66.

Kasson, John F. *Amusing the Million: Coney Island at the Turn of the Century.* New York, 1978.

Kaufman, Edgar, Jr. "Fine Years of Good Design." *Industrial Design* (August 1954): 23–29.

Kaufman, H. G. *Obsolescence and Professional Career Development.* New York, 1974.

Kennedy, Robert Woods. "The Style of Life." *Magazine of Art* 46 (March 1953): 99ff.

Kern, Stephen. *The Culture of Time and Space, 1880–1918.* Cambridge, 1983.

Kitson, Harry Dexter. "Understanding the Consumer's Mind." *Annals of the American Political and Social Science Association* 110 (November 1923): 131–38.

Kochman, Thomas. *Rappin' and Stylin' Out: Communication in Urban Black America.* Urbana, Ill., 1972.

Kowiniski, William S. *The Malling of America.* New York, 1985.

Kron, Joan. *Home-Psych: The Social Psychology of Home and Decoration.* New York, 1983.

Kron, Joan, and Suzanna Slesin. *High Tech: The Industrial Style and Source Book.* New York, 1978.

Kubler, George. *The Shape of Time: Remarks on the History of Things.* New Haven, Conn., 1962.

Kulikoff, Allan. "The Progress of the Quality in Revolutionary Boston." In Herbert G. Antman and Gregory S. Kealey, eds. *Many Pasts.* Vol. 1. Englewood Cliffs, N.J., 1973.

LaCour-Gayet, Robert. *Everyday Life in the United States Before the Civil War, 1830–1860.* New York City, 1969.

Larrabee, Eric. "Machines That Make Music." *Industrial Design* 1 (June 1954): 22–31.

Lears, Jackson. *No Place of Grace.* New York, 1981.

Le Corbusier. *The City of Tomorrow.* London, 1929.

———. *Towards a New Architecture.* Trans. Frederick Etchells, from 13th French ed. New York, 1927.

———. "What Is America's Problem?" *American Architect* 148 (March 1936): 17–22.

Lesieutre, Alain. *The Spirit and Splendour of Art Deco.* New York, 1974.

Liell, John. "Levittown: A Study in Community Development." PhD dissertation, Yale University, 1952.

Lippincott, J. Gordon. *Design for Business.* Chicago, 1947.

Lippincott, J. Gordon, and Walter Margulies. "We Couldn't Have Done It in Wichita." *Industrial Design* 7 (October 1960): 102–3.

Lippmann, Walter. *Drift and Mastery.* New York, 1914.

———. "Radio City." *American Architect* 143 (March 1933): 18.

Loewy, Raymond. *Industrial Design.* Woodstock, N.Y., 1979.

Loos, Adolf. "Ornament and Crime" (1908). In Ulrich Conrads, ed. *Manifestos of Twentieth Century Architecture.* Cambridge, 1964.

Lowe, David. *Lost Chicago.* Boston, 1975.

Lucie-Smith, Edward. *A History of Industrial Design.* New York, 1983.

Ludlow, William Orr. "Let Us Discourage the Materialistic Modern." *American Architect* 141 (April 1932): 24–25, 79.

Lukacs, Georg. *History and Class Consciousness.* Cambridge, 1971.

Lundberg, George A., Mura Komarousky, and Mary Alice McInerny. *Leisure: A Suburban Study.* New York, 1934.

Lynd, Helen Merrell. *On Shame and the Search for Identity.* New York, 1958.

Lynd, Robert S. "The People as Consumers." In Report of President's Research Committee on Social Trends, *Recent Social Trends in the United States.* New York, 1933.

McCanne, Lee. "Every House Will Have Its Own Theatre." *American Architect* 141 (May 1932): 46–47, 121.

McLuhan, Marshall. *The Mechanical Bride.* Boston, 1951.

Marcuse, Herbert. *The Aesthetic Dimension.* Boston, 1978.

————. *Eros and Civilization: A Philosophical Inquiry into Freud.* New York, 1955.

————. *One-Dimensional Man.* Boston, 1964.

Marx, Karl, and Frederick Engels. *The Communist Manifesto* (1848). New York, 1948.

Marzio, Peter C. *Chromolithography 1840–1900: The Democratic Art.* Boston, 1979.

Mayo, Elton. "The Irrational Factor in Human Behavior: The 'Night-Mind' in Industry." *Annals of the American Political and Social Science Association* 110 (November 1923): 117–130.

Mears, Charles W. *Salesmanship for the New Era.* New York, 1929.

Meikle, Jeffrey. *Twentieth Century Limited.* Philadelphia, 1979.

Mendelsohn, Eric. "Architecture in a Changing World." *Arts and Architecture* 65 (April 1948): 36–37, 54–55.

Merleau-Ponty, Maurice. *The Primacy of Perception.* Evanston, Ill., 1964.

Meyer, Grace M. *Once Upon a City.* New York, 1958.

Meyers, Marvin. *The Jacksonian Persuasion: Politics and Belief.* Stanford, Calif., 1957.

Mikkelsen, Michael A. "Two Problems of Architecture." *Architectural Record* 65 (January 1929): 65–66.

Miller, Perry. *The New England Mind: The Seventeenth Century.* Boston, 1968.

Mills, C. Wright. *The Power Elite.* New York, 1956.

————. *White Collar: The American Middle Classes.* New York, 1953.

Mintz, Sidney. *Sweetness and Power: The Place of Sugar in Modern History.* New York, 1985.

Mitarachi, Jane Fiske. "Harley Earl and His Product: The Styling Section." *Industrial Design* 2 (October 1955): 50–63.

Moholy-Nagy, Sibyl. *Moholy-Nagy: Experiment in Totality.* Cambridge, 1950.

————. *Native Genius in Anonymous Architecture.* New York, 1957.

Morgan, Edmund S. *Visible Saints: The History of a Puritan Idea.* Ithaca, N.Y., 1963.

Morris, William. *Selected Writings.* Ed. G. D. H. Cole. Bloomsbury, Great Britain, 1934.

"The Most Popular Builder's House." *Architectural Forum* 92 (April 1950): 134–37.

Mowry, George, ed. *The Twenties: Fords, Flappers and Fantasies.* New York, 1963.

Mowry, George E., and Blaine A. Brownell. *The Urban Nation: 1920–1980.* New York, 1981.

Mukerji, Chandra. *From Graven Images: Patterns of Modern Materialism.* New York, 1983.

Mumford, Lewis. *The Culture of Cities.* New York, 1938.

———. *From the Ground Up.* New York, 1956.

———. *Technics and Civilization.* New York, 1934.

Murphy, Emmett. "Louis Grubb." *Communication Arts* (May–June 1980): 58–62.

Museum of Modern Art. *The Design Collection: Selected Objects.* New York, 1970.

Musil, Robert. *The Man Without Qualities.* New York, 1953.

National Institute for Research Advancement Electronics Research Group. *NIRA Report* 2, no. 2. Tokyo, 1985.

Norberg-Schulz, Christian. *Meaning in Western Architecture.* New York, 1980.

North, Arthur T. "Houses Cannot Be Built Like Automobiles." *American Architect* 142 (December 1932): 18–20.

Norwich, Casmera. "Parts Plus." *Photo/Design* 4 (July–August 1987): 51–54.

Oeri, Georgine. "Aspen" (Report on the Fourth Aspen Design Conference). *Industrial Design* 1 (August 1954): 109–13.

Parker, Gail, ed. *The Oven Birds.* Garden City, N.Y., 1972.

Patten, Simon. *The Consumption of Wealth.* New York, 1892.

———. *The New Basis of Civilization.* Cambridge, 1968.

Pessen, Edward. *Jacksonian America: Society, Personality and Politics.* Homewood, Ill., 1969.

Platt, John Rader. "The Fifth Need of Man." *Horizon* 1 (July 1959): 106–11.

Poe, Edgar Allan. "The Daguerrotype." In Allan Trachtenberg, ed. *Classic Essays on Photography.* New Haven, Conn., 1980.

Powdermaker, Hortense. "An Anthropologist Looks at the Movies." *Annals of the American Political and Social Science Association* 254 (November 1947): 80–87.

———. *Hollywood: The Dream Factory.* Boston, 1951.

Pulos, Arthur J. *American Design Ethic: A History of Industrial Design to 1940.* Cambridge, 1983.

Quigley, Martin. "The Importance of the Entertainment Film." *Annals of the American Political and Social Science Association* 254 (November 1947): 65–69.

Rand, Ayn. *The Fountainhead.* New York, 1943.

Randall, Frank A. *History of the Development of Building Construction in Chicago.* Urbana, Ill., 1949.

Read, Herbert. *The Grass Roots of Art: Lectures on the Social Aspects of Art in an Industrial Society.* New York, 1955.

Reisman, David, W. Nathan Glazer, and Reuel Denney. *The Lonely Crowd.* New Haven, Conn., 1950.

Richards, J. M., and Nikolaus Pevsner, eds. *The Anti-Rationalists.* Toronto, 1973.

Rosenblum, Naomi. *A World History of Photography.* New York, 1984.

Rosenfield, Isadore. "The Architect in Soviet Russia." *American Architect* 144 (January 1934): 13–17.

Ross, Ishbel. *Taste in America: An Illustrated History.* New York, 1967.

Rudofsky, Bernard. *The Prodigious Builders.* New York, 1977.

Ruskin, John. *Seven Lamps of Architecture.* Boston, 1849.

Rybczynski, Witold. *Home: A Short History of an Idea.* New York, 1986.

Rydell, Robert W. *All the World's a Fair: Visions of Empire at American International Expositions, 1876–1916.* Chicago, 1984.

Rykwert, Joseph. *The First Moderns: The Architects of the Eighteenth Century.* Cambridge, 1980.

Sartre, Jean-Paul. *Being and Nothingness.* New York, 1956.

Schickel, Richard. *D. W. Griffith: An American Life.* New York, 1984.

————. *Intimate Strangers: The Culture of Celebrity.* Garden City, N.Y., 1985.

Schiller, Herbert I. *Information and the Crisis Economy.* Norwood, N.J., 1984.

Schindler, Pauline. "A Significant Contribution to Culture." *California Arts and Architecture* 37 (January 1930): 23, 74.

Schorske, Carl E. "Revolt in Vienna." *New York Review of Books,* 29 May 1986, pp. 24–29.

Schutte, Thomas F., ed. *The Uneasy Coalition: Design in Corporate America.* Philadelphia, 1975.

Schwartz, Hillel. *Never Satisfied: A Cultural History of Diet Fantasies and Fat.* New York, 1986.

Scully, Vincent, Jr. *Modern Architecture: The Architecture of Democracy.* New York, 1974.

Seale, Bobby. *Seize the Time.* New York, 1968.

Selz, Peter, and Mildred Constantine, eds. *Art Nouveau.* New York, 1975.

Shabecoff, Philip. "With No Room to Dump, U.S. Faces a Garbage Crisis." *New York Times,* 29 June 1987, B8.

Sheldon, Roy, and Arens Egmont. *Consumer Engineering: A New Technique for Prosperity.* New York, 1932.

Shepp, James W., and Daniel B. Shepp. *Shepp's World's Fair Photographed.* Chicago, 1893.

Sikes, Gini. "Art and Allegory." *Metropolis* (May 1986): 31–33, 40–41.

Silk, Leonard. "Economic Scene: Symbolism vs. Reality." *New York Times,* 9 January 1987, p. D2.

Silverman, Debora. *Selling Culture.* New York, 1986.

Smith, C. Ray. *Interior Design in 20th-Century America.* New York, 1987.

Sobel, Robert. *The Manipulators: America in the Media Age.* Garden City, N.Y., 1976.

Sombart, Werner. *Luxury and Capitalism.* Ann Arbor, Mich., 1957.

Sontag, Susan. *On Photography.* New York, 1978.

Sparke, Penny. *An Introduction to Design and Culture in the Twentieth Century.* New York, 1986.

Stephens, Harmon B. "The Relation of the Motion Picture to Changing Moral Standards." *Annals of the American Political and Social Science Association* 128 (November 1926): 151–57.

Steward, Ira. "Poverty." *Statistics of Labor,* no. 173. Massachusetts, March 1873.

Stowe, Harriet Beecher. "The Lady Who Does Her Own Work." *The Atlantic*

Monthly (1864). Reprinted in Gail Parker, ed., *The Oven Birds.* Garden City, N.Y., 1972.

Stowell, Kenneth K. "Small Houses, Unlimited." *Architectural Record* 103 (May 1948): 87.

Sullivan, Louis Henri. *The Autobiography of an Idea.* New York, 1956.

————. *Democracy: A Man's Search.* Detroit, 1961.

————. *Kindergarten Chats and Other Writings.* New York, 1947.

Suskind, Patrick. *Perfume: The Story of a Murderer.* New York, 1986.

Susman, Warren. *Culture as History.* New York, 1984.

Swartwout, Egerton. "Definition in Modern Architecture." *The American Architect—The Architectural Review* 125 (2 January 1924): 7–10.

Taylor, William R. *Cavalier and Yankee.* Garden City, N.Y., 1963.

Teague, Walter Dorwin. *Design This Day: The Technique of Order in the Machine Age.* New York, 1940.

————. *Land of Plenty: A Summary of Possibilities.* New York, 1947.

"They Want Television." *Architectural Forum* 92 (April 1950): 187–88.

Thompson, E. P. *William Morris: Romantic to Revolutionary.* London, 1955.

Thorp, Margaret Farrand. *America at the Movies.* New Haven, Conn., 1939.

Tocqueville, Alexis de. *Democracy in America.* 2 vols. New York, 1945.

Torrence, Kathy. *An Art Nouveau Album.* New York, 1981.

"The Trend of Progress in House Design." *American Architect* 143 (July 1933): 22.

"Trends." *Industrial Design* 2 (December 1955): 33–55.

Tzonis, Alexander. *Towards a Non-Oppressive Environment.* Boston, 1972.

Van Doren, Harold. *Industrial Design: A Practical Guide.* New York, 1940.

Walker, Ralph. "An Analysis of Order." *Pencil Points* 17 (December 1936): 689–90.

Wallace, Michael. "Visiting the Past." In Steven Brier, Roy Rosenzwery, and Susan Porter Benson, eds., *Presenting the Past.* Philadelphia, 1986.

Ware, Norman. *The Industrial Worker, 1840–1860.* Chicago, 1964.

Wharton, Edith, and Ogden Godman, Jr. *The Decoration of Houses.* New York, 1897.

Wiebe, Robert H. *The Search for Order, 1877–1920.* New York, 1967.

Williams, Eric. *Capitalism and Slavery.* New York, 1944.

Williams, Raymond. *Culture and Society.* New York, 1958.

————. *Keywords: A Vocabulary of Culture and Society.* New York, 1983.

Windsor, Alan. *Peter Behrens: Architect and Designer.* New York, 1981.

Wood, Michael. *America in the Movies.* New York, 1975.

Wright, Frank Lloyd. "America's Tomorrow." *American Architect* 141 (May 1932): 16–17, 76.

————. *The Future of Architecture.* New York, 1953.

Wright, Gwendolyn. *Building the American Dream: A Social History of Housing in America.* Cambridge, 1981.

Zavattini, Cesare. "Some Ideas on the Cinema" (1953). Reprinted in Richard Dyer MacCann, ed. *Film: A Montage of Theories.* New York, 1966.

Index

Beauty *(continued)*
as exclusive, 86; ideals for, vs. vitality, 180–81; photogenic, 89, 190–91
Beaux Arts school, 125, 127, 203–6
Behavioral psychology, 49
Behrens, Peter: Art Nouveau and, 132; corporate image and, 42, 211–12, 214, 215; *exact fantasy* and, 208; Gropius and, 140; modern style and, 42–43, 134, 137; transcendent abstraction and, 165
Being and Nothingness (Sartre), 102–3
Benjamin, Walter, 93, 154, 156, 239, 240
Benson & Hedges cigarettes, 16
Bentham, Jeremy, 200–3
Berger, John, 38, 190
Berkeley, George (bishop), 76
Bernays, Edward, 267–68
Bertherat, Therese, 182
Bicycle Thief, The (film), 153–56
Blake, Peter, 210
Blei, Franz, 42
Bloomer, Kent, 183–84
Bloomingdale's, 20, 270
Books of Hours, 28
Bourget, Paul, 119
Boyer, Paul, 204
Braverman, Harry, 80, 81–82
Breakdancing, 5–6
Breckenridge, Sophinisba, 76
Breuer, Marcel, 199
Bric-a-brac, 64, 65
Bricolage, 252
Brolin, Brent, 135
Brontë, Charlotte, 164, 205
Brown, Claude, 250
Brownson, Orestes, 65
Building construction, 34–35; *see also* Architecture; Skyscraper
Bulemia, 183
Burke, Kenneth, 156
Burlesque, 178
Burnham, Daniel H., 43, 127, 205–6
Buskirk, Martha, 205

Cabaret, 92
Calkins, Earnest Elmo, 45–47, 51–52, 143, 145, 242–43
Calvin Klein perfume, 106
Candie's shoes, 106
Capasa, Ennio, 16–17
Carnegie, Dale, 83–84
Casa Mila, 131

Celebrity: audience identification and, 92–93, 94–96; as commodity, 100–1, 155–56; consumption and, 96, 98–100; critical concerns and, 96, 97–98; image management and, 91–101
Centennial Exposition of 1876 (Philadelphia), 136
Century of Progress exposition of 1931 (Chicago), 228
Change: concept of style and, 4; consumer engineering and, 51–52; economy of waste and, 244; market economy and, 26; memorable images and, 247; modernism and, 145; modern style and, 23; politics of, and surfaces, 16–23
Changing Times magazine, 256–57
Chaplin, Charlie, 96, 97–98
Charisma, 105
Chase, Stuart, 78
Chernin, Kim, 182–83
Chivas Regal scotch, 16
Chromolithography, 37–39, 75
Chrysler, 216
CIA (Clandestine Service), 261
City: conception of self and, 72–77; fears of, 221; rural migration to, 71, 72; social control and, 203–9; style as tool and, 72–75; vs. suburb, 221, 224; waste generation and, 233–34
City Beautiful movement, 205–6
City planning, 203–6
Clark, Clifford Edward, Jr., 226
Class, 61, 62, 66, 68, 117; *see also* Middle class; Power relations; Working class
Clothing, *see* Fashion
Coca-Cola bottle, 179–80
Cohen, Samuel J., 250, 251
Coilliot House, 131, 132
Colbert, Jean Baptiste, 30–31
Colonialism, and luxury markets, 31–32
Columbian Exposition of 1893 (Chicago), 35, 37, 75, 122, 127, 167, 204–5
Commercial power, 196
Commodity self, 71
Conspicuous consumption: nineteenth-century industrialism and, 116–20; punk culture and, 251–53; status and, 27, 59; waste and, 233–39, 241
Constructivist movement, 141–42
Consumer culture: alienation and, 91; celebrity and, 91–101; ever-changing style and, 248; freedom and, 103–8; politics in, 268–71; promise of style and, 14; salesmanship and, 82–85; time perception and, 207; waste and, 236–37

Consumer democracy, 32
Consumer engineering, 43–47, 144–45; streamlining and, 149; and stylization of politics, 266–67; suburban housing and, 227
Consumer goods, suburban idea and, 230–31
Consumerism, *see* Consumer culture
Consumer psychology, 47–51, 82; *see also* Motivational psychology
Consumption: celebrity and, 96, 98–100; class and, 61, 62, 66, 68–71, 117; freedom and, 103–8; mass production and, 238–39; *nouveau riche* style of, 116–17; *see also* Conspicuous consumption
Corbett, Harvey Wiley, 169, 219
Corporate image, 22, 42–43, 112, 211–15
Countercultural trends, 248–50, 252
Country Music Hall of Fame (Nashville, Tennessee), 94–95
Courtship patterns, 74, 178
Covello, Leonard, 73
Craft, Christine, 264
Craftsmanship, 210, 214; *see also* Artisans
Credit: American dream and, 227; conceptions of wealth and, 159–60; 1980s middle class and, 276*n*18
Critical concerns, celebrity style and, 96, 97–98
Critical thought, 156; *see also* Thought, discouragement of
Crystal Palace, 136, 163–64, 205
Cultural conflict, 73–75, 81
Cultural symbols, 120
Cultural wage, 64
Culture, and industrialization, 41
Curtain wall, 34–35

Daley, Kevin, 261
Dawley, Alan, 59, 60
Dearborn, George Van Ness, 79
Decentralization, 220, 231
Deception, 227
Decline and Fall (Waugh), 212–13
Decoration, 33, 118, 122, 128
Decoration of Houses, The (Wharton and Godman), 122
DeMille, Cecil B., 89
Democracy: consumption and, 32, 60; diversity of style and, 111–12; and engineering of consent, 267–68; machine aesthetic and, 136

Democracy (Sullivan), 126
Demoralization, worker, 186–88
De Sica, Vittorio, 154
Design, vs. production, 33
Dickens, Charles, 91–92
Dietrich, Marlene, 89
Dior, Christian, 263
Disposable products, 38, 234, 236
Diversity: advertising and, 14–21, 22; democracy and, 111–12; mass-produced housing and, 229–30; standardized, 229
Division of labor, 101, 129–30, 278*n*40
Dreyfuss, Henry, 148, 196–99, 246
Drucker, Peter, 158

Earl, Harley, 46, 216, 245
Ecology movement, 251
Economic value, abstract vs. material, 157–61; *see also* Abstract value
Economy, as prevention of waste, 237–38, 239
Economy, U.S., 158
Economy, world, 158
Efficiency vs. aesthetics, 46–47
Eisenstein, Sergei, 91–92
Elements of Style, The (Strunk and White), 2–3, 273*n*3
Elite culture: access to style and, 29–30; burghers of late Middle Ages and, 29–30; consumer democracy and, 32; imagery of, 13–14, 16, 17; market in style and, 30–32
ELLE magazine, 16
Ellison, Ralph, 9–10
Emotion, 84
Engels, Frederick, 61, 62
Engineering, 137–38; *see also* Consumer engineering
"Engineering of Consent, The" (Bernays), 267–68
Enlightenment, 194
Environmentalism, 251
Equality, 65
Erenberg, Lewis, 92, 117, 177–78
Eroticism, 47–49, 128, 129–30
Esprit jeans, 17, 20
Estilo Gaudi, 131
Ethnic identity, 8
Europe, and modern aesthetic, 135–37
Evans, Randolph, 229
Everard, John, 90
Evian spring water, 191–92

Machine aesthetic: change in, in 1930s, 144–45; emergence of, 135–38; human body and, 188, 189–93; social relations and, 138–40, 141–42; society and, 206, 208–9; streamlining and, 145, 148–49
Machine age, 224
"Machine Age in America, The: 1918–1941" (Brooklyn Museum exhibition), 217–18
Machines for living, 221, 225–26; see also Housing; Suburbs
Madonna (Munch lithograph), 132–33
Manhattan skyline, 166, 169; see also Skyscraper
Mannheimer, Franz, 208
Manuscript books, 27–28
Manuscript workshops, 28
Marcuse, Herbert, 262
Market economy, 26–31
Market in style: industrial capitalism and, 32–37; mercantile capitalism and, 26–32
Marketplace, as term, 22
Marketplace style: adolescents and, 20–21; advertising and, 45–47; charisma and, 105; elite culture and, 13–14, 16, 17; immigrants and, 21–22; memorable images and, 247–48; self-identity and, 76–77; varied images of, 14–20
Marx, Karl, 61, 62, 224, 238
Marxism, 142
Masculinity, 129–30, 188–91
Mass media: celebrity and, 91, 92–94; consumption and, 99–100; and engineering of consent, 267–68; marketplace style and, 47; style obsolescence and, 244; see also Advertising; Television
Mass production: access to style and, 75–77; culture of abundance and, 237–39; embossed ornamentation and, 33; in fifteenth century, 28; geometric style and, 209–11; home building and, 229; of housing, 226–27; housing and, 232; pursuit of happiness and, 60–61
Mass reproduction, celebrity and, 93–94
Material goods, and economic value, 158–59
Mayo, Elton, 199
Meaning: commodity self and, 79; cultural symbols and, 120; impact of images and, 271; style market and, 251
Mears, Charles W., 83
Media, see Mass media; Television
Melville, Robert, 132
"Memory value," 246–47
Mendelsohn, Eric, 118
Men of Iron (Endore), 185–86, 187, 188

Mentzer, Mike, 190
Mercantile capitalism: abstract value and, 161–62; style market and, 26–32
Merchandising, see Advertising; Consumer engineering
"Microelectronics Revolution" (NIRA report), 186–88
Middle Ages, 26–30
Middle class: anxieties of, 66–68; credit and, 276n18; culture of abundance and, 239; emergence of idea of, 62–63; equality and, 65; nineteenth-century industrialism and, 59–61; value of history for, 235
Middle-class status: consumption and, 68–71; property ownership and, 225; "state of the art" technology and, 217
Middling class, 62
Military, 16, 194–96
Military-industrial complex, 216
Mills, C. Wright, 45, 92, 93–94
Minorities, 225
Mintz, Sidney, 31, 120
Mobile individualism, 75, 231
Mobro (garbage scow), 233, 234
Modern art movement, 143
Modernism: in Europe, 135–44; fashion and, 173; radical and commercial, 141–43; in United States, 144–49; see also Geometric modernism; Rational modernism
Modernismo, 131
Modern Merchandising Bureau, 99
Modern Times (Chaplin film), 97
Moholy-Nagy, Laszlo, 137, 141–42, 144, 166, 167, 171, 212
Moholy-Nagy, Sibyl, 166, 223, 237, 239
Money economy, 159–60
Monroe, Marilyn, 96
Moore, Charles, 183–84
Morgan, J. P., 124
Moriarty, Daniel, 249
Morris, William, 121, 122, 140
Motivational psychology, 82–85
Mumford, Lewis, 170, 219, 222
Munch, Edvard, 132

National Institute of Research Advancement (NIRA), 186–88
Nautilus equipment, 189–90
Neiman-Marcus, 14–16
Neomania, 51
Neorealism, 154–56
Neurasthenia, 67

New England, old money vs. *nouveau riche* in, 116

"Newspeak," 262

News programs, 264–66

New York City, 72, 166, 171; *see also* Manhattan skyline

Nineteenth century, evolution of style in, 121–34

Nineteenth-century industrialism: conspicuous consumption and, 116–20; culture and, 41; market in style and, 32–37; rationalism and, 124; social costs and, 59–61

NIRA, *see* National Institute of Research Advancement

Norberg-Schulz, Christian, 163

North, Arthur T., 229

North, Oliver, 269

Nouveau riche, 31, 116–17

Novelty, 52, 234, 236

"Now Generation," 249

Noyes, Eliot, 213

Obesity, 177–78; *see also* Human body

Obsolescence, *see* "Style obsolescence"

Ogilvy, David, 70

Oil paintings, 37–38

"Ornament and Crime" (Loos), 127–29, 135

Ornamentation: ideas as, 17, 20; modern style and, 23, 127–30; traditional cultures and, 22–23

Orwell, George, 258, 262

Packaging: memory value and, 246–47; power of style in, 22; waste and, 234, 241–42; *see also* Streamlining

Panic of 1857, 68

Panopticism: building design and, 221; functionalism and, 212, 215; skyscraper and, 220; social order and, 200–3, 206; suburbs and, 227; television and, 231–32

Panopticon (Bentham), 200–1, 208

Paper goods, 38, 234

Past, *see* History

Patten, Simon, 238–39, 243

Paxton, Joseph, 136, 163

Perception: reduction of social issues to, 269, 271; of time, 207

Period styles, 121

Personal computer, 160–61

Personal distinction, 57–59

Personality: photographic beauty and, 89; techniques for false, 82–85

Personhood, *see* Self

Pessen, Edward, 59, 266

Photography: commercial, 85–91; male image and, 190–91; power of image and, 24–26, 39–40

Planned communities, 229

Planned obsolescence, *see* "Style obsolescence"

Platt, John Rader, 234, 236

Play principle, 218

Politics: aestheticization of, 154; in consumer culture, 268–71; power of style in, 22; stylization of, 266–71

Pollution, 236

Pontiac automobiles, 104

Popcorn, Faith, 234

"Populuxe" ideal, 230–31, 244, 246

Portraiture, 39–40

Post, Emily, 130

Postmodernism, 218

Poverty: celebrity and, 94–96; industrialism and, 61–62; of middle class, 66–67; in modern economy, 159, 160

"Poverty" (Steward essay), 66–67

Powdermaker, Hortense, 93, 101

Power: aestheticization of, 196, 204, 209, 213; under feudalism, 26–27; industrialism and, 124–25; middle-class pretension and, 64–65; ownership of land and, 161–62; panopticism and, 200–3; product design and, 215–17; skyscrapers and, 220; style as element of, 23; wealth and, 100; *see also* Class; Power relations

Power relations: commercial images and, 156; consumer products and, 217; formal architecture and, 221; machine aesthetic and, 138–40; standards of beauty and, 172; style as embodiment of, 112, 114–20; *see also* Class

Presentability, 76

Product design: advertising and, 43–46; body ideal and, 179–80; corporate system and, 215–17; memory value and, 246; power of style in, 22; technological representation in, 215–17

Product improvement, and obsolescence, 245

Profitability, 43, 45–47

Progress: corporate image and, 215; Evolution Charts and, 147; individual freedom and, 79; market economy and, 26; modern industrial system and, 219; waste and, 234

Soloflex, 190–91, 193
Southern plantation life, 114–16
Space, organization of, 199–209
Speculation: abstract value and, 160–61; in material goods, 157; skyscrapers and, 166, 168, 169–71, 219–20; *see also* Abstract value
Spencer, Herbert, 135
Springsteen, Bruce, 92, 96, 97
Standardization, 197, 199, 229
Standardized diversity, 229
Status: art objects and, 27–28, 37–38; clothing and, 114; conspicuous consumption and, 27, 59; consumer goods manufacture and, 70; under feudalism, 26–27, 114; oil paintings and, 37–38; style industries and, 57–59; *see also* Class; Middle class
Stephens, James, 118
Steward, Ira, 66–67, 70, 73, 223
Stile Liberty, 131
Stile nuovo, 131
Store, as term, 46
Stowe, Harriet Beecher, 63–64
Streamlining, 145, 148–49
Strunk, William, Jr., 2
Stuyvesant Town (housing project), 222
Style: influence of, 20–23; notions of, 2–4
Style moderne, 131
"Style obsolescence," 51–52, 145, 147, 237, 242–46
Style Project, 4–10
Subliminal advertising, 48, 49–50, 51
Suburbs, 221, 223–25, 226–27, 229, 232
Sugar, 31–32
Sullivan, Louis, 125–26, 127
Sumptuary laws, 27
Superspectacle, 154
Surfaces, and politics of change, 16–23
Susman, Warren, 32, 74, 96, 238
Swartwout, Egerton, 169

Taut, Bruno, 218
TAXI magazine, 16–17
Taylor, Frederick W., 80
Taylorism, 80–82
Teague, Walter Dorwin, 44, 45, 226, 227, 229
Television: promise of style and, 13–14; style as information and, 264–66; suburban life and, 231–32
Things to Come (film), 166, 167
Thomas, Marcel, 28
Thompson, J. Kevin, 182

Thorp, Margaret Farrand, 98–99
Thought, discouragement of, 156, 263–66, 269, 271
Tiffany style, *see* Art Nouveau
Time perception, 207
Tocqueville, Alexis de, 59
Tong, Kaity, 264–65
Towards a New Architecture (Le Corbusier), 137–39
Trademarks, *see* Corporate image; Logos
Traditional societies, 21–23
Transcendence: in architecture, 165; capitalist aesthetic and, 163; celebrity and, 96; of machine as symbol, 142
Trivia, 247, 249
Truth: abstract value and, 168; vs. commercial truth, 264–65; images and, 25–26
Typography, 212, 215
Tzonis, Alexander, 211

Union of Soviet Socialist Republics (U.S.S.R.), 111–12, 113
United States, and modern aesthetic, 135–37
United Technologies, 158
Unity of form and substance, 122–24, 148
"Unity of opposites," 14–16
Urban architecture, *see* Skyscraper
U.S.S.R., *see* Union of Soviet Socialist Republics

Value, *see* Abstract value; Economic value
Values: as commodity, 255–56; disposability and, 234; mass-produced culture and, 232
Vanderbilt, William Henry, 119
Van Doren, Harold, 50, 148
Veblen, Thorstein, 27, 117
Vernacular community, 223–25, 237
Vernacular style, 3, 4–10, 210, 221
Virginia Slims, 180
Visual Display Terminals (VDTs), 187
Vitalis Men's Haircare products, 256
Vogue magazine, 181

Waldman, Bernard, 99
Walker, Ralph, 221
War, as beautiful, 18
Warhol, Andy, 97